REINTERPRETATION IN
AMERICAN CHURCH HISTORY

ESSAYS IN DIVINITY

JERALD C. BRAUER, GENERAL EDITOR

Reinterpretation in American Church History

BY R. PIERCE BEAVER, JERALD C. BRAUER

ROBERT T. HANDY, WINTHROP S. HUDSON

FREDERICK KIRSCHENMANN, MARTIN E. MARTY

SIDNEY E. MEAD, WILLIAM S. MORRIS

Edited by JERALD C. BRAUER

THE UNIVERSITY OF CHICAGO PRESS

CHICAGO AND LONDON

THE UNIVERSITY OF CHICAGO PRESS
CHICAGO AND LONDON

The University of Toronto Press, Toronto 5, Canada

© 1968 by The University of Chicago
All rights reserved. Published 1968

Library of Congress Catalog Card Number: 68–20186

Printed in the United States of America

General Editor's Preface

The present volume is the fifth in a series of eight books being published under the general title "Essays in Divinity." This does not appear, at first glance, as a particularly auspicious moment for such a formidable enterprise. At the very moment the so-called radical theologians announce that "God is dead," an eight-volume series investigating various dimensions of the study of religion or of theology is published. Is this not an ill-timed venture?

In point of fact, however, in America the discipline of theology was never in a healthier state. To be sure, there are no giants such as Tillich or Niebuhr on the scene, but there are many new and exciting factors in the picture. The very presence of the "God is dead" movement is evidence of a new vitality and ferment among the younger theologians. In no sense does such a movement herald the end of systematic theology or the impossibility of using God-language. It is but one of many significant attempts being made now at basic reconstruction and reinterpretation of Christian theology.

One primary fact marks this new age — the pre-eminence of dialogue in all aspects of divinity. Basic conversation between Roman Catholicism, Protestantism, and Judaism is just beginning, and its full effect on theological construction lies ahead. At the time systematic theology entered the preliminary phase of dialogue, Paul Tillich's last lecture pointed to the future of this discipline in relation to the world's religions. Dialogue is not to be understood as the "in" movement in religion today; it is to be viewed as providing a new base that will profoundly affect not only the systematic study of doctrines and beliefs, but every dimension of religious studies.

Another mark of the vitality of religious studies today is its dialogic relationship to other disciplines. Studies in divinity have never been carried on in complete isolation from other areas of human knowledge, but in some periods the relationship has been more fully explored than in others. The contemporary scene is marked by the increasing tempo of creative interchange and mutual stimulation between divinity and other disciplines. Several new theological disciplines have emerged recently to demonstrate this fact. The interplay between theology and literature, between theology and the psychological sciences, and between theology and the social sciences promises to reshape the traditional study of religion, as our major theological faculties are beginning rapidly to realize.

The emergence and increasing role of the history of religions is a case in point. Until recently, it has been a stepchild in the theological curriculum. Today it is developing a methodology that probably will prove influential in all areas of theological study. History of religions also appears to be the way that most state universities will introduce the serious and disciplined study of religion into strictly secular curriculums.

These are but a few of the factors that demonstrate the present vitality of the study of religion today. It makes both possible and necessary a series of books such as this. The particular occasion for the publication of "Essays in Divinity" is supplied by the one hundredth anniversary of the Divinity School of the University of Chicago and by the University's seventy-fifth anniversary.

The editor of this series proposed that this event be celebrated by the Divinity School faculty and alumni by holding seven conferences, each of which was focused on the work of one of the seven academic fields of the School. Out of these conferences have come eight volumes which will, it is hoped, mark the progress in the various disciplines of theological study and point to the ongoing tradition of scholarship in the University's Divinity School.

Though something may have been lost in thus limiting the roster of contributors to these books, this very limitation may have the effect of marking the distinctive genius of one theological center long noted for its production of scholar-teachers in American theology. Also, it will enable an observer to determine the extent to which several generations have been shaped by, and have shaped, a particular institution. It will be possible to note the variations of approach and concern that mark respective generations of that institution. Furthermore, it will help to assess the particular genius, if any, that a given institution possesses. It will demonstrate to what extent its graduates and professors are in the midst of contemporary theological scholarship. It is to be hoped that the series will provide both a bench mark for today's scholarly discussions and research in religion and a record from which future generations can assess the contributions of an institution at the turn of its first century.

None of these volumes pretends to be definitive in its area; however, it is hoped that each will make a useful contribution to its area of specialization and that the entire series will suggestively illuminate the basic tendencies of religious scholarship at the present moment. The intent has been to devote each volume to a particular issue or area of inquiry that is of special significance for scholarly religious research today, and thus to keep each volume from being simply a disconnected series of essays. It is hoped that these books will be found to have, each in its own terms, a genuine unity, and that the reader will note a cumulative effect as he moves from essay to essay in each volume.

It is not necessary to write a special introduction to the volume on *Reinterpretation in American Church History.* Such a paper would attempt to sketch out the development of the discipline and the several phases through which it went. However, at least two of the essays trace, in brief fashion, the emergence and achievements of the study of religion in America. There is no need for repeating.

A word is in order concerning the place of the discipline in the Divinity School of the University of Chicago. Many scholars have designated the late William Warren Sweet the father of American church history. It is clear that earlier scholars had taught individual courses in that area, and a number had written books. Sweet was probably the first man to be appointed as a professor of American church history with the specific responsibility of developing it as a field of inquiry.

In his charming retirement remarks, "Every Dog Has His Day and I've Had Mine," Sweet indicated that he was asked to come to "develop an entirely new field of history." He was given research funds, library funds to build up a source collection, and research assistants, to make the study of American church history "the best in the country." He had a context in which to work that provided him the kind of base on which to build. The work of his predecessor Peter Mode, though not devoted exclusively to American church history, was the most creative work in America. Sweet felt that when he came to Chicago it quickly developed a monopoly in research and theses in American church history, and he was gratified to note that general American historians now dealt openly and fully with the subject.

William Warren Sweet was, indeed, a pioneer in that field, and Chicago became the center of the discipline. That is why a special volume is devoted to the subject in this series. It is proper that the students of Sweet and their students appraise the present condition of that discipline. Clearly, it has come a long way. It is taught in all seminaries, in departments of religion, and in many history departments in the United States. Much important research and writing in American religious history has provided a rich resource for the study of American culture and civilization.

So widespread have these studies become that it is a good question whether the study of American church history can any longer exist as an isolated discipline. That is one major issue confronted in these essays. Each essay addresses itself to the problem of reinterpretation as it is now occurring in

American religious studies. At least four of the chapters confront the general problem of changing assumptions at work in the craft. The essays of Sidney E. Mead, Winthrop S. Hudson, Martin E. Marty, and Jerald C. Brauer present different analyses of this issue. The common theme runs throughout the series — we are in the midst of a period of reinterpretation in American church historical research, writing, and teaching.

The remaining chapters lift up the motif of reinterpretation as seen in specific areas of research in American church history. William S. Morris seeks to provide a new framework in which to interpret Jonathan Edwards, and Frederick Kirschenmann sets forth a reinterpretation of Horace Bushnell. R. Pierce Beaver traces through the changes in missionary motivation in these centuries of American experience and sets the stage for a reinterpretation of the nature of the missionary enterprise in the American religious communities. Robert T. Handy demonstrates how a badly neglected element in American religious history is only now beginning to receive adequate attention, and argues that proper regard for this dimension will have consequences for a reinterpretation of American religious history.

All of these authors are Chicago men either in their education or their present posts. All but one are former students of William Warren Sweet or are his academic grandchildren. Sweet carried through his special calling to the University of Chicago. Today American religious studies are commonplace. It appears as if the most exciting days of the discipline lie ahead. It is not a dormant area of research and writing. Perhaps some of the real excitement in the future will be the way the discipline understands itself and so seeks to relate itself to other disciplines — theological, humanistic, and social-scientific. That is the excitement that emerges in a period of reinterpretation.

JERALD C. BRAUER, *General Editor*

CONTENTS

1

Changing Perspectives on Religion in America
JERALD C. BRAUER

History is always written from a particular perspective. If it is good history, the perspective provides a point of view that illuminates and does not distort the data open to the historian. A perspective is not a source of propaganda, though it both opens a historian to certain views and limits what he can see. One perspective enables him to see things and to ask questions which another perspective fails to see; thus it is an enriching and enlarging factor of the historian's craft. On the other hand, a perspective inevitably misses certain possible angles or fails to note certain interconnections in historical data. Frequently the specific strengths and weaknesses of a given perspective are not discernible until a new perspective emerges through which a historian looks at data. The Reformation looks one way when studied from the perspective of Vatican I, but it looks another way when studied from the perspective of Vatican II.

Change in perspective marks the writing of the history of religion in America just as it is reflected in the various histories of America. It is evident that church history, as a discipline, is in the midst of a new phase of writing or interpreting the history of religion in America. It is the argument of this chapter that most of the writing now being undertaken still reflects the latest shift in perspective, which started in the 1950's. It is a further contention of this chapter that signs are now visible marking the end of this phase and that the discipline will soon be seen from a new perspective.

Three major perspectives have marked the writing of American church history. It is not proper to designate various

1

efforts prior to Robert Baird as histories of religion in America. His work marks the beginning of the effort to sketch out the nature and the development of the Christian community in America.[1] The perspective he employed held sway in modified form from the 1840's to the 1920's. Baird attempted to sketch out the history of religion in America in order to make sense of its peculiarities and role in American culture for European readers.[2] He laid a solid foundation for all future religious histories of America, and he worked out of a perspective that was to dominate church historiography for almost a century.

It is interesting to note that the primary title of his book reflected that perspective. He designated his book as religion in America, but the fact was that he wrote primarily about the various Christian groups. It was equally a fact that there was very little else in America to write about at that time. Baird wrote from the perspective of a Puritan-Pietist tradition that completely dominated the United States. Nevertheless, he did not engage only in chronicle. He developed a very useful typology of the denominations, and he clearly designated a central motif that determined the history of all Christian groups in America.

His typology was derived from the Puritan-Pietist ethos. All religious bodies were divided into two major groups — the evangelical churches and the non-evangelical. The former were those denominations that held the basic Christian doctrines of the Trinity and salvation through Christ alone by faith. Robert Baird had definite ideas about these basic Christian doctrines, and he thought some groups held them more clearly than others. In fact, Roman Catholicism could not be clearly designated as evangelical because it distorted, through bad practice, the true Christian doctrines it held. Catholicism was a special category.[3]

[1] Baird, *Religion in America; or an Account of the Origin, Relation to the State, and Present Conditions of the Evangelical Churches in the United States with Notices of the Unevangelical Denominations* (New York: Harper & Brothers, 1856). The book first appeared in Scotland in 1843 and was later published in the United States in 1844.
[2] *Ibid.*, pp. vff.   [3] *Ibid.*, p. 540.

On the other hand, those groups such as the Unitarians, Universalists, Swedenborgians, Jews, Deists, Atheists, and Socialists were classified as unevangelical religious groups. In short, for Baird, they were not Christian because they did not hold the basic evangelical doctrines. In this sense he felt justified in calling his book *Religion in America* rather than "Christianity in America." He admitted that some of these bodies started as Christian and still held Christian doctrines, but he charged that they failed to hold the basic Christian doctrines. They were, at best, distortions of Christianity and so part of the religious development in America.

This attempt at typology deserves credit from all historians interested in American culture. The first history of religion in America remains one of the very best because of its originality, insights, and comprehensiveness. Equally original and provocative was Baird's selection of voluntaryism as the central motif marking religion in America. It was the consequence of the separation of church and state, which threw all religious groups onto their own resources of persuasion and self-support. Baird correctly noted that this differentiated, in nature and role, religion in America from religion in Europe.[4] Through it he accounted for many unique features of American religion, particularly its activism. Also, he saw the revival system as especially related to and important for voluntaryism. Thus Baird provided the basic perspective from which the history of religion was viewed by scholars in America until the 1920's.

Two other men in this period must be mentioned. One, Philip Schaff, was the leading historian of Christianity working in America. A German by training, he delighted at the church life he found in America and wrote an eloquent and perceptive analysis in his book *America*.[5] Schaff agreed with Baird's two major assumptions concerning the centrality of

[4] *Ibid.*, pp. 78ff., 262ff.

[5] Schaff, *America: A Sketch of the Political, Social, and Religious Character of the United States of North America, in Two Lectures, Delivered at Berlin with a Report Read before the German Diet at Frankfurt-am-Main, September 1854* (New York: Charles Scribner, 1855).

voluntaryism and the continuity that extended through the spectrum of evangelical churches in America. By the 1890's, it was clear that detailed denominational histories had to be written in order to gather together source materials of the denominations and to demonstrate how each of them was integrally related to American culture. The American Society of Church History was founded in 1888, and its first major project was the writing in thirteen volumes, of the histories of the principal denominations in America, including a summary volume by Leonard W. Bacon. Schaff served as the general editor. The entire series operated with the perspective developed by Baird and embraced by Schaff.[6]

In 1888 there appeared Daniel Dorchester's *Christianity in the United States*, a massive volume of almost eight hundred pages.[7] He quite self-consciously built on Baird but sought to document fully the consequences of the voluntary system for church life and for American society. The result was a full accounting of missions, morals, reform efforts, education, and revivals. All this was tied together by a running account that employed Baird's threefold division of "Protestantism, Romanism, and Divergent Elements."[8] This was not a scholarly church history comparable to those produced under the editorship of Schaff; it was a filial labor of love by an ardent champion of evangelical Christianity. It was the primary example of what critics called the "scissors and paste" approach that marked this epoch. What Baird and Schaff developed as a stimulating perspective in the hands of creative and skilled historians provided only a handy framework for men who could not rise beyond chronicle to history. Much useful material was gathered, and a beginning was made in an attempt to relate religion to American culture, but the original insights of Baird were not developed imaginatively by his successors.

It was not until the 1920's that a major shift in perspective

[6] Schaff *et al*, eds., *The American Church History Series*, 13 vols. (New York: The Christian Literature Co., 1893–97).
[7] *Christianity in the United States from the First Settlement Down to the Present Time* (New York: Phillips & Hunt, 1888).
[8] *Ibid.*, p. 4.

developed and provided the second way of looking at the development of Christianity in America. This perspective prevailed for approximately thirty years and considerably improved the discipline of American church history. In fact, it marked the founding of the discipline itself, which did not quite develop in spite of Philip Schaff's valiant efforts. In the early 1920's, Henry K. Rowe published a short survey, *The History of Religion in the United States*. The book had a single theme, through which he attempted to sketch out religious developments in America.[9] That theme was the birth, development, and triumph of the principle of freedom in American religious history. This was neither a profound nor scholarly history: it was, rather, a popular apologia for what "mainstream" churches in America had become. It marked a new attempt at an overall generalization concerning religion in America.

Far more serious and of much greater consequence was the effort of Peter G. Mode at the University of Chicago Divinity School. In his brief tenure he produced two major works, which were fundamental in shaping a new perspective for the study of religion in America. His sourcebook, published in 1921, was the first serious effort to prepare a critical bibliographical work on American church history and laid the groundwork for the development of a new discipline in American theological institutions.[10] His successor, William Warren Sweet, built directly on that beginning. Henceforth, all serious study of American church history would be undertaken with the same method and rigor as that pursued in the best history departments in the country.

Of equal, if not greater importance, was Mode's provoca-

[9] Rowe, *The History of Religion in the United States* (New York: The Macmillan Company, 1924). Not to be overlooked is Thomas C. Hall, *The Religious Background of American Culture* (1930; reprinted, New York: Frederick Unger, 1959). This develops a different interpretation of the genius of American religion, and locates it in "Anglo-Saxon dissent" of late medieval England.

[10] Mode, *Source Book and Bibliographical Guide for American Church History* (Menasha, Wis.: George Banta Publishing Company, 1921).

tive book on the impact of the frontier on the development of religion in America.[11] As a member of the Chicago school of environmental historians, Mode was anxious to demonstrate how the American environment had shaped and changed Christianity in America. He readily adopted Frederick Jackson Turner's frontier hypothesis and applied it literally to the religious institutions in America. The results were provocative and stimulating. Unfortunately, Mode never had the opportunity of refining and developing in detail some of the insights he first sketched out in that highly original little book. He did, however, provide church historians and historians of religion and culture in America with a new perspective that proved as important as that provided earlier by Robert Baird.

It was William Warren Sweet, Mode's successor, who proved to be the leading historian who helped to shape the new perspective and who wrote out of it. A student of McMaster, he also adopted, in part, the Turner frontier hypothesis. In a masterful analysis of Sweet, Sidney E. Mead pointed out the incongruity of Sweet's combining McMaster and Turner.[12] At the same time Mead indicated how it was possible for Sweet to get away with it. For sheer output of books and monographs on American church history, Sweet was unsurpassed. All historians of American church history and life are in his debt for his superb surveys, topical histories, and collection of sources. Sweet set out to prove that the study of religion was absolutely necessary to understand American culture and it was necessary for churches to understand American history to interpret themselves.[13] He proved both points.

As is so often the case in the writing of history, it is at the very moment when a particular perspective is at the height of its productivity that it most fully documents its short-

[11] *The Frontier Spirit in American Christianity* (New York: The Macmillan Company, 1923).

[12] Mead, "Professor Sweet's Religion and Culture in America; a Review Article," *Church History*, 22 (March, 1953): 35.

[13] Sweet, "Every Dog Has His Day and I've Had Mine," *Divinity School News* (July, 1946), p. 6.

comings. Sweet rewrote American church history both in bulk and in interpretation. In the tradition of Baird and Schaff, he insisted that Christianity in America could not be judged by Old-World criteria. Unlike the two earlier historians, he sought to spell out in detail exactly what this meant. To do so he employed the frontier hypothesis, which enabled him to move beyond earlier generalizations. But this did not provide the main body of his work; what did, was the meticulous gathering of information and sources, "facts" in the McMaster tradition, combined largely with a chronological framework.

Sweet sought to explain why a form of Protestantism that barely existed in Europe came to dominate the American scene.[14] The frontier hypothesis, employed in its boldest form, enabled him to sketch the triumph of the "methodistic" type in American religion and culture. This was the predominant type of white Anglo-Saxon Protestantism up through the years of Sweet's writing and research.

Two consequences arose from this. First, this perspective held full sway among the American church historians throughout the twenties, thirties, and forties. It is even reflected in the encyclopedic work of Kenneth Scott Latourette, whether applied to his history of the American scene or to his analysis of the "great century" in missions, an Anglo-Saxon century.[15] This view was confirmed in the histories of Luther Weigle and Williard Sperry,[16] and it reflected itself in modified form in the work of Robert Hastings Nichols. It was even more evident in the writing of "secular" historians dealing with religion in America. Sweet's work set the pace for all.

Secondly, Sweet's reading of the American scene accounted

[14] Sweet, "The Frontier in American Christianity," *Environmental Factors in Christian History*, ed. John T. McNeill *et al* (Chicago: Univ. of Chicago Press, 1939), pp. 390–91.

[15] Latourette, *A History of the Expansion of Christianity* (New York: Harper & Brothers, 1941 and 1945), vols. 4 and 7.

[16] Weigle, *American Idealism* (New Haven: Yale Univ. Press, 1928); Sperry, *Religion in America* (New York: The Macmillan Company, 1946).

for the rise and triumph of the "methodistic" type, but it failed to establish a unifying thread or underlying theme, simple or complex, that made sense out of the history, role, and situation of all Christian groups in America, to say nothing of the various other religious bodies in American culture. The frontier could account for the triumph of one type, even a predominant type at the moment, but could it, in itself, account for the later success of groups such as the Roman Catholics or Lutherans? It could not. Nevertheless, Sweet forged the study of American church history into a responsible and respectable discipline of value both to theological schools and to history departments. He gathered a mountain of material for the use of future generations, and he risked an incongruous synthesis in the hopes of making both sense and clarity out of the American experience with Christianity.

Sweet's students and younger colleagues sounded the approach of a third and new perspective in the study of American church history. This perspective still dominates the writing of American church history, though there is ample evidence that a basic shift is underway. The Sweet legacy formed the basis for the emergence of the third perspective. Sweet shaped the central question that still dominates the discipline. What is unique about Christianity in America? His answer was not a radical break with Baird, but he asked the question more radically than Baird. As a result, Sweet broadened and deepened the answer to the question. He did not underplay or ignore religious liberty and voluntaryism, but he saw them, rather, as initial stages for the most important development in the American scene. The key to the uniqueness of religion in America was the triumph of the "methodistic" type made possible by the frontier; hence, the national period, 1789–1860, was the formative period in American church life.

A new generation of historians built upon Sweet but were dissatisfied with his explanation. They did not reject his question; they felt that his answer was not sufficiently profound nor adequate for the complexity of the situation. The basic unrest appears to have emerged simultaneously at two points. On the one hand, there was a feeling that Sweet totally overlooked the theological dimension, both in his method and in the content of the church history that he wrote. On the other hand, it was felt that he did not develop a sufficiently clear methodology to enable him to deal with the complexity of the answer to his question. A narrow interpretation of the frontier hypothesis combined with earlier generalizations on religious liberty and voluntaryism was not enough. The subtle interplay between geographical, psychological, economic, political, and theological forces was not sufficiently taken into account by Sweet. These two basic dissatisfactions were in no sense contradictory, and they appeared together, frequently in the same man.

The theological climate had changed, and so had the historical climate. Both changes affected the emergence of a new perspective in church history. Theology became deeply concerned about the uniqueness of revelation and the distance between religion and culture. It moved from a theology of culture to a theology of the Word. With it emerged a new concern for the church, an effort to redefine the nature of the Christian community and its role in society. This shift in theology had its effect on church historians. They became very much concerned about the concept of the church and the possibility of writing church history. Professor Sweet could not understand this concern and did not see what it had to do with writing American religious history. In fact, he looked upon the new mood as a European importation contrary to the genius of American developments.

A series of articles on methodology were written by church historians. Although they represented different points of view, all embodied a common question. What was the nature of church history? What was distinctive or unique about church history over against other historical disciplines? As early as 1946 James Hastings Nichols, of Chicago, addressed himself to this question and he was accompanied by his colleagues

9

Wilhelm Pauck and Sidney E. Mead.[17] Mead produced a series of provocative and brilliant essays on the nature of church history, and the theory he expounded soon found reflection in a series of superb and profound essays, which provided the turning point in the writing of American church history.

Sidney Mead sought a clear methodological base for his work and in so doing helped to develop a new perspective for the study of religion in America. He was concerned that the historian be conscious of the point of view from which he worked. One of his major criticisms of Sweet was that he thought his position was fairly objective but he in fact embodied a "Methodist" understanding of the church, religious life, and theology. This was reflected in Sweet's writings, which, in one sense, transcended a narrow denominationalism, but in another sense were an apologia for "methodistic" Christianity in America. Because this type of Christianity was predominant in America from the early nineteenth century to the mid-twentieth century, Sweet's work naturally appeared fairly objective. However, the more his history moved into the present century the more obvious became its inability to account for developments.

Because of Mead's acute sensitivity to the problem of perspective, he developed a point of view that was, for the first time in American religious studies, genuinely self-corrective. This led to a basic difference between Mead's interpretation of Christianity in America and that of his predecessors. Although he continued the quest for the uniqueness of Christianity in America, he was constrained to locate it in a very complex series of events and in a rich interplay between various forces. The result was the first genuinely sophisticated

[17] Nichols, "The Art of Church History," *Church History*, 20 (March, 1951); "Church History and Secular History," *Church History*, 13 (June, 1944); and "History in the Theological Curriculum," *Journal of Religion*, 26 (July, 1946). Mead, "The Task of the Church Historian," *The Chronicle*, 12 (July, 1949); Pauck, "The Idea of the Church in History," *Church History*, 21 (September, 1952).

analysis.[18] Mead did not eschew the sociohistorical approach of his predecessors, but he brought in a totally new dimension through his interest in the history of ideas.

In this respect Mead reflected not only the change in theological temper but equally the shift that had occurred in historical studies. The Turner frontier hypothesis was brought under stringent criticism, and it was modified at several important points. It was no longer to be seen purely as a geographical factor, and it was not to be understood as the unique formative force in the development of western democracy and so of American culture. Mead frequently quoted Benjamin F. Wright to the effect that "democracy did not come out of the American forest unless it was first carried there." [19]

Perhaps one of the most important developments in history at this time was the emergence of the history of ideas. Mead learned much from Alfred North Whitehead and from Arthur O. Lovejoy. It was Mead's synthesis of sociohistorical concerns with the fresh approach of the history of ideas that gave birth to the new perspective in American church history. Students of literature such as Perry Miller and F. O. Matheson demonstrated its richness in their studies of Puritanism and Transcendentalism in American culture. Mead was not satisfied with his mentor's almost exclusive concern with social forces, political institutions, and geographic environment. These were exceedingly important, but they were not enough.

Social forces and institutions live in, out of, and even create a matrix of ideas. The way people look at, feel about, and think over their institutions and society, determines in part what is done in and through that society. The inseparable relations between social forces and institutions and patterns of thought and belief provide the historian with his raw materials. Steam and democracy were the twin focuses of modern man, and under these rubrics much of American history could be written and understood. Thus Mead moved beyond the perspective of his predecessors.

[18] Mead, *The Lively Experiment, The Shaping of Christianity in America* (New York: Harper & Row, 1963).

[19] Mead, "Professor Sweet's Religion and Culture," p. 40.

There were four particular respects in which Sidney E. Mead moved beyond the perspective he inherited, and each of these reflects his effort to locate the genius of Christianity in America in a subtle interplay between ideas and the total social context. Perhaps one of his basic contributions was his definition of the church in the American context.[20] This has become a point of departure for most historians of American religious life. Mead was unwilling to settle for the implicit "methodistic" assumptions of Sweet concerning the church, and he did not find Baird's or Schaff's evangelical definition sufficient. The form the church took in America developed from European antecedents but became something quite unique in Christian history, the forerunner of the condition of the church everywhere in the modern world.

The denomination was a new organizational form of the church that developed in America. It was not theologically confessional nor territorial, as the church in Europe. Denominations were not like European sects, cut off from official churches, illegal or at best tolerated under the law, and at war with the culture of their day. All of these groups came to America, but none of them triumphed. Something new emerged, which built on many traditions and forged new ones. Religious liberty and the frontier provided the context in which the denomination came into being. Also there was a matix of ideas that dominated that context during the period of the origin and growth of the denomination. Out of this developed the denomination, "a voluntary association of like-hearted and like-minded individuals, who are united on the basis of common beliefs for the purpose of accomplishing tangible and defined objectives."[21]

Mead noted six characteristics which together mark, and help one to understand, the nature of the church in America as denomination. It is to be noted that these are not unknown in other Christian history, but they represent a unique constellation in the American scene. First is the element of historylessness or primitivism. Second is the centrality of vol-

[20] Mead, *The Lively Experiment*, pp. 103ff.
[21] *Ibid.*, p. 104.

12

untaryism, which accentuates the push for tangible goals and upgrades the role of laity and the constant search for consent. Third is the missionary outreach, the impulse to expand and grow or to die. Revivalism is a fourth mark of the denomination, which provided a technique for growth and shaped patterns of thought and action. Fifth is an anti-intellectualism based on the triumph of pietism and an avowed opposition to the Enlightenment, particularly its French variety. Finally, there is the spirit of competition, which works alongside a mitigating spirit of cooperation.

It is clear that Mead's concern was to develop a new understanding of the nature of the church in America that would enable historians better to understand its origins, development, and uniqueness. In short, it would enable them to write better history. Even a brief glance at all the post-Sweet survey histories of religion in America and many of the monographs reveals how profoundly this concept has influenced all such historical writing. Furthermore, such a concern demonstrates how Mead combined the socio-historical approach and that of the history of ideas (including theology), to move into the new perspective.

A second major contribution of Mead was his redefinition of the frontier. This was accomplished in several ways. In the definition of the denomination, he saw the European church and sect types thrust into the American frontier situation, where there was a "widespread reversion to primitivism." [22] Some of this was already present in the sects, some was forced on all groups by the situation. The emergence of the denomination he sees, in fact, as the rebuilding of the church in its new form, incorporating many new elements. This rebuilding Mead envisions as a continuing process.

Perhaps of greater significance was his redefinition of what frontier meant in terms of time and space.[23] He thus moved in a totally new direction from Mode and Sweet in assessing the impact of the frontier and in making possible a continuous application of that insight even to the present. Frontier meant

[22] *Ibid.*, p. 200.
[23] *Ibid.*, pp. 1ff.

that Americans never had time to spare, but they appeared to have infinite space. This shaped their character and institutions far more profoundly than the primitive conditions of the forests. Employing the frontier concept in this fashion leads to quite different conclusions from those advanced by Mode and Sweet on the basis of an unrevised Turner view. When frontier is understood primarily as the impact of limitless space and press for time, its psychological and spiritual consequences have to be carefully evaluated.

A third major difference from the perspective of the Sweet generation as well as from the Baird-Schaff generation, is supplied by Mead's much broader and more complex analysis of voluntaryism.[24] Again, his concern to interrelate the socio-historical environment with the complex flow of ideas is demonstrated. Previous historians were content to indicate how that principle differentiated American churches from all others and how it resulted in the many missionary, reform, and humanitarian activities of the churches. They did not seek to understand what this did to the concept and the nature of the church, the role of the clergy and of the laity, the place, content, and method of theologizing, and the way Christianity was related to culture. These were the issues in which Mead was interested as he analyzed the nature and consequence of voluntaryism. Earlier historians assumed voluntaryism's essential goodness and traced its achievements. Mead was not primarily interested in its goodness or its career. He was concerned with its nature and its consequences for the shape of Christianity in America. Others could trace out its history and development, and those who have done so show a decided dependence on Mead's analysis of voluntaryism.

A fourth point where Mead moved beyond his predecessors and contributed to the emergence of a new perspective was in his analysis of the Enlightenment in relation to Christianity in America.[25] Historians from Baird to Rowe, Mode, and Sweet tended to view the Enlightenment as a dangerous foe of the Christian religion in America. They assigned it only a

[24] *Ibid.*, pp. 96ff., 113ff.
[25] *Ibid.*, pp. 16ff.

negative role. The immediate predecessors of Mead assigned it a positive role but only insofar as it helped establish religious liberty in America or constitutional government. Mead built on this positive appreciation but went much further. He saw the Enlightenment as the only genuine intellectual tradition in America during its formative period. Mead states that the revolutionary epoch "is the hinge upon which the history of Christianity in America really turns." During this period rationalist philosophy and pietist Christianity found a common theological base from which they could cooperate in bringing about religious liberty against the wishes of traditionalist Christians. When disestablishment came, the alliance broke, and the combined Christian forces turned against the rationalists. This led to a schizophrenia in American religion and culture that has not been healed to this day, argues Mead. This he designated one of the taproots of American anti-intellectualism, and he assessed its consequences for American life. This insight of Mead has led to a reassessment of the relation of Christianity to the Enlightenment, but his basic generalization remains to be tested.

Most present-day historians of Christianity in America remain within the third perspective and exhibit a similar set of concerns to those of Sidney E. Mead. Each man does his work in his own unique way, but each operates within that perspective or is just beginning the search to move beyond it. Winthrop S. Hudson wrote two superb surveys of religion in America, in which he fully demonstrated the new perspective.[26] He too sought to develop the uniqueness of religion in America through a contextual approach that combined sociohistorical elements with the history of ideas. He shares the concept of the church as denomination, holds a more sophisticated view of the impact of the frontier, and generally views the entire development of religion in America integrally within American history. He is concerned with the interplay

[26] Hudson, *American Protestantism* (Chicago: University of Chicago Press, 1961), and *Religion in America: An Historical Account of the Development of American Religious Life* (New York: Charles Scribner's Sons, 1965).

of forces that moved the nation from a situation of Protestant domination to one of religious pluralism. Recently, Hudson has expressed reservations about the adequacy of the perspective that has prevailed through his generation of historians. He is now concerned to stress the continuity between religious life in Europe, particularly in England, and that in America.[27] It is clear to him that greater emphasis will have to be placed on this interdependence if an adequate history of religion in American is to be written.

The classic embodiment of the contemporary perspective is found in the two-volume work by H. Shelton Smith, Robert T. Handy, and Lefferts A. Loetscher, *American Christianity: An Historical Interpretation with Representative Documents*.[28] It is a thoroughly unified presentation of the development of Christianity in America from its beginning through 1960. It is comprehensive in its concern, contextual in its execution. Carefully interwoven are social, economic, political, religious and theological elements. No simple generalization underlies the work, but it incorporates that series of generalizations commonplace and basic to contemporary church historians. Its heart is the interplay between history of ideas and the complexity of a broadly defined environment.

It broke fresh ground in its periodization, seeking to find the dividing point from within the Christian movement in America rather than from the political watersheds in American life. This effort probably will not stamp future surveys of religion in America, but it was fully defensible in the light of the method and materials employed. Also, it was a refreshing breakaway from the stylized periodization that had prevailed so long. Aside from that particular attempt, however, the solid historical achievement of *American Christianity* epitomizes the perspective of this generation rather than embodies the first efforts for a new perspective. Its superb bibliography and excellent selection of sources will make it indispensable for years to come.

Several efforts by contemporary church historians docu-

[27] In this volume see chap. 6.
[28] New York: Charles Scribner's Sons, 1960–63.

ment the growing dissatisfaction with the prevailing perspective. Although none of them appear to have broken radically with the dominant perspective, they have evidenced sufficient unrest to move in new directions that might lead to the emergence of a new perspective. Sidney E. Ahlstrom exhibits particular concern with the development of theology in the American scene, but he does this in such a way as to lead one to a reassessment of the nature of religion in America. Reading his work, one is struck with the fact that Christianity in America has not been quite so anti-intellectual as has been frequently asserted.[29]

Ahlstrom reminds historians that they have frequently looked in the wrong places for evidence of theologizing in America and have often defined theology in too narrow a fashion. He makes these generalizations to establish his point, and he succeeds. The first mark of the American theological tradition is its diversity, which makes it virtually impossible to speak of an American theology; however, a good deal of theologizing was constantly taking place. Second, theology in America is derivative, unlike European theological traditions. Third, the first quarter of the nineteenth century is the watershed in the flow of various influences in American theology. Around these three themes Ahlstrom proceeds to sketch out the development of theology in America. His work calls for a reconsideration of one major generalization in American church history.

Another young historian working out of the present perspective but also calling for a reconsideration is Martin E. Marty.[30] He notes that church history is in the same kind of

[29] Ahlstrom, "Theology in America: A Historical Survey," *Religion in American Life, The Shaping of American Religion* ed. James Ward Smith and A. Leland Jamison (Princeton: Princeton Univ. Press, 1961), 1:234.

[30] In this volume see chap. 8. Not to be overlooked in the efforts at reconstruction are Edwin Scott Gaustad, *Historical Atlas of Religion in America* (New York: Harper & Row, 1962) and *A Religious History of America* (New York: Harper & Row, 1966), a survey history in the grand style, building on predecessors but moving beyond them in scope. In addition see Clifton E. Olmstead, *History of Religion in the United*

crisis as is all historical study, in fact, all humanistic studies. This is understandable because it is, in one sense, strictly a humanistic discipline. Nevertheless, he argues that it has the same kind of potential for contribution to theological study as history has for the humanities. He quotes with approval R. W. B. Lewis on the importance of having someone in scholarship prepared at particular times in history to look "backward with compensatory vigor."

Marty is interested in far more than that. Although he sees church history as part of historical studies in humanities as well as in a theological faculty, he notes several signs that point to a crisis in the discipline. Out of this crisis in the role of church history and its significance for study both secular and theological, he notes several new themes of reinterpretation emerging. One he designates as the move away from the pattern of interpretation stressing innocency. He interprets that in part as a preoccupation with the uniquely American and in part as an antihistorical bias in favor of simple, obvious explanations. In either case there is a distaste for the complex and a preference for the simple. He sees this as now passing. In fact, it passed shortly after Sweet concluded his work. A second new emphasis he designated as the attempt to move out of the isolation of American religious history and to locate it fully within a larger community such as the Atlantic community. Marty notes that this has not been overlooked, it simply has never been taken seriously. Marty is looking for a new and serious attempt to take "transverse sections of history in as many directions as possible." So he quotes Burckhardt.[31]

Finally, Marty argues that a new generalization might become the focal point for a fresh perspective on religious history in America. That theme is industrialization, and it ought to be seen as "an ecumenical event in the Western world," and a main theme in writing American religious history.[32] This will force historians to move beyond the perspectives of inno-

---

States (Englewood Cliffs, N.J.: Prentice-Hall, 1960), which does not break any fresh ground but builds well on the surveys that preceded it.

[31] In this volume see p. 211.

[32] *Ibid.*,

cence and isolation. The process of secularization could then be properly analyzed and understood. It too would be viewed as part of the grand theme of the modern western world. The study of church history would be closely related to the work of all historians, and what would differentiate the church historian would be his interest in the impact of industrialization on the Western Christian community. It is quite proper for a church historian to be working on only a part of that community, such as the American, but to understand it properly it will have to be seen in a wider community such as the Atlantic.

It is evident that a number of young historians are anxious to develop a new perspective through which to view the development and nature of Christianity in America. Both they and the discipline in which they work face a common problem, which appears to have no present answer. The partial answer will determine the future of American church history as a discipline. That answer will, as always, be only partial and temporary, but it will be sufficient to maintain the integrity and the momentum of the discipline. The question involves the uniqueness of American church history and, more broadly, the autonomy of all church history. Wherein does the study of American church history differ in method and content from the study of the history of American culture?

If there is something distinctive and unique about it, then it deserves to continue in a theological or religious curriculum. If it represents only a difference in focus on subject matter, it probably ought to be part of the history department. If most of the writing on church history subjects is now being done in history departments, why bother with departments of church history? Perhaps church historians should admit that they are like all other historians, save in one respect — they study religious institutions and ideas rather than political, social, or economic institutions and ideas. Historians of the Christian church must be concerned about the same complex interplay of forces and movements in culture and in society as are any other historians. The church historian simply focuses on this subtle interplay in relation to the Christian church.

If that is true, then it is hardly necessary to have departments of church history. An independent department of church history probably would be isolated from the rich context of a full history department within the social sciences or humanistic disciplines. If the church historian concentrates on a dimension of human experience not covered by fellow historians, and if this concentration plays a particular role in relation to theology as well as to history, then the church historian has a reason for existence. The problem is the particular dimension of human experience with which the church historian functions. The church as an institution is no different from any other institution in society. It may make special claims about its uniqueness; so do all other institutions. The history and role of the church as an institution is as open to the research of general historians as it is to church historians.

The assumptions on which the church historian used to function are no longer valid. His discipline developed at a time when it was a commonly held assumption that the church was a unique institution grounded in the supernatural and fulfilling a transcendent will in history. The church had a special role in society, and so it had a special history. The history of the church, though in and of history, was not like the history of any other institution; therefore, a special kind of historian was concerned about that history. There was sacred history and secular history, which, though intertwined and closely related, were clearly distinguishable.

No such distinction is any longer possible. This raises serious questions about the function of the church historian. Leonard J. Trinterud saw this problem with painful clarity but offered no solution.[33] He made it clear that church history could be written only of the Church Catholic. He defined the church as redemption through Christ in the circumstances of historical existence. This redemption expresses itself through institutional forms but is never confined to them. The church

[33] Trinterud, "The Task of the American Church Historian," *Church History*, 25 (March, 1956): 3.

historian assumes that the church exists as a community of people redeemed by God in history through Jesus Christ, argues Trinterud. Without that assumption there would be no church history, only the history of Christianity.

The problem is that the church historian ends by writing a history of Christianity that looks no different from that of historians who do not hold such an assumption about the church. Supposedly that controlling assumption should make his history look different, but does it? Finally, Trinterud rests his case in the fact that readers carry their own set of assumptions, and some of them will read church history where others do not.[34] That may be, but it does not make the slightest difference for the man writing the history. In short, Trinterud has made a case for historians of Christianity or for any historian writing about the churches or religion, but he has not made a case for the church historian.

Perhaps the day of the church historian, as he was long known, is now past, and we can speak only of historians of Christian religion. At this point the church historian becomes a particular kind of historian — a historian of religion, of the Christian religion in Europe or in America. Even this answer is too neat, and in a sense, is not an answer. What defines the historian of religions over against other historians? Does he operate with a content that is not handled by historians of political, social, or economic institutions, or by historians of culture? The historian of religion does, in fact, concentrate on a content quite different from other historians. He is not concerned simply with another institution, the church.

A historian of religion is concerned with the content, form, expression, and history of religion.[35] To do this he must have a method adequate to analyze and understand his subject matter. History of religions has developed a high degree of self-consciousness concerning its method and has moved far

[34] *Ibid.*, p. 13.
[35] Mircea Eliade, "Methodological Remarks on the Study of Religious Symbolism," in *The History of Religions, Essays in Methodology,* ed. Mircea Eliade and Joseph Kitagawa (Chicago: Univ. of Chicago Press, 1959), pp. 95, 97.

ahead in an effort to distinguish itself from other disciplines. Surprisingly little of this scholarship has been taken seriously by church historians. In the past, they could afford to ignore the research and methodological discussions in history of religions. That day is gone. Either the essential tasks of church historians can be done by regular historians or those essential tasks must be demonstrated as beyond the concern or the present competence of regular historians. An American historian is frequently interested in the history of the churches in American culture, and an occasional American historian is interested in the development of Christian thought in America. Such historians have not been trained and do not appear interested in analyzing the religious symbolism encountered in religion in America in order to understand the structure of the religious experience embodied.

The historian of religion is interested primarily in religious phenomena.[36] To be sure, he employs an empirical method similar to other historians, but both in his subject matter and in what he does with the results of his research, he differs from the historian of institutions or ideas. Because the historian of religions is concerned with the phenomenon of religion, he must first establish the possibility and reality of his subject matter.[37] That sounds strange, for what other historian must first demonstrate the reality and the shape of history before he pursues research in it? Religion offers a special problem. It is perhaps the only discipline constantly under threat of losing its subject matter.

The threat arises from two sides. On the one side are those who argue that religion as such really does not exist. It is perhaps a human projection of wishes or frustrations, the consequence of superstition, or camouflage for economic interests. If this is true, the study of religion is not worth the time or effort. At best, it should be detailed only in order to warn man of what he should not fall into. On the other side are

[36] G. Van der Leeuw, *Religion in Essence and Manifestation: A Study in Phenomenology* (New York: Harper & Row, 1963), 2:679ff.

[37] Joachim Wach, *The Comparative Study of Religions*, ed. Joseph M. Kitagawa (New York: Columbia University Press, 1958), pp. 9ff.

those who also feel that there is no religious phenomenon itself, but that what is called religion has its basis in a psychological, economic, or social dimension of the nature of man. It is very important to study religion in order fully to understand man; however, the proper way to study religion is through a discipline such as psychology, economics, sociology, or anthropology. In both cases there is no task for a historian of religion.

Thus the historian of religion constantly faces the task of defining the nature of religion and in that very process establishes, in part, his own discipline. He must demonstrate that there is a phenomenon, religion, that cannot be reduced to something psychological, social, or linguistic or to that which is a combination of all three.[38] The historian of religion is involved in both a normative and a descriptive task, which involves the results and materials from research in many disciplines, but he has a distinctive content and procedure of his own. The center of his work is concerned with religious experience, its reality, its content, its forms, and its history. No other historian is concerned precisely or primarily with that.

If the reality of the church as an institution no longer provides the church historian with a preserve immune from the poaching of fellow historians, research as a historian of religions does. If his concern is primarily with an institution taken for granted because of its historical existence, or primarily with abstract ideas in their historical continuity, then such a scholar might well be better off in a history department. He differs not a bit from those fellow historians, and he has nothing distinctive to offer. If the erstwhile church historian sees his essential task as the search to understand the nature of that religious experience called Christianity then he has a special task. His interest in the history of the church is not primarily institutional.

Religious experience, to be analyzed and understood, must be studied through the forms through which it expresses

[38] Eliade, "Methodological Remarks," p. 88.

itself. It does this uniquely through religious symbols.[39] These symbols are encountered in cultic rites, in thought patterns, in action, and in associational or institutional forms.[40] So the historian of religion investigates all of these in their historic expressions and development in order to understand that particular religious experience which is Christianity.

It is dubious whether church historians can or ought to become historians of religion in the full sense. That is, they can become self-conscious historians of one religion, Christianity, self-critically aware of the methods and concerns of the history of religions. A careful study of that discipline will reveal unique perspectives on the history of Christianity. It is amazing that church historians have not allied themselves with history of religions. There is a twofold explanation for their failure. First, they did not have to because they possessed a virtual monopoly on their discipline and were accepted uncritically. Second, at the very moment their discipline was being absorbed, the theological climate which might have provided resources for redefinition had no such resources and, in addition, sought to undercut history of religions. Dialectical theology drove a sharp wedge between God and the historical process, and it rejected the concept and the reality of religion. There was no such thing as religion, there was only Christian faith.

Both the theological and cultural climate have changed. The time is ripe for a reappraisal of the nature and the task of the church historian. To apply this to the present situation of the American church historian would demonstrate certain possibilities. It is clear that the historian of American religion is searching for a new perspective. Thus far, most of the evidence pointing toward a new perspective does not appear to establish anything unique or unusual for the historian of religion in America. He will be primarily another historian studying American culture and institutions but from a somewhat broader perspective than that presently employed. That

[39] *Ibid.*, p. 89.
[40] Joachim Wach, *Comparative Study*, pp. 59–143.

is not bad, but it means he is no longer a church historian nor a historian of religion in America.

If the perspective of history of religions were consciously adopted by historians of religion in America, would it make any difference? It would make a profound difference leading to a radical shift in perspective, which would usher in a new form of American religious history. A brief look at revivalism will demonstrate some of the possibilities. Revivalism has been one of the central themes in all histories of Christianity in America, notably those of Baird, Sweet, Mead, Hudson, Gaustad, Ahlstrom, and Marty and the classic new source history of Smith, Handy, and Loetscher. Numerous books on revivalism in America have been written.[41] Many of these studies are excellent, and some of the best have been written by general historians.

Is there no other way of analyzing the nature, role, and history of revivalism in America that would provide fresh insight both into revivalism and into the nature of the religious experience in America? There is, and studies in the history of religions provide the resources. One would ask the historian to begin his analysis of revivalism in terms of religious symbolism. To my knowledge, this has never been done. It would have to be done with great care and in such a way that the primary goal would be to understand the nature of the religious experience encountered through revivalism.

Revivalism was many things, but as one investigates the symbols encountered in it, several things become clear. It was a rite of initiation comparable to rites of initiation in other religions. Mircea Eliade says that initiation "denotes a body of rites and oral teachings whose purpose is to produce a decisive alteration in the religious and social status of the person to be initiated."[42] It also has the consequence of a profound existential change in an individual; he comes out

[41] An indispensable bibliography on revivalism is presented in Nelson R. Burr's *A Critical Bibliography of Religion in America* in *Religion in American Life*, ed. J. Smith and A. L. Jamison (Princeton: Princeton Univ. Press, 1961), 4:117–84, 677–91.

[42] Eliade, *Birth and Rebirth: The Religious Meanings of Initiation in Human Culture* (New York: Harper & Brothers, 1958), p. x.

a changed person, a new being.[43] Those who have not passed through the rites cannot attain this new state of being. Even a cursory study of revivalism indicates that it functioned as a rite of initiation in the American scene, particularly on the frontier.

There are many accounts from which one could select a description of the process of a revival. One of the fullest accounts is that of James Smith concerning the early work in the Cumberland Presbyterian revivals. He writes:

> Some were under the first awakenings on account of sin; and others were earnestly engaged in struggling for deliverance: in this state they continued all night. On Monday morning a glorious resurrection began to take place among the spiritually dead; for a considerable time praises and thanksgivings for the conversion of some newborn soul were heard almost every minute, until they became incessant: finally the whole congregation was filled with joy and gladness. Neighbors and friends, parents and children, brothers and sisters, were locked in each other's arms, praising God for redemption through the blood of the Lamb. Those who previously were bitter enemies now cordially embraced each other in the bonds of peace.[44]

Several things are absolutely clear. The revival appears as a rite of initiation. This was a ritual process that seldom varied in substance. The object was to put people through a particular kind of experience, one could call it a trial or test, in order that they might emerge as reborn or new. First, the person had to be convicted of sin in a profound way. He had to experience sin at such depth that he was ritually dead. Revival literature is replete with references to this fact. More often than not, on the frontier, this experience of death had a physical character to it. The person struck with

[43] Ibid., p. xiii.

[44] Smith, *History of the Christian Church From Its Origin to the Present Time . . . Including a History of the Cumberland Presbyterian Church* (Nashville: The Cumberland Presbyterian Office, 1835), pp. 8–9.

a deep personal sense of sin frequently went into a deathlike trance, or into utter physical stillness; some became rigid as in rigor mortis, while still others could do nothing but moan incoherently. Others were stricken with trembling, shrieking, violent physical leaping — all actions negating their usual life, as they departed their bodies, or were wholly possessed by evil.

It is clear that the believer first had to die to self, to be ritually dead after passing through fearful physical experiences. This death of self was followed by a "glorious resurrection among the spiritually dead." There is no doubt that this was a passage through death into life. The believer had a new perception of reality, of the cosmos and his place in it. He stood in an utterly new relation to the center of the universe and thus in a new understanding of his self and his fellow human beings. He moved from one sphere of life to a new sphere. He had been grasped by the holy, drawn into the sphere of the sacred; henceforth, he was a new man. He had been renewed, restored to a new beginning, a new life. There were very tangible consequences of the new life. There was not only a new view of life, of the self, there was also a new code of conduct, a new way of talking and acting, a belonging to a new society of believers and belonging to the old society in a new way.

Eliade also pointed out that initiation is a historical fact that is related to the structure of a particular society and its history.[45] It does not occur in a vacuum. Any initiation rite is both historical and transhistorical, and so it is with revivalism. It should be closely examined in the American context so that its particular historical expression and its transhistorical reality can be noted. This pays attention to the uniqueness of revivalism in the American scene, the special role it played and the particular forms it took. At the same time attention will be payed to its metacultural dimension. It is to be seen in relation to other rites of initiation and other patterns of revivalism. In this way the true nature of

[45] *Birth and Rebirth*, p. 130.

27

religious experience in America can be more clearly and accurately delineated.

This also provides the historian with a new perspective on revivalism. Was it by mistake that revivalism, though present in all areas of America, developed special forms and played a unique role in frontier communities? It would be worth investigating whether revivalism on the frontier was the special form of initiation into frontier society. It was not only a rebirth of the individual, it was also induction into the newly emerging stable form of social life on the frontier. A host of similar possible questions are posed by this approach. For example, did revivalism become the institution par excellence which embodied the process of *renovatio*? This was one of the distinctive motifs in the founding of America, and it became one of America's most persistent characteristics. What of the centrality of certain symbols in revivalism — hell, rebirth, sacrifice, and the millennium? What content did these have, and what role did they play? How did they, in particular, relate to the total American cultural and social milieu?

This brief analysis indicates some of the possibilities inherent in employing an approach from the history of religions to study the history of Christianity or of religion in America. A fourth perspective is just beginning to emerge among church historians of the American religious experience. It would be more accurate to call them historians of Christianity in America and to invite them to a careful study of the methods and findings of history of religions. It will provide them with a new perspective and an opportunity to function again as historians carrying out a special task, and in so doing will relate them even more closely to fellow historians. At the same time it will place historians of Christianity in a new dialogue with psychology, anthropology, and other social sciences. Above all, it will relate them to historians of religion.

2

The Genius of Jonathan Edwards
WILLIAM S. MORRIS

"Though his principles were *Calvinistic,* yet he called no man Father. He thought and judged for himself, and was truly very much of an original,"[1] wrote Hopkins of Edwards. But in what lay Edwards' originality? That question has received varied and contradictory answers. Lockean empiricism and scholastic logic have both been suggested as determining factors of his thought. His genius lay in a combination of both. He mediated between a philosophical and theological heritage which he treasured and a contemporary mentality which, critically, he shared. To exhibit this we shall set forth his early training and reading; exhibit his major conceptions, their origin and use; show the methods of reasoning and argumentation he employed; and, finally, evaluate the significance of his thought for his time and ours.

Early Training and Reading

In his second year at Yale, when fourteen, Edwards read Locke's *Essay* "with much delight." More than "the most greedy miser," he took "handfuls of silver and gold from some newly discovered treasure."[2] But a prior love remained, with influence: "the old logic" with which he used to be "mightily pleased."[3] This is the logic of Burgersdycke and Heereboord,

---

[1] S. Hopkins, "Memoirs" in vol. 1 of *The Works of Edwards*, 8 vols. (Worcester, Mass.: Thomas, 1850), p. 50.

[2] *Ibid.,* p. 12.

[3] H. G. Townsend, ed., *The Philosophy of Jonathan Edwards* (Eugene, Ore.: The University Press, 1955), p. 33: "One reason why, at first, before I knew other logic, I used to be mightily pleased with the study of the old logic was because it was very pleasant to see my thoughts, that

Dutch Calvinist Suaresian Aristotelian late scholastic logicians and metaphysicians. Part of Harvard's staple diet in 1701, when Yale was founded, it was still required reading as late as 1723. Most probably earlier, through his father, distinguished Harvard graduate and tutor of Edwards and other pre-college students, but certainly in his first year at Yale, Edwards gave intensive study to these logicians. Yale statutory provisions, signed by all students, required their

> beginning logick in ye morning att ye latter end of ye year unless their Tutors see cause by Reason of their Ripeness in ye tongues to Read logick to them sooner: they shall spend ye second year in logick with ye exercise of themselves in ye tongues: [4]

Edwards knew Latin before entering, was always proficient in languages, and had "first standing in his class." Thus he read logic in his first year, and probably sooner at his home. Logic was taught every morning in the first year, earlier or later, and throughout the next three years. Scholastic "Disputation" was required of all students, once every sixth week for beginners, increasing to "once every week" for "Commencers." For many years, Burgersdycke was a set textbook. Slightly previous to Edwards, "Sir Fiske gives them a taste of logic from the Leyden Latin manual of Burgersdicius so soon as their command of the language makes it possible."[5] A letter describing the course of study, 1713–14, almost certainly continuing in 1717, when Edwards began at Yale, lists "Burgers-

---

before lay in my mind jumbled without any distinction, ranged into order and distributed into classes and subdivisions, so that I could tell where they all belonged and run them up to their general heads. For this logic consisted much in distributions and definitions, and their maxims gave occasion to observe new and strange dependencies of ideas, and a seeming agreement of multitudes of them in the same thing, that I never observed before" ("The Mind," n. 17; references to this essay, to "Being," and to "Miscellanies" are hereafter cited as *Mind*, *Being* and *Misc.*, and are to note and page in Townsend).

[4] F. B. Dexter, *Biographical Sketches of The Graduates of Yale College, 1701–1745* (New York: Holt, 1885), p. 349.

[5] E. Oviatt, *The Beginnings of Yale* (New Haven; Yale University Press, 1916), p. 239.

dicius and Ramus's Logick, also Heereboord's [set?] Logic, & c" as being recited. Logic has probably increased, for now, "the two upper classes used to dispute syllogistically twice or thrice a week."[6] The Rector, not tutor Johnson, "approved" set books. Johnson spoke of the "scholastic cobwebs of a few little English and Dutch systems that would hardly now be taken up in the street, some of Ramus and Alstad's work was [*sic*] considered as the highest attainments." He disparaged the "distributions and definitions"[7] Edwards appreciated, and "introduced the study of Mr. Locke and Sir Isaac Newton as fast as they could and in order to this the study of mathematics." From this intense clash of ideas Edwards benefited, studying Burgersdycke and Heereboord during his first year, and Locke during his second.

Ramus is the other candidate listed. He, "by the time Edwards was doing his mature work had barely become moribund."[8] Probably, Edwards had read Ramus. But "the old logic" was not Ramus. Ramus' *inventio, iudicio, dispositio* are not found in Edwards, as terms or methods. Logic for Edwards is concerned with terms, their connections in propositions and strict syllogistic reasoning. Ramus rejects the Aristotelian categories and predicables. Burgersdycke reintroduces them, in protest against Ramus, and in terms of them makes his definitions, distributions, and distinctions. Edwards clearly follows Burgersdycke. For Ramus, logic is the "Art of Disputing well." For Burgesdycke and Edwards, it is the art of *"Definitions, Divisions, Syllogisms* and *Method,"*[9] which is far wider than the Ramist definition, *"ars bene disserendi,"* and includes a necessary ontological and philosophical part which Ramus and many Puritans who followed him rejected. Ramus' conception of method belongs to rhetoric. It is "orderly pedagogical presentation of any subject by reputedly

[6] Dexter, *Biographical Sketches*, p. 115.
[7] S. Johnson, *His Career and Writings*, ed. H. & C. Schneider (New York: Columbia University Press, 1929), 1:6, 8 ff.
[8] P. Miller, *The New England Mind* (Cambridge, Mass: Harvard University Press, 1954), p. 176.
[9] [Franciscus] Burgersdicius, *Monitic Logica* (London: R. Cumberland, 1697), 2:46; 1:31 (hereafter cited as "Burg.").

scientific descent from 'general principles' to 'specials,' by means of definition and bipartite division."[10] Burgersdycke warns against this bimembrous division. "Often the Nature of the Dividend refuses *a Dichotomy, or Bimembrous Division . . .* to seek always for *Dichotomy,* is a sort of *accurate Vanity.*"[11] Edwards follows Burgersdycke and not Ramus, both early and late. Method, for Burgersdycke occupies one short last chapter. It is largely concerned with natural and not artificial method, especially speculative "synthesis" and practical "analysis." Edwards uses both methods, reinterpreted by Descartes and Arnauld. He studied Burgersdycke on definition carefully. Like Burgesdycke, he distinguishes between definition of the name, and definition of the thing. Definition of the name, or synonymous definition — which Locke disparages — Edwards uses with great effect, defining volition by seventeen near-synonyms, "whatever names we call the act of the will by — choosing, refusing, approving, disapproving."[12] This is, as Burgersdycke directs, preliminary to "definition of the thing,"[13] where Edwards defines choice as "the determination of the will by the strongest motive."[14] For Burgersdycke logic "*searches out the Meanings of Words and Things.*"[15] Edwards begins *Freedom of The Will* and *The End for which God Created The World* by explaining "*Various Terms and Things Belonging to the Subject of the Ensuing Discourse,*" noting that many things are "entirely different in nature and kind." In *God Glorified,* he "distributed" "good." The marks whereby common and special grace may be "distinguished" are set forth, respectively, in *Distinguishing Marks,* and *Religious Affections.* Burgersdycke sets out clearly the function of the ten Aristotelian categories in a passage (cf. Footnote 3 *supra*) to which Edwards' note on

[10] W. J. Ong, *Ramus* (Cambridge, Mass: Harvard University Press, 1958), p. 30.
[11] Burg., 2:19.
[12] Jonathan Edwards, *Freedom of The Will,* ed. P. Ramsey (New Haven: Yale University Press, 1957), p. 137 (hereafter cited as *FOW*).
[13] Burg., 2:1–2.
[14] Edwards, *FOW.,* 141 ff.
[15] Burg., A:3.

"the old logic" has a strong resemblance. Burgersdycke talks of "Forms and Classes," and Edwards of "classes and subdivisions." Burgersdycke says that by categories we "may survey them at one View or Glimpse." Edwards says that "I could tell where they all belonged and run them up to their general heads." Burgersdycke says that "we observe how this or that may be compared with any other thing." Edwards says that they gave "new and strange dependencies of ideas, and a seeming agreement of multitudes of them in the same thing." Thus we may conclude Edwards studied Burgersdycke as an integral part of his training.

Major Conceptions: Their Origin and Use

Edwards used many major Burgersdyckian concepts. Burgersdycke holds an "Aristotelian" realist view of "universals." "A Universal is that which is apt of its own Nature to be predicated of many things, as *Man, Horse, Plant*,"[16] either actually or potentially existing. For Locke, unlike Burgersdycke, universals are not necessarily constitutive of things or knowledge:

> The Perception of the agreement or disagreement of our particular ideas, is the whole and utmost of all our knowledge. Universality is but accidental to it, and consists only in this, that the particular ideas about which it is are such as more than one particular thing can correspond with and be represented by.[17]

"All things that exist are only particulars." Universals are man-made, because "of reason and necessity." Man must think brachylogically. Universals are formed by abstraction from particulars by making one particular representative of many, and by deriving general meanings from them. Locke maintains that our general ideas of substances have a "foundation in nature." Our mind here "only follows nature; and puts none together which are not supposed to have a union in nature."

[16] *Ibid.*, 1:3.
[17] John Locke, *An Essay Concerning Human Understanding*, ed., A. C. Fraser (Oxford: Clarendon Press, 1894), bk. 4, chap, 17, para. 8; vol. 2, p. 404.

But neither are there fixed unalterable species in nature, as monsters and crossbreeds show, nor such universals in the human mind, but merely those of convenience and use. There are no "substantial forms" to constitute the essence of species. We know only the "nominal essences" of substances, that is, the groups of ideas generally found together in particular things, and not their "real essences," that is, their inner constitutions. Where morals and mathematics and other "mixed modes" (man-made "complex ideas") are concerned, we know both their "real" and "nominal" essences. Man constructs both particular ectype and its identical universal archetype. The universal, "parricide" has no opposite "son-killing." Moral and religious "universals," that is, "mixed modes," vary remarkably from one culture to another. They are entirely "made by the understanding," "perfectly arbitrary," and "without patterns or reference to any real existence." Here, as with substances, "supposed real essences" cannot be "the essences we rank things into." "Species are as men, and not as Nature, makes them." All universals are "inventions and creatures of the understanding, made by it for its own use, and concern only signs, whether words or ideas," not real things or universals in our thought.

Edwards rejected this Lockean conceptualism. The starting-point of much of his epistemological analysis, it was not the origin of his fundamental logical and metaphysical ideas. He agrees with Locke that our knowledge begins in particular ideas, but these ideas themselves convey universals to us. Universals — which are not arbitrarily man-made — characterize both things and our knowledge of them. Edwards holds a penultimate epistemological conceptualism (near to "Aristotelian" realism), grounding it in a Calvinistic theistic idealism. Real Platonic universals, not existing apart from God, characterize the expression of His will and wisdom in Himself, and in and to the world. Rejecting Locke's basic abstraction from metaphysical grounding, Edwards rescued his epistemology from the profound skepticism at the heart of it. God reveals universals gradually by particular ideas, in and through the things which, by God's will, they constitute. Real

34

essences and archetypes are, in degree, and gradually, made known to us, in and through particular substances. The real natures of mathematical and moral entities, being purely intelligible, are clearly revealed to us in and through their concepts. The vacuum created by Locke's rejection of "substantial forms" is filled by the immediate presence of the divine power and activity. God makes things to be, to us, as ectypes, what they eternally are in the divine understanding and will as universal archetypes. Universals *in re* and *in mente* are real and correspond to each other because both are grounded simultaneously in the divine mind and divine power, at work *in re* and *in mente*. They are the immediate direct expression of His essence, of His will and wisdom. "Since where His power is exercised there His essence must be, His essence can be by nothing excluded."[18]

Retaining Locke's general analysis of human understanding in terms of ideas, simple and complex (a distinction already found in Heereboord), and not rejecting the active functions of the mind in knowledge, Edwards gives ideas a new metaphysical character, function, status and grounding as expressions of God's mind, presence, and purpose. The Immediacy of God in "the sense of the heart" is only a particular application of this general epistemological position. Here, where God acts not upon man's mind through the external structures of nature, but internally within the mind of man by His spirit, the true nature and union of outer world and inner mind, are revealed as one in the new simple idea of the divine.

The realism and rationalism of Edwards' training in Burgersdyckian logic and metaphysics, the belief in the "natures of things," constituted by God and knowable by man, transmuted Locke's more epistemological analysis of experience, divorced from real knowledge of nature and direct knowledge of God, into a metaphysically grounded analysis of existence in which God, man and the world are united:

> That which truly is the substance of all bodies is the infinitely exact and precise and perfectly stable idea in

[18] "All that is real is immediately in the first being." *Being*, p. 16.

God's mind together with His stable will that the same shall gradually be communicated to us and to other minds according to certain fixed and exact established methods and laws.[19]

Things are "copies" of God's archetypal universals. "Things as to God exist from all eternity alike,"[20] both in His mind, and in the world, and in our minds, correspondingly to both. He guarantees things, the knowledge of things, and the correspondence of one with the other. "The foundation of the most-considerable species, or sorts in which things are ranked, is the order of the world — the designed distribution of God and nature."[21] "He designed such and such particulars to be together in the mind," and "by His making such an agreement in things"[22] universals exist.

This is the philosophical basis for Edwards' anti-Lockean presupposition that there is a real, objective, not man-made, nature of true virtue, of morals and religion, and of the will and understanding, intelligible to, and susceptible of, the mind's precise analysis. They exist "in the necessary nature of things," not just as arbitrary human constructs. They are subjects of strict demonstrative reasoning, and of universal and necessary rational criteria. As subjects of "science," strict certain knowledge exhibiting necessary and universal connections, particular phenomena can be interpreted and coordinated, and what is not so characterizable, rejected as "accidental." Edwards fulfills Locke's mathematical ideal of morality, with universal and necessary features, *proportionately* related in real and objective and not purely subjective real and nominal essences.

Edwards acknowledged that "all universals, therefore, cannot be made up of ideas abstracted from particulars, for color and sound are universals as much as man or horse."[23] Locke

[19] *Mind*, n. 13, p. 32.
[20] *Ibid.*, n. 36, p. 41.
[21] *Ibid.*, n. 47, p. 50.
[22] *Ibid.*, n. 43, p. 47.
[23] *Ibid.*, n. 42, p. 46.

had admitted that "substance" also is non-abstractable and Edwards took seriously the Burgersdyckian "transcendents" of *"Being, Thing, One, True, Good,* which by their Community exceed all the degrees of *Categories."* [24] Locke eschewed "the vast ocean of Being," but "Being" dominated Edwards' thought in his eulogy of his future wife and in his conversion experience. Everything was characterized as Being, and, though abstract, Being was capable of a priori proof from the principle of non-contradiction, as well as inferable from contingent existence by the casual principle. God, man and the world, and everything in and of them exhibit consent or dissent of Being to Being. It was this metaphysical premise of Being, as, eminently speaking, necessary substance and universal predicate, *"subsistens per se, et esse in subjecto"* found in Burgersdycke, Heereboord, Turretin and Spinoza, that Edwards brought to his study of More, Newton and Locke, and found in them particular empirical determinations of it. Also, "thing" structures Edwards' "metaphysical logic" in the same manner and in a far wider sense than that of phys-ical thing or substance. Thus, when he says that "all things that begin to be," "that whatsoever begins to be" must have a cause, he means that everything, abstract and concrete, uni-versal and particular, must have a necessary and sufficient reason why it is, and is as it is.[25] Edwards here, and generally, uses "causality" in its widest "transcendent" rational sense, in Burgersdyckian manner.[26] So also his realizing Locke's "math-ematical morality" is grounded in the "transcendent" use of the category of quantity as *"the Quantity of Perfection, and Quantity of Vertue."* This underlies his idea of "excellence" and "the nature of true virtue" where virtue consists in the proportional response of Being to Being, quantitative and qualitative.

Locke almost resolved substance into relations, qualities and causal powers. We need "substance" but "have no idea what it is." Replying to Stillingfleet's charge of *"almost dis-*

[24] Burg., 1:6.
[25] *FOW*, pp. 180 ff.
[26] Burg., 1:20; 1:13.

carding Substance out of the reasonable part of the World,"
Locke quotes Burgersdycke's definition of it as *"Ens* or *res
per se subsistens* & *substans accidentibus."* [27] Thus God is substance in the most general, unrestricted, sense. Burgersdycke
calls God "substance" in an "equivocal" sense.[28] Edwards,
answering Locke's skepticism, and grasping the logic of Burgersdycke's position, calls God the only substance. Others —
for example, spirits and bodies — are substance in a less
proper sense, differing in degrees of Being. God alone sub-
sists of Himself, not being subject to accidents. All other
things subsist in Him, as ideas. All so-called accidents of
bodies are not, as accidents, in independent substances (except in the usual non-metaphysical way of speaking), but
exist only in the divine substance as His ideas. Here "substance" in its "transcendent" sense is given the primary defining meaning, as equivalent to Being and fullness of Being.
"Bodies have no substance of their own . . . there is neither
real substance nor property belonging to bodies; but all that
is real is immediately in the first being." [29] Locke complains
"the secret abstract nature of substance in general" is unknown.[30] Edwards replies: "the secret lies here: that which
truly is the substance of all bodies is the infinitely exact and
precise and perfectly stable idea in God's mind." [31] Locke's
second definition of substance as "substratum," "support,"
"something" which "we know not what," [32] Edwards refers to
God. The "latent substance, or something that is altogether
hid, that upholds the properties of bodies, . . . that something is He 'by whom all things consist.' " [33] A metaphysical
referent is supplied to transform a skeptical Lockean episte-

[27] *The Works of John Locke,* 3d ed; (London: Bettesworth, 1727),
1:345.
[28] Burg., 1:5,8.
[29] *Being,* p. 17.
[30] *An Essay Concerning Human Understanding,* bk. 2, chap. 23, para.
6: vol. 1, p. 396.
[31] *Mind,* n. 13, p. 32.
[32] *An Essay Concerning Human Understanding,* bk. 2, chap. 23, para
1 f.: vol. 1, p. 390 ff.
[33] *Mind,* n. 61, p. 63; cf. P. Miller, ed., *Images or Shadows of Divine
Things* (New Haven: Yale University Press, 1948), p. 115.

mological analysis into an affirmation of faith. The epistemological analysis is accepted but the metaphysical conclusion is
denied, on non- , even anti-Lockean premises. In Edwards,
"substance" is banished from the reasonable world, only in
the sense of being found everywhere in God, and in a lesser
analogical sense in spirits and bodies.

The category of "quantity" structures Edwards' thought
about Being and its degrees. "Transcendent" "quantity" as
proportionality of Being and response of Being to Being finds
its exemplification in the "excellence" of moral and aesthetic
values and the exact mathematical sciences equally as in
the Newtonian laws of gravity and motion which give order,
harmony, regularity, and beauty to the created world, pre-
venting any "bifurcation of nature." So also, the category of
"quality" furnished an important concept for Edwards' dis-
positional as against Locke's non-dispositional account of
knowledge, in an attempt to correct their common "rationalistic psychology." Locke's analysis of knowledge is almost
entirely in terms of present content of consciousness. He
briefly discusses habit only as a function of memory in recall-
ing intuitive and demonstrative truths, and custom as the influence of frequent perceptions upon our usual perceptual
judgments. Edwards found in Burgersdycke a scholastic version of the Aristotelian *hexis* much to his need:

> A Habit is said to be an *adventitious* Quality, because
> not flowing from the Essence of the Subject, or its Prin-
> ciples, but from elsewhere; and is either infus'd by God,
> as *Faith, Hope, Charity, Prophecy, Gift of Tongues,* & c.
> or acquir'd by frequent Acts." [34]

For Edwards, religion is not "the act, exclusive of the habit,"
"but holy love . . . and an habitual disposition to it." [35] It is
the "infusing" of "a new, divine and supernatural principle,"
a *superdonitum*.[36] It is by reference to the "fixedness and

[34] Burg., 1:15.
[35] J. Edwards, *Religious Affections*, ed. J. E. Smith (New Haven:
Yale University Press, 1959), p. 107 (hereafter cited as *RA*).
[36] *RA*, pp. 207, 239.

strength of the habit . . . whereby holy affection is habitual," rather than "by the degree of the present exercise" that
religion is real. It is not present in any "exact proportion to
the degree of affection, and present emotion of the mind." [37]
It is a "new principle," [38] and like a principle is "ally'd in Sig-
nification" to "*Element* and *Cause*" and means "the *First
from whence any thing is, or exists, or is known.*" [39] It is not
an "indwelling principle, they don't derive any denomination
or character from it; for there being no union it is not their
own." [40] It is of grace, not nature. It is not engendered by
religious or moral habituation. This concept enables Edwards to resist Stoddardean "means," "sincere endeavours,"
"moral efforts," "Half-Way Covenants" and "Converting Ordinances," as not engendering the "habit" of true religion.

That Edwards is analyzing an essential relationship and
not an accidental one, underlies his whole use of the Burgersdyckian doctrine of signs. Although Locke's doctrines of
signs has influence in the epistemology of the "sense of the
heart," it was of no use as a criterion by which to distinguish
"certain" from "no certain" signs, true from false in religion.
Locke's doctrine is psychological, not logical. Words are
signs of ideas, and ideas of things, but there can be no certain logical relation in either case. Edwards needed firm
criteria to distinguish "certain" from "no certain" signs. Burgersdycke distinguishes a "*certain*" from "uncertain *Indica-
tion of a Thing.*" The certain is "Natural . . . *signifies of its
own Nature,*" is not "arbitrary," and "*belongs almost to the
Doctrine of Causes.*" It may be "*Antecedent, Consequent*" or
"*Conjoyn'd*" as "Cause of *the thing signified, or the Effect,*"
but must be "*Necessary*" not "*Contingent.*" [41] An uncertain
sign is "accidental" as Edwards repeatedly calls it. This doctrine of signs helped Edwards to correct his early, uncritical
evaluation of the revival phenomena, governed too much by
Locke's psychological approach and doctrine of "nominal

[37] *Ibid.*, p. 118.
[38] *Ibid.*, pp. 205 ff.
[39] Burg., 1:48.
[40] RA, p. 201.
[41] Burg., 1:75 ff.

essences." The criteriological account advances from *The Distinguishing Marks* (1741) through *Some Thoughts* (1742) to *Religious Affections* (published in 1746), under the attacks of Chauncy (1742, 1743). The defining characteristics and non-accidental properties (that is, those which flow from and always and only accompany it) are necessary features and distinguish a thing from all else. "Of its own nature," they are not arbitrary.

With this rational doctrine of essences and of excellence as proportionality, concordant with his mathematical ideal of knowledge, virtue and religion, Edwards could apply Burgersdycke's criteria. In human as in non-human nature and mathematics, necessary relations obtain, and are deducible from the metaphysical ground of their Being. The affections "do not only necessarily belong to the human nature, but are a very great part of it." [42] Edwards' thought is consistent throughout. He pours Lockean empirical content into a non-Lockean rational framework, realizing Locke's unrealized mathematical ideal. He early rejected Locke's doctrine, though not terminology, of "mixed modes," thereby refusing an arbitrary character to religion and morality. Signs must indicate some "necessary connection in the nature of things" if there is to be "known and certain connection at all" [43] There are absolutely necessary relations "in the nature of things," moral and religious, as in mathematics. "God hath established," "contrived and constituted" things such. [44] The logic of signs depends upon a logic of real "natures" and essences, and is the logic of Burgersdycke, and not of Locke, who denied objective real essences in morality and religion.

Burgersdycke's fifth and sixth categories, "action and passion," differ from those of Locke, and structure Edwards' thought.

> When an Action has a Subject or Patient, it is not in the Agent, but Patient. For Action (as we have said) is a Flux of the Effect, and therefore ought to be in that

[42] *RA*, p. 101.
[43] *Ibid.*, p. 160.
[44] *Ibid.*, p. 179.

Subject in which it is effected; but the Effect is in the
Patient, and therefore the Action *ought* to be in the Patient *also*."[45]

This is Edwards' doctrine, informing his use of the word,
"principle." Where God savingly acts, he acts not only *upon*
but *in* the soul. "In the soul where Christ savingly is, there he
lives. He don't only live without it, so as violently to actuate it;
but he lives in it; so that that also is alive."[46] His doctrine of
conversion is structured in these terms. "A Divine and Supernatural Light" is "*Immediately* imparted to the Soul."
Likewise, also, his doctrine of the will, in language remarkably similar, if not identical, stresses, against his Arminian
opponents, that action and passion are relative terms, each
applicable to the same subject. Burgersdycke's other distinctions, within this category, between immanent and transient,
perficient and corrupting are also found in Edwards.

Freudenthal discovered that the eightfold Burgersdyckian
distinction of efficient causality structured Spinoza's thought.
The same scheme of efficient, and the further threefold Burgersdyckian distinction of final causality is reproduced in Edwards. He rejects Locke's repudiation of final causes for
"productive efficacy," and from his earliest days replaces the
latter with Burgersdycke's sufficient condition, or "reason
why."[47] He subsumes Locke's under Burgersdycke's concept.
A rationalistic concept replaces one empirically derived and
characterized. It becomes one of Edwards' major two or
three "middle terms" which enter into all of his thinking.
Cause is "any antecedent" that "truly belongs to the reason
why the proposition which affirms that event is true."[48] The
full cause of a thing is thus the sum totality of prior conditions, and a cause of it, any part of that totality. Burgersdycke's concept is that of sufficient reason for existence, "that
by which a thing is, *that is*, which confers somewhat towards

[45] Burg., 1:26.
[46] *RA*, p. 342.
[47] Burg., 2:99 ff., the middle term of a demonstrative syllogism. Cf.
S. E. Dwight, *The Life of President Edwards* (New York: Carvill, 1830),
pp. 760–61.
[48] *FOW*, p. 181.

the thing's *Existence*."[49] For Edwards, it is "the ground and reason, either in whole, or in part, why it is rather than not; or why it is as it is, rather than otherwise."[50]

Burgersdycke's axiom is that "the Cause is before its Caused, both in *Nature and Knowledge*"[51] and cause in its most proper sense is immediately next.[52] Edwards accepts this maxim though he applies it to both potential and actual causes. Metaphysically, it accounts for his rejection of a causative material world of secondary cause *proper* intervening between God and man; epistemologically, it accounts for his rejection of Locke's theory of representative perception with its *tertium quid* between the knowing mind and what is known, in favour of a direct causal theory of perception in terms of God's immediate causal activity. As does Burgersdycke, Edwards distinguishes order of nature from order of time, and order of nature from order of knowledge which it causes. The other two types of order, "Disposition, Dignity," are also important structuring elements in Edwards' thought. Burgersdycke's axiom, "Nothing *lastly*, acts without *Design*: there is therefore *an End for whose Sake the Cause Efficient acts*,"[53] governs Edwards' interpretation of action, divine, human, animal, and non-animate. The close relation of efficient and final causality in Burgersdycke and Edwards offsets them sharply from Locke's purely efficient type of causality as force. Burgersdycke's "essential" and "accidental" causes become Edwards' real positive, and negative occasional causes. Burgersdycke's accidental cause is when "one depends upon another, but *not when*, or *in as much as it causes*."[54] Likewise, Edwards uses Burgersdycke's distinc-

[49] Burg., 1:49.
[50] *FOW*, p. 181. From earliest "Notes on Natural Science," cause was consistently, "reason why": Dwight, *The Life of President Edwards*, p. 760. Edwards is anti-Hume: *Misc.*, n. 1297, p. 216.
[51] Burg., 1:49. Cf. Francis Turretin, in J. W. Beardslee III, ed., *Reformed Dogmatics* (New York: Oxford University Press, 1965), pp. 340–43 and *Misc.*, n. 749, pp. 83 ff.
[52] Burg., 1:51. Edwards' earliest thought agrees: Dwight, *The Life of President Edwards*, 760 f.
[53] Burg., 1:49.
[54] *Ibid.*, p. 50. "Such suggestions may be the occasion, or accidental cause of gracious affections" (*RA*, p. 228).

tion between the "next Cause . . . *that which immediately constitutes the Caused,*" distinct from all of the rest which are more remote, to reject Locke's distinction between preference and choice.[55]

These concepts of "Cause and Caused in general" are given further systematic treatment in Burgersdycke, in his chapters on each of the four Aristotelian causes. Like Maimonides, Edwards regarded the efficient, formal and final causes as identical. The formal cause, or defining characteristic of a thing is part of its "reason why." Indeed, it is the close relation of formal and efficient cause, under the concept of cause as reason why, and the oft coextensiveness of "the Cause Efficient Internal *of the Predicate, and Form of the Subject*"[56] which on many occasions leads Edwards into a virtual identification of the two. When Edwards says that "the will always *is* as the greatest apparent good, or . . . is *determined* by the greatest apparent good," he identifies efficient with formal cause, because both are definable as what makes a thing to be, and "the ground or reason why."[57] While Edwards does not make great use of material cause, it is sometimes found as offset from formal cause.[58]

The first distinction within efficient causality, in Burgersdycke, is that of active and emanative causality. The former proceeds by action upon something else; the latter is *"that from which a thing immediately flows and proceeds* without any Action."[59] Edwards agrees that, where action is upon another, it proceeds by action mediating its effect. "An active being can bring no effects to pass by his activity, but what are consequent upon his acting."[60] This distinction, as also its opposite in the pair, *emanativa*, is exactly reproduced in Edwards. Thus, in *God Glorified*, there is "participation," "communication," "effusion," "diffusion" of the "fulness" of God,

[55] Burg., 1:51; *FOW*, pp. 138 ff.

[56] Burg., 2:104.

[57] *FOW*, p. 144.

[58] *The Works of Jonathan Edwards* (London: Westley and Davis, 1834), II, 15 (hereafter cited as *Works*).

[59] Burg., 1:58.

[60] *FOW*, p. 187.

in and upon man.[61] In *Spiritual Light,* without the aid of "second causes," knowledge of God is "a participation of the Deity: it is a kind of emanation of God's beauty."[62] In *The End,* "This propensity in God to diffuse himself, may be considered as a propensity to himself diffused; or to his own glory existing in its emanation.[63]

Burgersdycke's next distinction between cause immanent and transient, in oneself and upon another,[64] is found throughout Edwards. He distinguishes between "an active being" which "produces an effect in another being," and one in which "his activity is conversant about himself, to produce and determine some effect in himself."[65] Often, this distinction is expressed in terms of cause *ad intra* and *ad extra.*[66]

Freedom, for both Burgersdycke and Edwards is part of the doctrine of rational causality.[67] For Locke it is psychologically derived power, which is related to causality as inner nexus between cause and effect. Its restoration, full-center, to this position offsets Edwards' general position against that of Locke, and gives it its greater strength. Hence Edwards' attack on Arminian non-caused freedom, as an inner psychological power known to "experience." Edwards agrees with Burgersdycke's general doctrine of freedom *a coactione,* and *a necessitate naturae,* but not of freedom from moral necessity.[68] The fourth "efficient" causal distinction between cause *per se* and *per accidens,* is found throughout Edwards, and is often called "occasional cause" or, in one place, "*causa sine qua non,*" that is, a necessary indirect, negative condition, necessary but not sufficient to produce a given effect.[69]

[61] *Works,* 2:3–7.
[62] *Ibid.,* 2:16.
[63] *Ibid.,* 1:100.
[64] Burg., 1:49–50, 58–59.
[65] *FOW,* p. 187.
[66] *Misc.,* n. 1218, p. 152.
[67] Burg., 1:59; *Misc.,* n. 342, p. 157: "Let this be laid down first as a postulate before treating of those doctrines about free will: that whatever is, there is some cause or reason why it is; and prove it." Cf. *FOW,* pp. 180 ff., and P. Ramsey's denial of this in *FOW,* pp. 23 ff., and A. E. Murphy's rebuttal, "Jonathan Edwards on Free Will and Moral Agency," *Philosophical Review,* 68 (1959): 189 ff.
[68] Burg., 1:59–60; *FOW,* pp. 164 ff.
[69] Burg., 1:61.

The fifth distinction is between principal and less principal cause. Under the first is stated the principle of sufficiency of cause to effect found in Descartes, Locke and Edwards.

> A Principal is *that which produces the Effect by its own Virtue.* . . . The Principal Cause, is *either equal to, or nobler, never worse than the Effect* . . . when the Virtue of the Cause is *such* as that it contains *in it*, whatever is in *the Effect*, it is said to be a *principal Cause*. The Effect is said to be contained in the Cause, either *formally* or *eminently*. When *formally*, or the Effect is of the *same Nature* with the Cause, the Cause is said to *be univocal*, and is *equal to* its Effect; . . . When *Eminently*, or the Cause by a *Nobler Sort* of Virtue produces the Effect, it is said to be *Aequivocal*, and is *better than its* Effect.[70]

Edwards uses this principle, and that of proportionality, to structure the relation of God, man and the world in terms of degrees of Being. For Edwards, as for Turretin, the world is eminently, not formally in God, and with the Suaresian sharp distinctions between finite and infinite, Edwards is clearly saved from the charge, often made, of pantheism. God "communicates of the goodness of his nature, it is doubtless his peculiar work, and in an eminent manner, above the power of all creatures."[71] The world is in God who is above it, a higher Being, not merely in it, or of it.

Less principal causes are procatarctical, "*that which Extrinsecally* excites," in terms of "*Object, Occasion, Author or Merit*;" proegumenal, "which *inwardly disposes*, or also *excites*;" and "*Instrumental*."[72] Edwards is clear that "to excite is to be a cause." The whole notion underlies Edwards' treatment of "inducements" and "motives." It structures his whole argument on the relation of God to man. As object, God is "objective good" and "objective ground" of man's *nisus* towards Him. He is occasional, but not proper cause of sin. By his being absent, man is excited to sin. He is "Author"

[70] *Ibid.*, 1:62–63.
[71] *RA*, p. 203.
[72] Burg., 1:63.

or "Moral Cause," for throughout, "it is not of him that willeth," but of God, the author of all. He is "Meritorious Cause," for as supreme giver of "Reward and Punishment, Praise and Blame," He *"moves the Agent to a Requital,* and that either in *good or evil things."*[73] The proegumenal or disposing cause structures the relation of God as creative cause, producing the world *ex nihilo,* caused to do so, of his own disposition alone:

> Merely in this *disposition* to cause an emanation of his glory and fulness — which is prior to the existence of any other being, and is to be considered as the inciting cause of giving existence to other beings — God cannot so properly be said to make the *creature* his end, as *himself.*[74]

Thirdly, instrumental cause as *"that which subserves the principal cause in its Effecting"*[75] becomes Edwards' "means and endeavours" through which God acts and man responds.[76] Of these three lesser causes, Edwards' apparent nature and circumstances of the objects viewed "corresponds to the procatarctical," and "the manner of the view" and the "frame and state of the mind," to the proegumenal.[77]

Burgersdycke's sixth distinction of efficient cause into first and second[78] exactly corresponds with that of Edwards. "He is the *first* cause of it; and not only so, but he is the *only* proper cause."[79] Sometimes He acts, concurring with "second causes," but sometimes without them. First cause is distinguishable into first "absolutely" and "in its own Genus."

[73] *Ibid.*

[74] *Works,* 1:100; cf. *Ibid.,* 1:98 and Burg., 1:26: "Creation is nothing else but the producing of something out of nothing; *that is,* out of *no subjected matter."*

[75] Burg., 1:65.

[76] *FOW,* pp. 365–71; *RA,* p. 378. The affections need "proper means and endeavours." Grace's "exercises should have some degree of connexion with means, after the manner of a principle of nature" (*Works,* 1:409).

[77] *FOW,* p. 147; cf. p. 198. "Procatarctical" *"Extrinsically* excites," and proegumenal *"inwardly disposes"* (Burg., 1:63, 65; *Works,* 2:5, 16; *RA,* p. 224).

[78] Burg., 1:65.

[79] *Works,* 2:3.

"The Cause absolutely First, is only *One*, to wit, *God*."[80]
Edwards agrees with this so well, that he rarely talks of "first
causes" natural or moral, and virtually abolishes all secondary causes, metaphysically strictly speaking. "GOD, *the original of all being, is the* ONLY *cause of all natural effects*."[81]
Seventhly, universal is distinguished from particular cause:

> Universal is *that which concurrs* with other Causes, with
> the *same Efficiency*, to the producing of *many Effects*.
> A Particular *only* which by its Efficiency produces but
> one Effect . . . God concurrs with particular Causes *to
> all Effects*.[82]

So in *God Glorified*, Edwards persistently speaks of God as
absolute and universal cause, upon whom all things depend
universally and absolutely. Throughout his thought, He is
universal cause in this sense. Burgersdycke's eighth distinction between cause next and remote has already been noted.

Throughout his work, Edwards explores in highly original
fashion the relation of final and efficient cause. His doctrine
of final causes is based on Burgersdycke's three distinctions
and is reproduced in *The End*. First, final cause is "cui" or
"cujus." "The End *of which*, is that which the Efficient desires." "*For* which, for whose sake, or for which the Efficient
desires such an End."[83] Edwards' title is studiedly, "the End
for which God created the World." He created it for Himself
and His own Glory. Section II of his Chapter One elabo-
rates on the end *"of which"* — "*those things which reason
leads us to suppose God aimed at in the creation of the
world*." Section III proceeds from thence to ask the question *"for which*," and thus is entitled, "*Wherein it is considered how, on the supposition of God's making the fore-
mentioned things his last end, he manifests a supreme and
ultimate regard to himself in all his works*." This answers the
question, "for whose sake" God created the world.[84] Burgers-

[80] Burg., 1:65–6.
[81] *Works*, 1:223 (*Original Sin*); *Being*, 16–20.
[82] Burg., 1:66.
[83] *Ibid.*, 1:68.
[84] *Works*, 1:94 ff.

dycke's second distinction states: "the Principal End is that which the Agent *first, or also, principally* intends. The Secondary, which the Agent *so intends* as that it may *enjoy it* with *the Principal*." Thirdly, "A Subordinate *End* is that which is referred to *some farther End*. The *Last*, to which *all other Ends are referred*: that it self to no farther." Edwards exactly reproduces these distinctions at the outset of *The End*. "A *chief* end is opposite to an *inferior* end: an *ultimate* end is opposite to a *subordinate* end." [85] Here "chief" translates Burgersdycke's "principal," and "inferior" his "secondary." Edwards builds on this three-fold distinction, elaborating upon it, but never departing from it.

In his chapter on "Conveniency of Things," [86] Burgersdycke precurses Locke's agreement of ideas, and discusses the ways in which things agree with each other. The relation of analogy is one form of agreement, and is a form of identity, that is, identity of ratios. Locke defines identity only in terms of *numerical identity*, barely mentions *analogy* and other "proportional" relations, and disparages *logical identity* as a principle of argument. Burgersdycke notes two kinds of ways in which things "*are united amongst themselves*." In simple agreement, things are united "*one thing with another in the same Third*." [87] The second kind is complex, the "*Analogy, of many, in the same Habitude*." [88] Edwards took seriously Burgersdycke's statement that analogy may be attributed to all things in general. He applied it radically both in *The Images* and in his doctrine of proportionality and excellence. Locke's ideal of a mathematical morals is fulfilled in Edwards' "proportionality" which governs "consent of Being to Being" in divine and human love as much as it does the laws of gravity, the beauty of art, and the integrity of religion. "Some have said that all excellency is harmony, symmetry, or proportion; but they have not yet explained it." Edwards explains proportion in terms of "identity of rela-

[85] *Ibid.*, 1:95.
[86] Burg., 1:77. "Conveniency" is obsolete for "convenience" or "agreement."
[87] *Ibid.*, 1:77.
[88] *Ibid.*, 1:78.

tion." As Burgersdycke, he analyzes it into simple and complex, which, respectively, are "equality" and "likeness of ratios; so that it is the equality that makes the proportion," that is, the simple "equality" is the foundation of the complex (the proportion, or analogy) or "likeness of ratios." "Thus if there be two perfect equal circles or globes together, there is something more of beauty than if they were of unequal, disproportionate magnitudes." [89] This last is an example of Burgersdycke's agreement of "one thing with another in the same third," that is, simply identity of relation. Proportion or analogy is a construct from this simple, and, is in Edwards' phrase, "likeness of ratios." This is identical with Burgersdycke's and Euclid's definition. Edwards argues from the same example, in concrete, as Burgersdycke cites from Euclid in the abstract; following Burgersdycke, he develops complex analogies far beyond the usual four-term analogies. He probably uses Burgersdycke's term, "proposition," for the antecedent in an analogy. [90]

Methods of Reasoning

There are two poles to Edwards' method, the rational and the empirical. The rational functions according to the strict norms of Aristotelian deductive logic, as "synthetic," and to those of Cartesian and Lockean intuition and demonstration, proceeding from what is "analytic." As with Locke, the empirical pole begins with simple and compound ideas of sensation and reflection as providing the *data* of knowledge, which the mind uses in making affirmations in propositions which, in themselves and their connections, are subject to the strict criteria of logic. Reason is concerned with truth, and *aisthesis* or "sense" with perception, in the five senses, in general, and in the "sense of the heart" in particular.

The two methods are correlative and convergent, because of the pre-established harmony of sensible and intelligible in the understanding and will of God who gradually reveals

[89] *Mind*, p. 21.
[90] Townsend, *The Philosophy of Jonathan Edwards, Mind*, p. 23; cf. Burg., I:80.

the universal and intelligible world through the sensible and particular. Logic gives and tests truth of general, impersonal description; perception, especially the "sense of the heart" in religion, gives and tests particular personal knowledge of acquaintance with that of which logic speaks. Reason suggests what sense confirms, in personal experience and scriptural testimony; and sense gives what reason corrects and explicates. Both are necessary, and neither of itself is sufficient. Descriptive truth without personal acquaintance gives only notional, not real knowledge; personal acquaintance without descriptive generalization is pre-logical and prior to judgment and questions of objective truth. Aristotelian and Cartesian canons of logic structure and control Lockean epistemology, and correct Lockean psychology. Edwards follows Burgersdycke's methodological logic of "directing the understanding in the Knowledge of Things." [91] It is true that the syllogism, as in Descartes and Locke is somewhat psychologized, subjectively perceived inference being essential for discovery in knowledge. Yet, Edwards appeals to objectively valid formal implication for testing truth, more so than does Locke. Probable evidence, on the one hand, and certain self-evidence on the other, "material" features of the premises, constitute criteria for distinguishing dialectical and probable from apodeictic and certain arguments. In the latter, where true conclusions are validly drawn from two true premises, scientific demonstration, the ideal of knowledge, is present. Rules and criteria are given for the assessment of probable evidence and certain self-evidence. This comprehensive concept of logic was eminently suitable for Edwards' rational-empirical approach.

Edwards' method of doctrine and proof as distinct from that of empirical discovery is that of rational deduction. This proceeds *"from Universals to Particulars, and in that Progress all the parts are to be connected together by apt Bonds of Transition."* [92] *Religious Affections* traces the "necessary" logic of the impact of Transcendent upon human being; the

[91] Burg., 1:1.
[92] *Ibid.*, 2:135.

psychology of *The Will* explicates the necessary implications
of Being for what constitutes beauty and virtue as proportional consent; theology discusses what necessarily follows
for created Being from uncreated Being. "The Questions of
the *Inferiour* are to be demonstrated by the Principles *of the
Superiour Science.*" [93] The will's determinism is an example
of "metaphysical or philosophical necessity,[94] for "we have
no strict demonstration of anything, excepting mathematical
truths, but by metaphysics." [95] Edwards, like Spinoza — who
was also influenced by Burgersdycke — reproduces all four
parts of the geometrical method in his early writings.[96]
Firstly, first principles, "divided into definitions, postulates,
and axioms or common notions," are set apart from the dem-
onstrations. These are Burgersdycke's self-evident "praecog-
nitions" and Locke's despised *"praecognitis."* Secondly, "the
conclusion which is to be established by the demonstration,
is summarized apart from the demonstration, in the form of
a proposition." This is the meaning of "proposition" [97] in
Edwards, which he first states and then demonstrates. Like
Euclid and Burgersdycke, Edwards calls these "theorems,"
indicating his highly geometrical conception of method.[98]
Thirdly, the geometric method "reasons from the known,
that is, the first principles, to the unknown, that is, the conclusion." Hence we proceed from self-evident causality to its
particular instances in human willing, by "those self-evident
maxims by which they are demonstrated." [99] Fourthly, "sup-
plementary deductions, explanations and propositions are
given in the form of corollaries, scholia and lemmas." So

[93] *Ibid.,* 2:111.
[94] *FOW,* pp. 151 ff.
[95] *Ibid.,* p. 424.
[96] As outlined in H. A. Wolfson, *The Philosophy of Spinoza* (New
York: Meridian, 1958), 1:40 ff., from which the following quotations
are taken.
[97] *Being,* pp. 3–4, 14.
[98] *Being,* p. 3; cf. Resolution II: *"Resolved,* when I think of any
Theorem in divinity to be solved, immediately to do what I can towards
solving it, if circumstances do not hinder" (Dwight, *The Life of President Edwards,* p. 69).
[99] *Being,* p. 9.

Edwards writes, "Let there be always laid down as many Lemmata, or preparatory propositions, as are necessary, to make the consequent proposition clear and perspicuous. When the proposition allows it, let there be confirming Corollaries and Inferences, for the confirmation of what had been before said and proved." [100] Edwards' use of "lemmas," "corollaries," geometic diagrams, "Q.E.D." conclusions, "disputations and questions" indicate fulfillment of his resolve "always, when I have occasion, to make use of mathematical proofs." [101]

The demonstrative syllogism, as Burgersdycke notes, is an extension of the geometrical method into discursive reasoning. Edwards' early resolve and practice, "to explain by way of objection and answer, after the manner of Dialogue," [102] is developed in *The Will*. Here Edwards accepts Burgersdycke's ideal of certain scientific demonstration as against the "Syllogism Dialectical or Probable." This Aristotelian ideal of self-evident intuition and demonstration proceeding from the known to the unknown characterized the Cartesian method. This basic unity of Aristotelian and Cartesian method was argued by Heereboord. Descartes' novelty lay in stressing the analytic rather than the synthetic pole. *Inventio*, discovery of simple truths must precede *enumeratio* or *inductio* to conclusions. We must begin with clear and distinct simple ideas and only then move along a "chain of reasoning" with a lively consciousness of every intuitive link in a lineal series; "lest our reason should go on holiday," there is to be no reliance on memory or syllogistic rules. Cartesian method was well known in the colony, and Edwards knew it, certainly, through Arnauld. There is convincing evidence that Edwards adopted Descartes' four rules of method. Edwards

[100] Dwight, *The Life of President Edwards*, p. 703.

[101] *Ibid.* The mathematical a priori character of his ideal of proof is evident: "A state of nothing is a state wherein every proposition in Euclid is not true, nor any of those self-evident maxims by which they are demonstrated; and all of the eternal truths are neither true nor false" (*Being*, p. 9).

[102] Dwight, *The Life of President Edwards*, p. 703. Cf. *Being*, p. 19, "Objection" "Answer"; *FOW*, pp. 342, 384 ff.; cf. *Misc.*, 1208:140 ff.

accepted the Cartesian and Lockean conception of demonstration as a lineal series of self-evident intuitions, each perceived self-consciously by the mind, without the aid of memory. But he did not reject the belief that we know and can only know some truths by syllogistic argument indirectly. Such self-evident perceptions may be either of sensation or of reflection. Reasoning about things not immediately present must approximate to the clarity and distinctness of immediate perception. For "reasoning does not absolutely differ from perception any further than there is the act of the will about it." [103]

Edwards agrees with Descartes and Locke that knowledge consists in clear and distinct intuitions and demonstration therefrom, and that syllogistic reasoning without this is not demonstrative knowledge. Intuition differs in degree, as in kind, in sensation, in intellectual intuition into the necessary connection of terms in a proposition, and of the steps in a syllogism. It is keenest in aesthetic, moral, and religious perception, in the "sense of the heart," which is a "sort of intuitive evidence," "seeing rather than reasoning." [104] "'Tis not by discourse, neither is it by intuition as other intuitions." [105] Edwards is here distinguished from Descartes and Locke who merely inferred God by the causal principle. Edwards finds Him immediately intuitable by "sense" in "a new simple idea" and not *only* arguable to by complex ideas, though He *is* such. This is knowledge by acquaintance, not *of* "ideas" and "their agreement and disagreement," but *by* idea of the real.

This concept of knowledge offset Edwards, on the one hand from the existential skepticism of Descartes' rationalism, and, on the other, from that of Locke's empiricism, in a highly original rational-empirical synthesis of ideal and real. Truth is not ultimately Locke's "perception of the relations there are between ideas," but "the consistency and

[103] *Mind*, n. 58, p. 56. This is thoroughly Lockean in stressing mind's activity.
[104] *Misc.*, n. 201, p. 247.
[105] *Ibid.*, aa:245.

agreement of our ideas with the ideas of God . . . with the things as they are," [106] for "God and real existence are the same." [107] By identifying knowledge of existence with knowledge of God and his ideas, Edwards overcame Locke's various dichotomies between: knowledge of agreement *between ideas* and knowledge of the *agreement of ideas with things*; real and nominal essences; ideas of primary and secondary qualities — all are ideas immediately caused by the divine presence and activity. Logical truth, coherence of ideas and consistency of thought is a *criterion* of real truth, whose *nature* is correspondence of empirical ideas and their agreements with fact and their "union" in fact. Coherence and logical consistency constitute the *nature* of logical, mathematical, and metaphysical truth; they are only the *criteria* of empirical truth, where *truth is* correspondence of our external ideas with those of God, in His immediate presence to us. But in God, rational coherence and consistency constitute the *nature* of truth, in His perfect idea, and correspondence obtains between particular ideas given to us and "His perfect Idea" in accordance with His purpose gradually to reveal things to us as they are. Thus, sensible experience is implicitly rational, and the ultimate correspondence and *nature* of truth is that between the coherence of our ideas, intelligible and sensible, with the coherence of God's ideas, themselves ultimately intuitable in one simple perfect undivided Idea of God in an act of intuitive vision.

Logic must be tested by reference to fact, as to adequacy and applicability (where it concerns the empirical). Likewise, what is asserted as fact, or putative self-evident empirical intuition, must be tested by its coherence with other fact and generalization from fact, by the canons of logic. We cannot solve a logical question, for example, the so-called self-determinism of the will (involving logical contradiction), by appeal to logically unanalyzed psychological experience; but we can appeal to experience and analyze it to find that it confirms and demands what reason suggests, that is, that

[106] *Mind*, 10:30–31.
[107] *Ibid.*, n. 15, p. 33.

there is and can be no uncaused act of volition. Nor may we solve a question of fact, for example, whether there is a "sense of the heart," by appeal to logic. This is to turn from the logical, not to the a- or anti- but to the pre-logical. The gap between sensible and intelligible within the Platonic notion of participation and imitation by the first of the second is closed by God's constant purpose gradually to reveal the intelligible through the sensible. Ideas are not *tertia quid* separating us from God and existence; they are *media* by which we know God in the world.[108] We experience immediately and directly, his constitution of things (of, for example, genera and species) in and through the order, harmony, analogies and resemblances of our given ideas. The logic of abstraction is applicable because it reproduces explicitly the logic implicit in immediate experience when God acts in and upon the mind. In conveying universals, He arouses there an "innate" capacity to form universals, intuit principles of argument (for example, causality), and incline to modes of argumentation (for example, to God). Particulars mediate universals, even the universal of Being, which universals we abstract in our logic and metaphysics. Thus Edwards prevents the reduction of metaphysics to logic, of logic to epistemology, and of epistemology to psychology — agnostic and skeptical tendencies all too evident in Locke. He avoids the various reductionisms of Hume and other eighteenth-century thinkers. He retains a severely "metaphysical *logic*."

The two forms of demonstrative method open to Edwards were the "synthetic" and the "analytic." Burgersdycke sets forth both, and Descartes advocated the latter, which Locke practices in an epistemological and psychological mode. Arnauld noted that they are convertible as reversible, and both usable in one discipline, for discovery or presentation.

---

[108] The world of particular sense *and* universal idea is as in Augustine and Berkeley, the "divine language." This is the burden of *Images*. Edwards displays Locke's early notion of idea as *medium*, which changed to *tertium quid* later. "Thus it is in things that we know by our external senses, by our bodily sight for instance. We first see them or have a clear idea of them by sight, before we know their existence by our sight" (*Misc.*, n. 1090, p. 252).

Locke's advocacy of "analytic" intuition of ideas and their relations and demonstration thereby, with syllogistic reasoning for teaching and controversy, is similar. Edwards uses the "analytic" method in the service of the "synthetic." *Distinguishing Marks* and *Religious Affections* are analytical. In the latter, twelve putative signs are shown to be "not certain," because they have only an accidental relation to religion. Part Three shows how twelve constitutive characteristics of religion — offset in a one-to-one contrary relation to the first twelve uncertain signs — are certain signs, because they are all defining features, or necessary properties and exhibit various aspects of religion analyzed as intellectual illumination, emotional enlivening, and practical living. An analytical definition into these three constitutive parts precedes the twelve-fold analysis of its structure. Likewise, the analysis of terms in *The End*, "Notes on Mind," and "Miscellanies" are metaphysical, epistemological, and psychological analyses, later used in a synthetic context. Lockean analyses subserve a non-Lockean deductive metaphysics and method of argument.

Edwards used two principles of argumentation, identity and contradiction, and causality, as necessary connection or "reason why." Locke had little use for arguments conducted by the first. Edwards makes frequent use of *reductio ad absurdum* argument, which is a form of "reducing things to a contradiction." Thus, Edwards proves a priori the solidity or inseparability of body by assuming the contrary and following out the logical consequences from the "propositions" and "postulates." With the aid of "axioms," etc., he shows that these consequences contradict what reason must suppose by its axioms, etc. Edwards also frequently uses the method of reducing two things to an identity by making each equal to some third. There is an argument of identity from the sameness of contraries, very much like the topical arguments of Burgersdycke. The whole of Edwards' essay "On Being," which lays a priori the foundations for all of Edwards' thought, proceeds by the method of identity and contradiction. Edwards' thought begins analytically, with the notion of Being; analyzing it, he finds it impossible to think non-Being without contradiction. He goes on to identify Being with consciousness and its ideas, "consciousness and being are the same thing exactly." [109] He explicates and "illustrates" his contention by five arguments, each of which supposes the contrary, and reduces to a contradiction. It presupposes Being as definable in terms of ideas and consciousness, and analytically deduces the consequences of that presupposition, thus appealing to the principle of identity and contradiction. The positions thus established are consistently maintained through his later thought, and other points are deduced therefrom in a deductive linear fashion. But metaphysical "strictness and abstraction" permits that "we may speak in the old way, and as properly and truly as ever," [110] and thus, the "idealism" is often, though still there, implicit rather than explicit.

For Edwards, experience must always be subject to the rules of reason and Scripture. Yet particular truths of sense and Scripture may go beyond what reason — without or undirected by sense or revelation — may comprehend. But the "sense of the heart" appeals to an alogical element requiring the principle of causality to account for it, not as a principle of argumentation but as a principle of interpretation. The "new simple idea" of God is clear and distinct, true, adequate, and real in Locke's sense. It is immediately self-evidencing. But beyond its self-evidencing immediacy, when subjected to judgment, it becomes subject to rational norms. As immediate idea, we are aware of it as non-self–caused, and as characterized by a quality which man could not give it. It is this pre-logical element which supplies Edwards with the data which cannot dispense with logic and argument but for which logic and argument are no substitute. It is *super-* and *supra-* not *anti-*rational. It is, throughout, subject to rational criteria, and works through rational means. No separation or opposition is possible between it and reason. It provides the first-hand data and the *power* of reason to

[109] *Being*, p. 6.
[110] *Mind*, n. 34, p. 39.

have insight into these data. "By this sense or taste of the mind, especially if it be lively, the mind distinguishes truth from falsehood." [111]

The principle of causality, not as a principle of interpretation, but as a principle of scientific argument, dominates *The Will*. How informed Edwards' whole thought is with the syllogistic forms of reasoning is evident from his sermons and from his use of the practical syllogism of faith [112] and of prayer [113] to test the claims of particular persons with respect to their having faith or rightly exercising prayer. It can be a negative test, though not a positive transmitter of faith. It can indicate the problematical hypothetical character of every particular empirical religious or moral statement. Not that there is anything probable about religion or morality themselves, or the universal objective tests to which experients are subject, with their "necessary" criteria. The Gospel is "beyond all mere probability," unlike "arguments fetched from ancient traditions, histories, and monuments." [114] "Internal evidence" gives "a sight of its glory." [115] Rules of interpretation of Scripture must be transformed from being external, extrinsic, and informative to becoming internal and intrinsic, informing experience. Yet argument has its fourfold functions of awakening unbelievers, forcing them to give rational consideration, confirming the faith of believers, confuting errors, and establishing objective rational truth.[116]

It is this last function that *The Will* performs, to establish by "strict demonstration" [117] what is "essential" to freedom in "the science of the will." It is "necessary" not "probable" reason; that is, it uses the apodeictic, certain, not dialectical probable syllogism. It attacks the middle term of the Arminians, "self-determinism," as the logical *proton pseudon* and

[111] *Misc.*, n. 397, p. 249.
[112] E.g., "Eternity of Hell's Torments," *The Works of President Edwards*, (Worcester, 1808), 7:397 ff.; cf. RA, pp. 268, 294, 502 ff.; cf. Turretin in Beardslee, ed., *Reformed Dogmatics*, pp. 393 ff.
[113] *Works*, 1:405 (Thoughts on the Revival).
[114] RA, pp. 304–5.
[115] RA, p. 307.
[116] *Ibid.*
[117] FOW, pp. 424, 429, 430, 431, 433, 435.

replaces this "medium" by one of strict "philosophical necessity," logical in character, which, as "necessity of connexion
and consequence" is exhibited first in the connection between the terms of a certain proposition, and then in the
connection between the premises and conclusion of a strictly
necessary syllogism. Exhibited now as mathematical and
now as causal necessity, the distinction between mathematical certainty (of identity and contradiction) and causal
certainty often disappears under the notion of both as forms
of sufficient reason why. This new "medium" of demonstration, that is, middle term in a strict demonstrative syllogism,
is laid down at the beginning and structures the reasoning
which, when not conducted as *reductio ad absurdum* or
reductio ad infinitum by the principle of identity and contradiction, is syllogistic throughout with causality, in one form
or another, as the needed middle term in the syllogism. The
argument proceeds first from effects to causes and then from
cause to effect, in strict accordance with the rules governing
these complementary forms of demonstrative argument,
"reason why" and "reason that," in the "Regress Argument."
No closer application of demonstrative syllogistic method
could be possible than that which sustained with great vigor
and power in *The Will*. But this is but the contrary pole to
that acute penetration of direct immediate experience in *Religious Affections*. Head and heart are married together in
one true union where true rationality and piety inform one
another, and the false abstractions of pietism and rationalism
fail to effect their divorce.

Significance of His Thought

The significance of Edwards' indebtedness to the concepts
and methods of Burgersdycke and Locke is clear. It enabled
him to fashion a philosophy and theology which is best described as one of spiritual realism. God as a divine Being is
alone real, and other minds and spirits are real only as dependent upon and upheld by Him. Ideas are real as mind-
dependent, and universals as real essences are eternally present in and to the divine mind, and wheresoever else His stable

wisdom and will uphold them in being. This theistically grounded "realism" enabled Edwards to overcome the nominalistic tendencies in Locke's thought, and to transpose the inherited thought of Calvinism from a formal scheme of doctrine into an account of experiential reality. Because the universal is present and known in and through the particular, he can existentialize the intellectual and universalize the institutional. He demanded that the nominal be grounded in the real, the legal in the moral, the ascribed in the achieved, the potential in the actual, and the rational in the empirical. With the concepts and methods he evolved in his youth out of his "Aristotelian" and "Lockean" background, he was able to give this demand philosophical formulation and instantiation in his earlier and later writings. He thus heralded and initiated a new age of philosophical theology in America, an age which was to bear fruit — theoretical and practical — for well over a century. This was needed to counter the growing tendencies to institutional formalism and rationalistic dogmatism from within the Church; and from without, the self-confident assurance of man in his own intellectual and moral powers which constituted what Edwards called "Arminianism." Thus, "justification by faith" loses its character of imputed righteousness and forensic justice and becomes a knowledge by acquaintance of He who is. It is not primarily intellectual assent, doctrinal apprehension, voluntaristic will-to-believe, nor even mere personal trust, but knowledge of God in the heart and response of the heart in the interior life and the external expression of that life of love to God and neighbor in deeds of charity. Assurance can ultimately be grounded only in the assurance of the good conscience that God is working savingly in our hearts and lives, by faith active in love. Original sin likewise becomes a real sharing by all mankind in Adam's first rebellion by virtue of our real essential identity with him. In our participation in him, by our common humanity, we shared in his original act of rebellion. At the Fall, we were there, in Adam, as universal man. As faith is near to love, and both are consent of being to Being, so sin is their opposite. It is dissent of being from

Being. It results in privation of being and response to being, and tends to nothingness and self-destruction. The Church becomes essentially those who are bound in a real relationship to God in and through Christ. Any supposed covenant relationship not grounded in this real relationship becomes suspect. Any "means," "endeavours," or "converting ordinances," which are not appropriately instrumental to or expressive of this real relationship of personal being to God's Being through union with Christ must be rejected. An outwardly lived good life must not be confused with an inwardly converted heart. Man-centered morality is no substitute for God-centered piety. The imputed and ascribed cannot take the place of the actual and the real. Attempts to do so in doctrine or institutional practice only express or lead to formalism, deceit, and hypocrisy. The Church is ultimately an ontologically grounded community, not a voluntaristic society. Its visible appearance must be grounded in invisible substance. It is grounded in God's Being and activity in Christ, and only secondarily in man's response in mind and heart. It is grounded in the truth of religion and virtue, and not in the pragmatic efficacy of preaching. Likewise the Great Awakening was for Edwards the first contemporary sign of the coming Kingdom of Christ. The Kingdom of Christ's love would come certainly and come soon. Edwards gives contemporary embodiment to eschatological prophecy, and finds its fulfillment in the realization of a real kingdom of love and virtue here on earth. The elect are those who respond to Being with consent of their being; and the damned are those who respond negatively with dissent of being from Being. Thus, Edwards grounds theological terms and doctrines in his philosophy of Being. What is referred to in it is not so much some salvation scheme as some moral or religious condition which has an experiential grounding, not just in the subjective psychological features of the experient but in these as grounded in some apprehension by and of Being itself, both withal exemplifying scriptural precedent and rule.

Edwards was a man of his age. He is an Enlightenment

thinker. But he finds enlightenment not in the self-confident powers of man's reason to discover truth for himself, or the unaided power of his morality to live the good life. True enlightenment is the illumination of heart and mind by the power of God penetrating to the core of one's being as one opens oneself to its influence. Edwards filled the thought forms of the moral and aesthetic sense of Shaftesbury and Hutcheson with the Augustinian, Calvinistic *sensus divinitatis*. Religious insight is continuous with moral and aesthetic insight, but all three are grounded in the activity of the divine in and upon the soul. He corrects thereby the humanist presuppositions of those whom he would controvert. Morality is not the exhibition of man's autonomous self-determining powers, but a continual response to the divine initiative and imperative. Ought implies can, and man is responsible for his acts. But his will needs the constant direction and support of the divine if it is to be determined to do the right thing. The good will is the only unconditional good; but the good will is within the power of God alone to create; "it is not of him that willeth."

Edwards accepts wholeheartedly the appeal of the eighteenth century to reason and experience. He widens the concept of experience from the natural perception of ideas of sensation and reflection of Locke and Hume to include perception of the divine. This experience given in the "sense of the heart," is both pre- and post-logical. It gives the data upon which reason can work; and when the ratiocination of man's unaided reason becomes perplexed by paradoxes and antinomies, it makes evident both the reality and mystery of the divine Being. Reason is the subject and not the cause of man's enlightenment. It is enlightenment which man needs, and which God alone can supply in the immediate sense of His presence. Thus, the concepts of both reason and experience are widened and deepened and both are grounded in the sovereign working of God's Being. But this is only one aspect of Edwards' effort to follow the eighteenth century in its demand that theology be anthropologically centered. "The proper study of mankind is man." Hence Edwards, in his writings, published and unpublished, starts with an analysis of the will and understanding, morals and religion. This teleological conception of human nature matches that of Bishop Butler; Edwards in his stress on the good will above and against all natural inclination which is not subservient to the universal rule of love, while akin to Kant, betters him in finding a resolution of the conflict in the distinction between consent to, relative and absolute, partial and whole. The genius of Edwards is that he sets the problems in terms of eighteenth-century thought that he might give answers relevant to its condition, though not typical of the Enlightenment mind itself.

Edwards has much to teach us in our contemporary scene. Firstly, he teaches us that while we need to understand the historical in terms of the contemporary, we nonetheless need to estimate the contemporary in terms of the historical. Edwards was deeply grounded in the thought of the past; it is the dimension of the historical which is often lacking in contemporary philosophical and theological thought. Secondly, Edwards illustrates that in our ecumenical discussions, the divisions between Protestant and Catholic are often artificial and conceal larger agreement of outlook and concern. Edwards' background of Suaresian scholastic thought determines his fundamental theological outlook. He has "a practically Roman conception of the place of love in justifying faith,"[118] while echoing Luther's faith active in love. There would be more hope of mutual understanding if our debates were more historically grounded. Thirdly, our concern for the union of the Church must be grounded, as was Edwards', in prayer and work for the extension of Christ's Kingdom into the hearts of all men, that is, the growth of real faith active in real love of God and man in those bound together in Christ. Fourthly, by using the concepts and methods furnished him by Burgersdycke, Locke and others, Edwards was able to generalize his religious experience into the meaning of the Enlightenment and be-

---

[118] T. A. Schafer, "Jonathan Edwards and Justification by Faith," *Church History*, 20 (1951):61.

yond. Fifthly, Edwards illustrates, as all great theologians have illustrated, that there can be no consistent, comprehensive theology without a developed philosophy in whose terms it may be coherently expressed. Sixthly, Edwards shows that, if we are to avoid the dead formalism of rationalism, on the one hand, and the aberrations of pietism and enthusiasm, on the other, both thought and feeling, in their full range and depth, must find their true place in any interpretative theological outlook. Edwards clearly saw this over half a century before Schleiermacher, and in many ways has a juster estimate of the place of reason in religion than does the latter. It is in his combination of the rational and empirical that Edwards' greatness lies; and his genius consists in his union of the old and new necessary to effect that synthesis.

3

Horace Bushnell: Cells or Crustacea?

FREDERICK KIRSCHENMANN

Interpreters of Horace Bushnell from Theodore Munger to William A. Johnson, have been guilty of misrepresenting Bushnell's theology. Several reasons exist for the development of this tradition of misinterpretation and it will be instructive to list them before attempting a reconstruction of the methodology Bushnell actually employed. From the perspective of that methodological stance, we shall then be in a position to interpret the substance of Bushnell's theology more accurately.

The misinterpretation of Bushnell's theology began with Theodore Munger who, unfortunately, was the first major disciple and interpreter of Bushnell's thought. Munger was one of the creators of the "new theology" in Amercia, a theology which looked to nature as the ultimate source of authority, a theology which asserted a doctrine of divine immanence that identified God and the world, a theology which maintained a moralistic doctrine of sin that carried with it a belief in historical progressivism and utopianism. It was that theology which Munger tried to read back into Bushnell.

That Bushnell's theology could not be fully reconciled with the "new theology" was, of course, obvious to Munger, but he insisted that Bushnell had set the tone that was now being fully explicated by the proponents of the "new theology." Apparent inconsistencies with that tone could be accounted for, explained Munger, in that Bushnell was a man born out of season. Nature was not yet willing to give up the secrets which Bushnell needed to substantiate his vision. It took another generation. Hence, Bushnell was a lonely prophet,

as Munger saw it, ". . . sitting in the dark, waiting for dis-
closures in nature that would substantiate what he felt was
true in the realm of the spirit."[1] Munger comfortably maintained that it was only natural that some inconsistencies
should appear, since Bushnell could not find sufficient support for his views from nature in his own time. The one matter,
however, that Munger found impossible to dismiss or explain
was Bushnell's consistently dark and severe view of sin. This
Munger could only lament.[2]

Given Munger's peculiar approach to Bushnell's theology,
it was impossible for him to understand either the spirit or
substance of Bushnell's thought. From the context of his
erroneous perspective, Munger was led to maintain that the
"secret" to Bushnell's theology lay in "his relation to nature."[3]
Whether or not a thing agreed with nature, Munger contended, was the ultimate criteria by which Bushnell mea-
sured truth. As I shall demonstrate later, this was anything
but a key to understanding Bushnell's theology.

The fact is that both friends and foes of Bushnell were
unable to comprehend his methodological stance because it
was so far removed from their own presuppositions. Leonard
Bacon, a friend, observed that Bushnell was "so far removed"
from the "mental habits" of his contemporaries that "they
could only misunderstand him."[4] Bushnell's contemporaries
had come to think of the discipline of theology in terms of
precise definitions and logical exactness. Words were regarded as being capable of conveying truth literally, with
the result that theological controversies raged over the length
and breadth of New England, each party claiming that its
creed was the truth incarnate. Bushnell maintained that none
of their thimble formulas or creeds could contain the truth

[1] T. T. Munger, "Horace Bushnell," *Christian Literature*, 4 (1896):
411.
[2] T. T. Munger, *Horace Bushnell Preacher and Theologian* (Boston:
Houghton Mifflin and Co., 1899), p. 219.
[3] T. T. Munger, *Essays for the Day* (Boston: Houghton Mifflin and
Co., 1904), p. 157.
[4] L. Bacon, "Concerning a Recent Chapter of Ecclesiastical History,"
The New Englander, 38 (1879):710.

of God. No language could make such claims. A new view of language was needed, one which would properly perceive the function and limitations of language. It was this new view of language which Bushnell fostered that distinguished him from his contemporaries, but it also made it impossible for his contemporaries, steeped in the old mental habits, to understand him. Munger, similarly unable to comprehend the function which Bushnell's theory of language performed, proceeded to read his own theological methodology into Bushnell, and since Munger was universally considered the man upon whom the mantle of Bushnell had fallen, it was almost inevitable that his interpretation of Bushnell should become authoritative for American theology. Accordingly, the first reason for the developing tradition of misinterpretation of Bushnell, simply stated, was Theodore Munger.

A second reason was that Bushnell was destined to be interpreted from secondary sources because few men dared to read him in the original for fear of being associated with his alleged heresies. Washington Gladden reported that few clergymen bought or read Bushnell's books because "Bushnellism was a name with which no ambitious minister could afford to be branded."[5] This — coupled with the fact that Munger's interpretation of Bushnell was sustained by other "new theology" enthusiasts, such as Washington Gladden and George Gordon — made Munger's exposition of Bushnell seem all the more credible, with the result that almost everybody who wrote anything about Bushnell from that day to this seems to have been destined to write about him from Munger's perspective.[6]

[5] W. Gladden, *Recollections* (Boston: Houghton Mifflin and Co., 1909), p. 120.

[6] In 1902 George B. Stevens tried to show that Bushnell's theology was comparable in its essential points to Albrecht Ritschl's; see G. B. Stevens, "Horace Bushnell and Albrecht Ritschl, A Comparison," *The American Journal of Theology*, 6 (1902):35–56. Five years later Foster praised Bushnell for "banishing" the doctrine of original sin and maintained that he used the "method of intuition" (F. H. Foster, *A Genetic History of New England Theology* [Chicago: Univ. of Chicago Press, 1907], pp. 405–6, 412). In 1913 Benjamin W. Bacon (Munger's biographer) parroted Munger, declaring that Bushnell "led over from con-

A third reason for the developing misinterpretation of Bushnell is that few interpreters of his thought have recognized the important role which tradition played in Bushnell's thinking. It was between the writing of *God in Christ* and *Christ in Theology* that Bushnell's interest in historical theology and his appreciation for the thinking of men in the Church's past developed.[7] Consequently, contrary to the

---

ceptions of transcendence and supernaturalism to conceptions of immanence and evolution," and that he stressed the "conception of the soul as innately kin to God" (B. W. Bacon, *Theodore Munger: New England Minister* [New Haven: Yale Univ. Press, 1913), pp. 305–6]. Six years later J. W. Buckham presented a similar picture of Bushnell, lamenting the fact that Bushnell cluttered up his writings with orthodox doctrines because they served only to reopen the "chasm between the divine and the human, which he [Bushnell] had closed by declaring man himself a supernatural being" (see J. W. Buckham, *Progressive Religious Thought in America* [Boston: Houghton Mifflin and Co., 1919], p. 28). Such is the interpretation which became normative. The same interpretation appears in W. Burggraff, *The Rise and Development of Liberal Theology in America* (Boston: Houghton Mifflin Co., 1919); W. S. Archibald, *Horace Bushnell* (Hartford, Conn.: Edwin Valentine Mitchell, 1930); W. M. Horton, *Realistic Theology* (New York: Harper and Brothers, 1934); A. J. Wm. Meyers, *Horace Bushnell and Religious Education* (Boston: Manthorne and Bureck, 1937); George Hammar, *Christian Realism in Contemporary American Theology* (Uppsala, Sweden: A.-B. Lundeguiltska, 1940), and others. Current interpreters such as Donald Meyer, who recently wrote that Bushnell dismissed the problems of sin and declared that "a good environment is itself the grace of God," reflect the same interpretation (in A. M. Schlesinger and Morton White, eds., *Paths of American Thought* [Boston: Houghton Mifflin and Co., 1963], pp. 80–81). And in his recent monograph on Bushnell, William Johnson reiterates the same interpretation, declaring that Bushnell "had not taken seriously the doctrine of original sin" (W. A. Johnson, *Nature and the Supernatural in the Theology of Horace Bushnell* [Lund, Sweden: CWK Gleerup, 1963], p. 132). The chain of interdependence among some of these interpretations is interesting and revealing. Horton, for example, admits his dependence on Buckham, and Hammar footnotes practically all of his references to Horton and Burggraff.

[7] There is ample evidence that Bushnell did some intensive reading in historical theology between the writing of *God in Christ* and *Christ in Theology*. In a letter to Dr. C. A. Barton, he said that the writing of the second volume cost him "five times the labor which the other [*God in Christ*] cost, because it has put me to the investigation of others . . ." (M. B. Cheney, *Life and Letters of Horace Bushnell* [New York: Charles Scribner's Sons, 1903], p. 273). Leonard Bacon confirmed this. "For my own part, I was surprised — and I have not yet ceased to

proponents of the "new theology," Bushnell was always concerned that his theology be orthodox according to the ancient
standards. In fact he insisted that his theology was really a
return to an older orthodoxy than the orthodoxy which the
New England theologians who accused *him* of heresy embraced.

Finally, Bushnell was misinterpreted because he refused
to make his own theological methodology explicit. In keeping with his new approach to the discipline of theology and
his new theory of language which inspired that discipline,
he did not wish his views to become an ironclad system which
others could appropriate and proclaim as the truth incarnate.
Consequently, Bushnell purposely employed a certain amount
of vagueness and elusiveness so that his readers would not
make a definitive system out of his methodology. He had
hoped in this manner to lead his contemporaries out of their
old mental habits of seeing truth only in neat formulas and
into a new, dynamic method which would only catch at
glimpses of truth. He instructed his readers accordingly:

> If we find the writer, in hand, moving with a free motion,
> and tied to no one symbol, unless in some popular ef-
> fort, or for some single occasion; if we find him multi-
> plying antagonisms, offering cross views, and bringing
> us round the field to show us how it looks from different
> points, then we are to presume that he has some truth

wonder — at the thoroughness and insight with which he had studied
the history of theology as related to the subjects in question . . ."
(Bacon, "Concerning a Recent Chapter of Ecclesiastical History, p. 710).
Bushnell reported the double surprise which he experienced as a result
of this intensive reading program, "first, that I am so much nearer to
real orthodoxy than I supposed, and secondly, that the New England
theology, so called, is so much farther off" (H. Bushnell, *Christ in
Theology* [Hartford, Conn: Brown and Parsons, 1851], p. 247). From
this point on, Bushnell always expressed concern on behalf of his orthodoxy, insisting that "I really had done nothing more than to revive, in
a modern shape, the lost orthodoxy of the Church" (Cheney, *Life and
Letters of Horace Bushnell*, p. 284). Bushnell's daughter confirmed
this statement: "We must remember that Dr. Bushnell had never ceased
to consider himself orthodox according to the ancient standards; in
fact, that he felt it to be his mission to rescue certain important truths
of orthodoxy from the mire into which they had fallen" (*ibid.*, p. 338).

in hand which it becomes us to know. We are to pass round accordingly with him, take up all his symbols, catch a view of him here, and another there, use one thing to qualify and interpret another, and the other to shed light upon that, and, by a process of this kind, endeavor to comprehend his antagonisms and settle into a complete view of his meaning.[8]

But the mental habits of Bushnell's contemporaries were too firmly entrenched for them to see this. Only a very few, like S.D.F. Salmond, ever really understood the method Bushnell employed.[9]

Be that as it may, Bushnell's new methodology, informed by his theory of language, cleared the way for him to affirm a new, dynamic and ecumenical approach to the nature and task of theology. In his *Christ in Theology* he stated that approach succintly.

But if we speak of the actual results of theologic study and exercise, — the forms of truth, or opinion, or system prepared by it, — we need to distinguish between a close or merely reasoned system, and an open free system that waits for the discovery always of God; between an incrustation on the outside, to keep and imprison the life, and a cell or point of embryonic tissue begun at the center of life itself. They tell us that when the crustacea have grown a shell so thick and old that the life can no longer pierce through it and keep it on the footing of a living substance, it begins to be a foreign matter constringing [sic] the vital action, and the animal dies, suffocated by the tomb it has built. So it is when our theological crustaces are coffined in the close system we

[8] H. Bushnell, *God in Christ* (Hartford, Conn.: Brown and Parsons, 1849), p. 67.
[9] S. D. F. Salmond, "The Theology of Horace Bushnell, *The London Quarterly Review*, 95 (1901), 133–58. This article is unquestionably the finest interpretation of Bushnell's methodology in this early period. Salmond perceived all the essential elements of Bushnell's thought.

speak of. Since it is no longer *of* them, but a cerement of dead and strange matter *about* them, not quickened by their faith, they die of strange doctrine in it.[10]

The crucial question, then, is whether theology ought to have the character of a cell or a crustacea, and for Bushnell it had to be the former, a "living state," "an open state," "a condition of germinative force and ever extending growth."[11] Whenever theology became a dead, reasoned system, confined and closed, it strangled the very life of faith it was attempting to explain and communicate.

By this, Bushnell did not mean that he was opposed to systemization as such. Although there would inevitably be much "hay and stubble"[12] in any system, yet the discipline of systemization was invaluable. The systems produced were always of necessity "flimsy as soap-bubbles,"[13] yet "system is the instinct of intelligence, and to crucify the instinct of system is, in one view, to crucify intelligence."[14]

Furthermore, systemization is invaluable despite error because errors themselves make a contribution to the theological discipline. Bushnell held that errors in theological systems, like errors in creeds and Scripture, performed a valuable service. He advocated the writing of creeds even though they were always false because it was precisely the errors in creeds that led men to look beyond the creeds to the truth to which the creeds pointed. Similarly, imperfections in Scripture led men to look beyond the forms and symbols of the written word to the truth to which the symbols pointed. "How necessary, often, all their conflicting representations are to a full and well-rounded Christian doctrine, — practiced in this way, he will begin to have a more exalted sense of the truth."[15]

Consequently, far from recommending that the discipline

[10] Bushnell, *Christ in Theology*, p. 73.
[11] *Ibid.*, p. 83.
[12] *Ibid.*, p. 84.
[13] *Ibid.*, p. 72.
[14] *Ibid.*, p. 64.
[15] *Ibid.*, p. 52.

of theology be discarded, Bushnell insisted that theologizing was essential, but that the task be performed with a clear understanding of its limitations. Here, again, his position was informed by his theory of language.

> If all language is found to be under conditions of form, while truth itself, being spiritual, is out of form, or has no form, it does not follow that Christian doctrine is to be despaired of, or treated with indifference. It is only to be sought with greater patience, a more delicate candor, and a more ingenious love.[16]

The statement that ". . . all language is found to be under conditions of form, while truth itself, being spiritual, is out of form . . ." reveals, in a succinct manner, the way in which Bushnell interpreted the function of theology. Once Bushnell became convinced that language (which was part and parcel of the finite world of forms) could not literally communicate truth (which was out of form), he was faced with a crucial question. How can truth be communicated? Is man doomed to be forever cut off from any insights into or revelation from the truth?

It was this question, in part growing out of his observation of theological controversies in New England, that led Bushnell, with the help of insights from Coleridge, to scrutinize the whole nature and function of language in human discourse and to apply his theory of language to the discipline of theology and finally to his description of the Christian faith itself.

The theory of language which Bushnell finally arrived at has four constituent parts. However, before I delineate these distinctive parts, it will be instructive to attempt a seminal description of Bushnell's theory, and how he interpreted the Christian faith in terms of it.

It is clear that Bushnell obtained the initial insights for his theory of language from Samuel Taylor Coleridge.[17] How-

---

[16] *Ibid.*, p. 65.

[17] Bushnell was very clear about his indebtedness to Coleridge. "By-and-by it fell to me to begin the reading of Coleridge. For a whole half

ever, it has not always been noted that Bushnell departed quite radically from Coleridge's philosophy. The philosophy of Coleridge was essentially Kantian, establishing a radical dichotomy between "imagination" and "fancy," between "reason" and "understanding." These dichotomies, said Coleridge, were founded upon the more basic division between spirit and nature.

> I have attempted, then, to fix the proper meaning of the words, nature and spirit, the one being the *antithesis* to the other; so that the most general and negative definition of nature is, whatever is not spirit; and *vice versa* of the spirit that which is not comprehended in nature. . . .[18]

Once Coleridge had established this dichotomy between nature and spirit, he declared that the only way one could know anything about the spirit level was through direct intuition. "The faculty of reflection" was operative on the level of "understanding" (the level of material and sense objects), but on the level of "reason" (the level of the spiritual) one could only know through "a direct aspect of truth, an inward beholding having a similar relation to the intelligible or spiritual, as sense has to the material or phaenomenal [*sic*]."[19]

Bushnell did *not* borrow this scheme. While Bushnell appropriated the two-level concept and maintained the same

---

year I was buried under his 'Aids to Reflection,' and trying vainly to look up through. I was quite sure that I saw a star glimmer, but I could not quite see the stars. My habit was only landscape before; but now I saw enough to convince me of a whole other world somewhere overhead. . . . Shortly after, a very strong lift in my religious experiences came as a waft upon my inspirations, to apprise me more distinctly of their existence, and of the two-world range that belonged to me. . . . In this mood of exigency, I discovered how language built on physical images is itself two stories high, and is, in fact, an outfit for a double range of uses" (Cheney, *Life and Letters of Horace Bushnell*, p. 209). In this brief statement, Bushnell intimates that it was the idea of the two-storied universe, and not the total philosophy of Coleridge, that interested him.

[18] S. T. Coleridge, *Aids to Reflection* (Burlington: Chauncey Goodrich, 1840), p. 236.

[19] *Ibid.*, p. 217.

radical dichotomy between them, he did *not* follow Coleridge in maintaining that one could only apprehend the truth
of the spirit level by direct intuition. Direct intuition was
impossible according to Bushnell. Rather, the truth of the
spirit level was always communicated through the powerful
dialectic that was carried on between the two levels.

What Bushnell in fact did, was to take insights concerning the dichotomy between reason and understanding from
Coleridge, after which he then returned to the New Testa-
ment, and this led him to conclusions quite different from
those of Coleridge.

One of Bushnell's favorite passages of Scripture was the
first chapter of the Gospel of John. Here Bushnell found all
the ingredients for a theory of language that made communication of truth under the conditions of finitude possible. "In
the beginning was the Word . . . All things were made
through Him . . . He was in the world and the world was
made through Him, yet the world knew Him not." These
words now had new meaning for Bushnell. The creative
agent of God gave to the world a *logos* structure, a "form"
through which God continually communicates His truth to
man. Yet man can never know His truth, for the truth itself
is infinite, "out of form," while man and his world are finite,
"in form." Hence, language is always going on "under the
guidance of the Word or Divine 'Logos', in the forms, images,
activities and relations of the outward world. . . . It speaks
in words He gave, and under a grammar that He appointed
and yet it knows Him not."[20]

It will now begin to become apparent how Bushnell related
language to the incarnation and how that interpretation at
once became the heart of his methodology and the foundation for his understanding of the Christian faith.

For Bushnell, the theory of language built upon the *logos*
concept now became the basis for interpreting salvation-history, which, in turn, became the context for understanding
the Christian faith. From the first moment of creation God
has continually been revealing His truth to men so that lan-

[20] Bushnell, *God in Christ*, p. 32.

guage, the sum of all the organic mediums God uses to communicate Himself, is itself a kind of incarnation. "All words are, in fact, only incarnations, or insensings of thought."[21] All of history is therefore a history of revelation, and revelation is God speaking to us through the *logos* structure of the world (form), and that is language. It was no accident that Bushnell's early lecture on revelation was largely devoted to the subject of language.[22]

Some of the more significant moments of our salvation-history have been recorded in Scripture; creation, the forming of the nation of Israel, the development of the law, the prophets. All of these were moments in the continuous process of divine self-communication through organic forms. Then God "crowns the revelation process by the incarnate life and life-story of His Son . . . . We can say nothing of Christ so comprehensively adequate as to call Him the metaphor of God; God's last metaphor!"[23]

It was a source of constant dismay to Bushnell that while it required an incarnate life for God to communicate Himself to man, New England divines were under the illusion that they could hold the truth of God in their tiny formulas.

> It is a great trouble with us that we can not put a whole scheme of redemption, which God could execute only by the volume of expression contained in the life and death of his incarnate Son, into a theologic formula or article of ten words.[24]

On the assumption, then, that truth itself is always out of form and that we to whom the truth must be communicated are always in form, Bushnell next concluded that all language for us must have a physical base. Herein lies the basis for Bushnell's departure from Coleridge.

> . . . It is impossible . . . that any terms of language for mental notions, things of the spirit, unseen worlds,

[22] See Cheney, *Life and Letters of Horace Bushnell*, pp. 88–89.
[21] *Ibid.*, p. 56.
[23] H. Bushnell, *Building Eras in Religion* (New York: Charles Scribner's Sons, 1881), p. 259.
[24] Bushnell, *Christ in Theology*, p. 33.

beings invisible, should ever exist save as there are physical images found to serve as metaphoric bases of the
necessary words. . . . So we see . . . that all the truths
of religion are going to be given to men by images; so
that all God's truth will come as to the imagination.[25]

Accordingly, all language of spiritual things "must get its
power to express the unknown by drawing images and figures
from the known."[26] This was the purpose of salvation-history.
Through the centuries God had always used the images of
the known to lift the vision of men to the unknown—from
creation to the calling of a chosen nation, from a holy nation
to the law, from the law to the prophets, from the prophets
to a Son—and the biblical maxim "that it might be fulfilled"
is nothing more than "the systematic fact of language itself."[27] When the fullness of time finally came (that is, when
men had been sufficiently trained by being led from the
known to the unknown) God was able to "disburden his
whole heart's love and be known by what he can bear and
do for the world of mankind."[28]

Thus God had been "preparing, even from the first, to be
finally known as the Lord and Savior of the whole world,"
but had He used the symbol of the Son before men had been
prepared to receive this unknown, it "would not even have
been remembered in history."[29] Knowledge by direct intuition is not possible, it must always have a physical base in
what is already known.

Consequently, Bushnell (far from following Coleridge)
maintained that while there was a radical dichotomy between the two levels, there was also a powerful dialectic
between them; that far from affirming the concept that one
could only apprehend the truth of the spirit level intuitively,
Bushnell insisted that one could only peer into the spirit

[25] Bushnell, *Building Eras*, p. 255.
[26] *Ibid.*, p. 258.
[27] *Ibid.*, p. 256.
[28] H. Bushnell, *The Vicarious Sacrifice Grounded in Principles of Universal Obligation* (New York: Charles Scribner and Co., 1869), p. 67.
[29] *Ibid.*, p. 66.

level *through* finite forms. However, we must always remember that the finite can only serve as an image, a medium of communication; it can never embody the infinite, nor can it be its imperfect copy.

It was on this basis that Bushnell insisted that all systems, creeds, sacred writings, etc., were not only inexact but false.

> Words of thought or spirit are not only inexact in their significance, never measuring the truth or giving its precise equivalent, but they always affirm something which is false, or contrary to the truth intended. They impute form to that which is really out of form. They are related to the truth, only as form to spirit — earthen vessels in which the truth is borne, yet always offering their mere pottery as being the truth itself. . . . Therefore, we need always to have it in mind, or in present recollection, that they are but signs, in fact, or images of that which has no shape or sensible quality whatever; a kind of painting, in which the speaker, or the writer, leads one through a gallery of pictures or forms, while we attend him, catching at thoughts suggested by his forms. In one view they are all false; for there are no shapes in the truths they represent, and therefore we are to separate continually, and by a most delicate process of art, between the husks of the forms and the pure thought presented in them.[30]

So language, all organic forms or mediums of communication including theological systems, is like a painting. A painting is never identified with the message it is intended to convey. The message is not the color and design. But if we become receptive to the combination of color and design the painting can suggest a message to us. We can catch at the message suggested by the forms. This is why it is futile to argue over fine points of logic. The impressions which a painting intends to create will not be discerned by artists who scrutinize the shading, balance, and chemistry with a magnifying glass and dispute them. The message will be dis-

[30] Bushnell, *God in Christ*, pp. 48–49.

cerned by the connoisseur with an appreciative soul who allows the impressions to pour into his heart. Similarly, the truth which language is intended to communicate will not be perceived by logicians and grammarians who argue about the consistency, logic, and definitions of words, trying to discover an exact indisputable meaning but by those who allow word combinations to stir their imaginations and catch at the truths they suggest.

It was in this sense that the attitude of reception was more important for Bushnell than the preciseness of the composition. "Let us only take the attitude of reception; let us cease from our foolish endeavor to make universes of the truth for God out of a few words and images that we have speculated into wise sentences."[31] The emphasis which Bushnell placed on the attitude of receptivity makes it apparent, again, how radically he departed from Coleridge. Coleridge, following Kant, maintained that the mind was "creative." "We receive but what we give" is the way Coleridge liked to put it. It is true that Coleridge asserted a "primary" level of imagination which was a sort of automatic creativity by which the mind naturally created daily visions of prosaic occurrences without any real effort, which is not far removed from receptivity. But the poet and the seer had to go beyond this to the "secondary" level of imagination, straining to create a more real and a more elaborate vision of the truth.[32]

Bushnell's accent on the attitude of receptivity did not mean, however, that he paid no attention to creative writing and composition. Quite the contrary, he took great pains to compose the forms very carefully so as to free the imaginations of men which had become imprisoned by the "mental habits" of seeking truth in precise formula. Again, Bushnell did not suggest an end to systematic thinking, but a new attitude toward systems. We must constantly shun the trap of believing that our preciseness of composition and defini-

[31] Bushnell, *Christ in Theology*, pp. 33–34.
[32] See B. Willey, *Nineteenth Century Studies* (New York: Columbia Univ. Press, 1949), pp. 14 ff. Cf. I. A. Richards, *Coleridge on Imagination* (Bloomington: Indiana Univ. Press, 1960).

tion will produce literal conveyances of the truth. It is precisely that attitude which invites preoccupation with logical calculus, arguments over fine points of consistency, and wranglings over precise definitions. These are the sources of unnecessary conflict which only blind us to the truth which is trying to break in upon us through the forms of language. Given the attitude of receptivity, however, proper composition, composition which excites the imaginations of men, was very important. It was for this reason that Bushnell commended the task of constantly rewriting theology. We always need new forms to hold the minds of men in the orthodox truths; otherwise they begin to affirm the form rather than the truth to which form points them. As Bushnell put it, "It may even be necessary to change the forms, to hold us in the same truths."[33]

Consequently all language, including theological systems, is relative, inexact and false, and therefore all language, including creeds and Scripture, should never be expected to convey truth literally. Language can only hint at truth, only arouse the mind of another to catch at it.

> Words . . . are legitimately used as the signs of thoughts to be expressed. They do not literally convey, or pass over a thought out of one mind into another, as we commonly speak of doing. They are only hints, or images, held up before the mind of another, to put *him* on generating or reproducing the same thought; which he can do only as he has the same personal contents, or the generative power out of which to bring the thought required. Hence, there will be different measures of understanding or mis-understanding, according to the capacity or incapacity, the ingenuousness or moral obliquity of the receiving party —. . . .[34]

And thus theological systems must be cells, not crustacea, living centers which constantly change their forms to invite the minds of men to catch at the truth to which they point,

[33] Bushnell, *God in Christ*, p. 80.
[34] *Ibid.*, pp. 45–46.

not closed systems which imprison the mind and prevent it
from seeing beyond the form and glimpsing at the truth to
which the form points.

Now let us analyze the four constituent parts of this theory
of language. First, there is an analogy between mind and
matter. By this Bushnell meant that there is a mysterious,
analogous relationship between that which is in form and
that which is out of form. What is in form is somehow prepared to present that which is out of form to us. It is this
analogous relationship that makes it possible for form to lead
us beyond form. Consequently, while we are in the historical situation of being led from known forms to unknown
forms there is always the existential occurrence of insight
(the breaking through of that which is out of form through
our receptivity to that which is in form) by virtue of the
analogy between mind and matter.

Frederick Ferre, Paul Van Buren, and others have recently
questioned the whole use of analogy, and perhaps rightly so,
but Bushnell did not concern himself with the philosophical
problems connected with the use of analogy. For him, such
analogy was implicit in the doctrine of the incarnation and
he rested his case on that. The creative agent, he insisted,
had left His stamp, a *logos* structure, on reality. He "speaks
in words he gave and under a grammar he appointed." Like
fragments of mirror perfectly fitted together, the world of
form had been perfectly constituted to reflect that which
is out of form to us. Bushnell therefore insisted that form
was never to be depreciated. Form was absolutely essential
to any apprehension of the truth. Accordingly, Bushnell consistently affirmed the dialectic between mind and matter,
never sacrificing the one for the other as they were in Swedenborgian mysticism.

. . . All the terms of language, in which thoughts and
spiritual truths are presented, all the instruments of expression by which God is set before men, must be taken

out of the world of form, and will offer truth and God to us only under analogies or conditions of form.[35]

Accordingly, while Bushnell maintained, with Coleridge, that there is a radical disjunction between that which is in form and that which is out of form, he nevertheless affirmed a powerful, mysterious dialectic between them which riveted the connection between them in such a manner that form always contained in it the capacity to point man beyond it. Form, therefore, was always indispensible to revelation.

> The revelation . . . whether it is a proposition of language, a vision, a burning bush, or a divine life in the flesh, will have *something* in it *which puts it under the conditions of forms, and something which pertains to its intellectual and spiritual significance.* And then the account must ever be liquidated between what belongs to the form and what to the significance, . . . constant care being had not to manufacture truth by inferences drawn out of the forms, but to find truth in them by a simple and delicately receptive contemplation of them, or insight of what they express.[36]

The assertion that an analogy exists between mind and matter is, by itself extremely important for arriving at a proper interpretation of Bushnell. It invalidates the contention that Bushnell was an intuitivist. It demolishes Munger's argument that Bushnell was a naturalist. It makes the thesis that Bushnell was a Swedenborgian untenable. And since Bushnell interpreted the Christian faith in terms of the analogy between mind and matter, it fully dissociates him from the theologies of divine immanence, the moralistic doctrine of sin, and the ethical or psychological relationship to Christ. Similarly, it points out the fallacy of writing Bushnell off as a subjectivist just because he once blurted out that he would hold by his heart rather than his head.[37] Bushnell certainly

[35] Bushnell, *Christ in Theology*, p. 39.
[36] *Ibid.* (italics mine).
[37] Even Sidney Mead gave his support to this view. See S. Mead, *The Lively Experiment* (New York: Harper & Row, 1963), p. 172.

preferred his heart to logical gymnastics, but he never sub-
stituted his heart for his head. The whole man needed to
be receptive to organic forms so that by virtue of their analogy to that which was out of form men might be led to
glimpses of truth.

The second constituent in the edifice of the theory of language is that all language is figurative. Bushnell's primary
concern under this assertion was to clarify the distinction
between the literal and figurative use of words. Bushnell
maintained that a great misconception lay in the fact that
most people regarded the distinction between the literal and
figurative use of language to be limited to the use of certain
words. For example, the word "heart" may refer to an organ
of the human anatomy or to the seat of the emotions, the
former use being literal and the latter figurative. But people
who limited the distinction between figurative and literal to
these few peculiar words never perceived the basis upon
which the literal became the symbol for the figurative. If
they had, they would soon have discovered that all words
for thought have a physical base. The real distinction between the figurative and the literal "runs through the very
body of language itself, making two departments; one that
comprises the terms of sensation, the other the terms of
thought."[38] Accordingly, the only literal language there is,
is that consisting of mathematical symbols, or words used as
names for physical objects. "Pen," for example, is a literal
symbol for a writing instrument. But all words for *thought*
are figurative, having their bases in some physical phenomenon. Hence, all words which are used to describe thought are
words which find their origin in some physical form, and that
form is intended to lift the mind beyond the form itself to
a formless, non-physical thought or truth which is perceptible to the mind.

Precisely here lay the fatal error of New England's theo-

After all, Bushnell did say that "the heart and the head must be as
two that walk together, never so truly agreed as when they agree to
help each other." Bushnell, *God in Christ*, p. 316.
[38] Bushnell, *God in Christ*, p. 40.

logians, as Bushnell saw it. They had assumed that there
were both literal and figurative words in the realm of *thought*.
They readily admitted that there were metaphors in theological language. "Shepherd" and "sheep" were metaphors for
Christ and the faithful. But, they went on to assume that
there was also an exact language which set forth theological
truths exactly and literally, and on that basis they asserted
that creeds and doctrines, if carefully formulated, could be
literal expressions of the truth, and the Scriptures could
be verbally inerrant.

> Just here is the fruitful source of imposture in theology.
> Reducing the truth of scripture into forms of abstract
> statement, under figures so effectually staled by time
> and familiarity that they seem, instead, to be literal and
> exact names of the ideas intended, it calls the product
> certainty. . . .[39]

On the contrary, all words representing thought were
"forms" which somewhere in their history had their origin in
physical objects or actions. "Influence," for example, had its
root in physical nature in a literal, physical in-flowing of a
river and its tributaries. The term, however, is only a figure, a
symbol which is meant to suggest a mental world of non-physical, or formless, thoughts, ranging from that phenomenon
which sways a person in a certain direction by argumentation, to the belief in the effect of the mysterious workings of
God in the holy Trinity. But as long as we assume that such
forms carry absolute truth within them, our minds will be
constantly boxed in by these forms and we will be given a
false and suffocated concept of the truth. Besides, such
absolutized finite truths will always be thought to be synonymous with God and therefore of necessity involve us in
idolatry.

The third constituent of Bushnell's theory of language is
that it is impossible to escape form in human language.
"Whoever attempts to bring any truth out of form, into an
exact, literal, abstractive language clear of form, begins in a

[39] Bushnell, *Christ in Theology*, p. 42.

delusion at the outset, and is very certain to be deeper in delusion at the end."[40] It is impossible to escape form in language, first because the moment we think of anything ". . . the subject must be clothed in forms that are only signs or analogies and not equivalents to the truth."[41] This is a point stressed equally by Walter J. Ong. Father Ong observes that even when words are not audibly spoken they take on form for they become conversation within us. To think is to converse with ourselves, consequently words take on form; ". . . in so far as words are formed within us, they are destined for externalization."[42] It is also impossible to escape form in language, according to Bushnell, because language takes on added form when words are put into sentences. Individual words may eventually lose the physical roots from which they were derived but when they are put into a sentence "there will yet be some particles of relation or transition which carries the whole idea of the sentence into a setting of form . . ."[43]

We note here that Bushnell's refusal to discard the task of systemization was again rooted in one of the constituents of his theory of language. All language takes on externalization — form. So to think is to systemize. Hence, one can never escape systemization; he either systemizes conscientiously and carefully or unconsciously and indiscriminately, but systemize he does. One can, however, have either proper attitudes toward systemization (viewing it as a cell, an open, living, dynamic process) or improper attitudes toward it (seeing it as a crustacea, a closed, dead, imprisoning status).

The fourth constituent, which completed the edifice of Bushnell's theory of language, was that paradox is necessary in human language! Since words are only suggestive symbols and therefore always subject to misrepresentation, Bushnell deemed it necessary to use symbols of opposites and

[40] *Ibid.*, p. 51.
[41] *Ibid.*, p. 15.
[42] W. J. Ong, *The Barbarian Within* (New York: Macmillan, 1962), p. 50.
[43] Bushnell, *Christ in Theology*, p. 50.

contradictions in order to move the mind to a more adequate picture of truth.

> Thus as form battles form, and one form neutralizes another, all the insufficiencies of words are filled out, the contrarieties liquidated, and the mind settles into a full and just apprehension of the pure spiritual truth. Accordingly we never come so near to a truly well rounded view of any truth, as when it is offered paradoxically, that is, under contradictions; that is, under two or more dictions, which, taken as dictions, are contrary one to the other. . . . So also . . . poets express their most inexpressible or evanescent thoughts, by means of repugnant or somewhat paradoxical epithets; as, for example, Coleridge, when he says, —
> The Stilly murmur of the distant sea
> Tells us of silence.[44]

Again one of the constituent parts of Bushnell's theory of language inspired one of his propositions: that error and contradiction in creeds and Scripture are good, for they pry the mind loose from the old mental habits of neat logical consistency and exactness and free it to catch at the truth which always lies beyond form.

Accordingly, it was the theory of language, not nature, that was the "key" to Bushnell's theological methodology.[45] And language, thus interpreted, gave to systematic theology

[44] Bushnell, *God in Christ*, pp. 55–56. Coleridge's lines are from "The Eolian Harp."

[45] The fact that the theory of language is the "key" to Bushnell's theology is confirmed by Bushnell himself as well as all those who knew him best. See the following: Bushnell, *God in Christ*, p. 102; Bushnell, *Christ in Theology*, pp. 15, 63; Cheney, *Life and Letters of Horace Bushnell*, p. 203; H. Clay Trumbull, "Reminiscences of Dr. Bushnell," *The Sunday School Times*, 61 (September 2, 1899): 498; C. Clever, "Horace Bushnell, Preacher and Theologian," *The Reformed Church Review*, 4th Ser. 4 (1900): 73; W. Walker, "Dr. Bushnell as a Religious Leader," *Bushnell Centenary* (Hartford, Conn: Case, Lockwood and Brainerd Co., 1902), p. 25; A. S. Chesebrough, "Horace Bushnell, the Theological Opinion of, as Related to his Character and Christian Experience," *The Andover Review*, 6 (Aug. 1886): 114.

a sense of aliveness and dynamics for Bushnell; it made the task of systemization an exciting and stimulating adventure.

Systematic theology thus conceived had real ecumenical possibilities. Contradictory propositions in disparate systems were not to be seen as occasions for enmity and divisions but opportunities for new insights which break in upon the minds of men as they look beyond the contradictions to the truths which always lie beyond the formulas of men. Bushnell would have agreed wholeheartedly with Alfred North Whitehead that "A clash of doctrines is not a disaster—it is an opportunity."[46] Bushnell had hoped that his insights would bring an end to the enmity which existed between theological parties in New England.

Thus conceived, the systems which systematic theology produces are living cells, ever growing, ever taking on new forms, ever changing. They are not crustacea, always becoming more entombed, hardened, and static smothering the dynamic faith which they imprison.

Viewed from this perspective, Bushnell's theology takes on an entirely different character from that which is usually attributed to him. When we take his methodology seriously we soon discover that he did not foster a moralistic doctrine of sin. Rather, he saw sin as an ontological distortion, a fragmentation of the perfect order of forms, destroying the original communication between God and man which had existed by virtue of the logos structure of existence. We soon discover that Bushnell did not proclaim a doctrine of Christ in ethical and psychological terms. Rather, Christ was a real power of being "new-crystalizing the soul." Christ is an ontological power which reestablishes communication between God and man, not a moral or psychological influence that appeals to man's emotions and moral sensitivites.[47] And we also discover that Christian nurture is not a gradual process of natural growth and education. Rather, it is a process of

[46] A. N. Whitehead, *Science and the Modern World* (New York: Macmillan, 1926), p. 266.
[47] See Bushnell, *The Vicarious Sacrifice*, pp. 169–71.

communication which takes place between parent and child by virtue of the ontological ties which exist between them.

Accordingly, when we take Bushnell's own theological methodology seriously, we discover that his assessment of himself was correct when he said

> . . . I wish you to be notified of the confidence I have that, when the smoke of these agitations is blown away, it will be discovered by any competent scholar and critic in Church history who may undertake to settle the precise merit or relative import of my supposed defections, that I was really closer in agreement of doctrine and a closer sympathy of evangelic sentiment with the acknowledged fathers and teachers of the Church, than my brethren who are testifying so great concern on my account. The verdict will be, not that I raised any banner of revolt against orthodoxy, but that, on the contrary, I only sought to restore its equilibrium. . . .[48]

[48] Cheney, *Life and Letters of Horace Bushnell*, p. 259.

4

Negro Christianity and
American Church Historiography
ROBERT T. HANDY

There has been much comment about the rather impressive productivity in the field of American church history in the 1960's.[1] An atlas, a bibliography, a source book, several basic texts, and collections of interpretative essays — all these have appeared so far in this decade.[2] There has also been published a number of books and many articles dealing with particular denominations, conspicuous figures, and special problems. Some of these writings deal directly with Negro Christianity in the United States.[3]

[1] See Henry F. May, "The Recovery of American Religious History," *American Historical Review*, 70 (1964): 79–92; William A. Clebsch, "A New Historiography of American Religion," *Historical Magazine of the Protestant Episcopal Church*, 32 (1963): 225–57.

[2] Edwin S. Gaustad, *Historical Atlas of Religion in America* (New York: Harper & Row, 1962); Nelson R. Burr, *Religion in American Life*, vol. 4, *A Critical Bibliography of Religion in America* (Princeton, N. J.: Princeton Univ. Press, 1961); H. Shelton Smith, Robert T. Handy, and Lefferts A. Loetscher, *American Christianity: An Historical Interpretation with Representative Documents* (2 vols.; New York: Scribner, 1960, 1963); Winthrop S. Hudson, *Religion in America* (New York: Scribner, 1965); Edwin S. Gaustad, *A Religious History of America* (New York: Harper & Row, 1966); Sidney E. Mead, *The Lively Experiment: The Shaping of Christianity in America* (New York: Harper & Row, 1963); James W. Smith and A. Leland Jamison, eds., *Religion in American Life*, vol. 1, *The Shaping of American Religion* (Princeton, N.J.: Princeton Univ. Press, 1961).

[3] See E. Franklin Frazier, *The Negro Church in America* (New York: Schocken Books, 1964); Donald G. Mathews, *Slavery and Methodism: A Chapter in American Morality* (Princeton, N. J.: Princeton Univ. Press, 1965); Andrew E. Murray, *Presbyterians and The Negro — A History* (Philadelphia: Presbyterian Historical Society, 1966); David W. Reimers, *White Protestantism and the Negro* (New York: Oxford Univ.

On the whole, however, American church historiography has regarded the history of Christianity among Negroes as a "special topic," to be treated in connection with certain definite crises or to be handled by those with a particular interest in that subject. In the main general historical interpretations of American church life, Negro Christianity has been treated rather incidentally, even casually. A recent extensive survey article dealing with "The History of Christianity" as studied in America — one-third of which focuses exclusively on American church history — does not even mention Negro Christianity as such. Three titles dealing with anti-slavery and pro-slavery thought in the nineteenth century are listed, but the extensive and rapidly growing body of literature on the various aspects of the religion of Negroes is not otherwise mentioned.[4] Readers of the basic introductory writings in the field gain little overall knowledge of Negro Christianity. Yet the materials for the study are vast, though admittedly uneven. The leading bibliographer of religion in America, Nelson R. Burr, has devoted a solid chapter in his massive work to "The Negro Church," as well as contributing important sections to other aspects of Negro religion — in all some sixty pages of his narrative bibliography.[5] The realities with which these materials deal, however, have not yet been sufficiently considered and worked into the general treatments of American church history.

This study of Negro Christianity and American church historiography may suggest that the story of Christianity in America has been generally told too much from the viewpoint of the "main-line" denominations, without enough attention to the religious movements of various minority groups and of the "disinherited" elements of the population. There have been some good studies of these matters, but have they been given sufficient attention in the general inter-

Press, 1965); cf. Elizabeth W. Miller, comp., *The Negro in America: A Bibliography* (Cambridge, Mass.: Harvard Univ. Press, 1966).

[4] James H. Nichols, in Paul Ramsey, ed., *Religion* (Englewood Cliffs, N.J.: Prentice-Hall, 1965), pp. 155–217.

[5] Nelson R. Burr, *Religion in American Life*, vol. 4, pp. 346–81, 610–14, 683–93, 839–46, 940–43.

pretations? The argument of this essay may have wider application, though it will focus on the tendency of American church historiography to minimize specifically Negro Christianity.

It may be of some helpfulness to speculate on the reasons for this lack, in the effort to try to overcome it. The subject of the history of Christianity among Negroes is one with deep emotional overtones for almost everyone. In his stimulating book *Slavery*, Stanley M. Elkins notices that "there is a painful touchiness in all aspects of the subject; the discourse contains almost too much immediacy, it makes too many connections with present problems."[6] Touchiness is also present in the discussion of the religious and church life of Negroes; the immediacy and the connections with present problems are much in evidence. For white Christian historians of religion, especially if they have been influenced by contemporary trends in social ethical thought and action, there may be certain feelings of guilt to contend with as the fuller meaning of what white Christians have done to blacks in the past (and present) come home to them. As Kyle Haselden has put it, "The white Christian is and has been an oppressor and exploiter of his darker-skinned fellowman. He is guilty and no white man should attempt to hide that guilt or to apologize for it."[7] The story of the dealings between Christianity and Negroes is a long one, and much of it makes hard reading. As Frank Tannenbaum has explained, British-American civilization, in part because of lack of precedent and experience, allowed extremely harsh patterns of chattel slavery to be developed and identified with the African — with the general consent and often active support of the churches.[8] By the later eighteenth century, however,

[6] Stanley M. Elkins, *Slavery: A Problem in American Institutional and Intellectual Life* (Chicago: Univ. of Chicago Press, 1959), p. 1.
[7] Kyle Haselden, *Mandate for White Christians* (Richmond, Va.: John Knox Press, 1966), p. 10.
[8] Frank Tannenbaum, *Slave and Citizen: The Negro in the Americas* (New York: Knopf, 1947).

much Christian and Enlightenment humanitarian thought was hopeful that slavery was a dying institution. But in the early nineteenth century this expectancy was crushed. For example, a Committee on Slavery made this report to the General Conference of the Methodist Episcopal Church in 1816:

> The committee to whom was referred the business of slavery beg leave to report, that they have taken the subject into serious consideration, and, after mature deliberation, they are of opinion that, under the present existing circumstances in relation to slavery, little can be done to abolish a practice so contrary to the principles of moral justice. They are sorry to say that the evil appears to be past remedy; and they are led to deplore the destructive consequences which have already accrued, and are likely to result therefrom.[9]

One cannot help but wonder if they would have spoken differently—and if it would have made any difference—had they had any inkling of the "destructive consequences" to come.

The Presbyterians at that time seemed to be doing better; in 1818 their General Assembly published a remarkable statement on slavery as "a gross violation of the most precious and sacred rights of human nature."[10] But the very next year, in endorsing the American Colonization Society with its racialist overtones, the Assembly said, "In the distinctive and indelible marks of their colour, and the prejudices of the people, an insuperable object has been placed to the execution of any plan for elevating their character, and placing them on a footing with their brethren of the same common family."[11] With few exceptions, the churches retreated in the

[9] *Journal of the General Conference of the Methodist Episcopal Church, 1796–1836*, (New York, 1855) 1:169–70.
[10] *Extracts from the Minutes of the General Assembly, of the Presbyterian Church, . . . 1818* (Philadelphia, 1818) p. 29.
[11] *Ibid.*, . . . *1819* (Philadelphia, 1819), p. 163. On the Colonization Society, see P. J. Staudenraus, *The African Colonization Movement, 1816–1865* (New York: Columbia Univ. Press, 1961).

face of popular opinion; more than that, many of them as makers of opinion industriously promulgated views of Negro inferiority in both North and South.

When he comes to deal with the rise of the Negro congregations and denominations, the white Christian scholar is hardly relieved of his discomfort, for he must face the fact that the isolation of vast numbers of his fellow Christians came because of white Christian discrimination against Negroes. Twin motifs run through the story of the separation of black from white Christianity. First, as Benjamin E. Mays and Joseph W. Nicholson have explained, "The Negro church began as a means of separating an unwanted racial group from common public worship; that is, it had a social and psychological origin." [12] The details of separation varied from denomination to denomination; many particulars are gathered up in Mays' and Nicholson's summary paragraph:

> The whites have stimulated Negroes to build or purchase their own churches by direct acts of discrimination against them; by financially aiding them to purchase or build churches or to start new work; by separating the Negroes under white supervision; by giving church buildings to Negroes or encouraging them to remain at old sites when the whites moved or built new churches; by willingly granting the request when Negroes desired their own church; or by friendly counsel and advice.[13]

Negroes were simply not wanted in most white churches. Nor were they wanted in white society in general. Negroes often could see little if any difference between white Christians as citizens and other white citizens as he found himself systematically excluded from many aspects and opportunities of American life.

The other motif then displayed itself. Forced to accept the situation, Negro Christians seized the opportunity and made the most they could out of it. So, "the church was the first

[12] Benjamin E. Mays and Joseph W. Nicholson, *The Negro's Church* (New York: Institute of Social and Religious Research, 1933), p. 37.
[13] *Ibid.*, p. 6.

community or public organization that the Negro actually owned and completely controlled."[14] Congregational and denominational starts had been made by free Negroes before the Civil War; after Emancipation there was rapid development. Here the Negro was institutionally freest; here he could take over and manage his own affairs. Hence, both because he was excluded from white church and because he found freedom in his own, the division of white and Negro Christianity came about.[15]

In the later nineteenth century, as the freed slaves flooded into the churches, the denominations — chiefly Baptist and Methodist — were very much like the churches from which they divided; they reflected fairly accurately the patterns of pietistic evangelicalism of the two largest Protestant denominations. According to Carter G. Woodson, "the [Negro] Baptists used the same polity, the same literature, and sometimes the same national agencies as the white Baptists."[16] But then, as the churches lived apart for many decades, and were deeply involved in the lives of people of quite different cultural settings, they moved in different directions. How far apart they have grown has been sharply clarified in recent years. Many people were jolted when Gerhard Lenski, on the basis of his detailed sociological examination of religion in Detroit, found four major religious groupings in the population: white Protestants, Negro Protestants, Roman Catholics, and Jews. Lenski explained:

It may seem surprising that the Protestant population has been divided by race rather than denomination. This was done for the simple reason that the denominational groups within Detroit Protestantism no longer constitute self-contained socio-religious groups to any degree, while the racial groups do. Both the religious

[14] *Ibid.*, p. 279.
[15] For further discussion of this point, see Reimers, *White Protestantism and the Negro*, pp. 12–13, 29–31, 56–60, 146–47.
[16] Carter G. Woodson, *The History of the Negro Church* (Washington: Associated Publishers, 1921), p. 201.

and secular activities of Protestants in Detroit are highly
segregated along racial lines. . . .

In the Negro Protestant group the communal bond
is extremely strong, owing to the discriminatory practices of the whites. . . . In the realm of primary-type
relationships — intimate relations of kinship and friend-
ship — segregation tends to be the rule in the urban
North almost as much as the rural South.[17]

In terms of political and economic behavior, Lenski found
that Negro Protestants were usually closer to Roman Catholics than to white Protestants. The difficulties of Negro
Protestant life as seen from the sociological perspective are
reflected in one of his summary paragraphs:

The Negro Protestant group is in an especially interesting situation, sharing as it does much of the social
heritage of white Protestantism, but existing in a totally
different environment. For roughly the first two-thirds
of its existence, Negro Protestantism was a religion of
slaves in an agrarian setting. Currently it is becoming
the religion of a depressed urban proletariat. In short,
it has been obliged to exist in environments which provided minimal opportunities for development. In many
ways Negro Protestantism resembles a tree growing on
a mountain close to the timber line, and hence having
characteristics which do not reveal its potentialities.[18]

Some students of Negro Christianity have made the point
even more sharply than that, and have found that the exclu-
sion of the Negro from the larger sphere of Christian faith
and community has meant that Negro religion is a separate
type. Joseph Washington, Jr., has put it this way:

. . . Negro religion is an attempt to develop fraternalism
in response to the paternalism of white Protestantism.

[17] Gerhard Lenski, *The Religious Factor: A Sociological Study of
Religion's Impact on Politics, Economics, and Family Life* (Garden
City, N.Y.: Doubleday, 1961), pp. 20, 36.
[18] *Ibid.*, p. 318.

> Although it is intended to imitate Protestantism, it developed solely into a racial fellowship with no other reason for existence. . . . Negro and white Christians are not on opposite ends of the same faith, but rather are expressions of two different ultimate concerns.[19]

Washington's startling thesis has not been without its critics, of course. Charles R. Lawrence writes that there has been a triumph of faith despite the unhappy picture of segregation. "This writer is convinced," he exclaims, "that the major argument of *Black Religion* is essentially true but that our allegedly twice-fallen Darker Brothers are still nourished by a deep understanding of the Gospel and the faith — often vaguely perceived and too frequently distorted by a defensive race consciousness."[20] My own study and limited observation inclines me to follow Lawrence here, for I believe that the Gospel has often broken through the limitations of institutional Christianity, whether the latter be cast primarily in a white, a Negro, an Oriental, or some other pattern. One could even turn Washington's argument around and suggest that it may be easier for the Gospel to triumph in the churches of minorities than in those of the majority. The Christian emphasis on the love of God for all his creatures has broken through institutional limitations again and again, without reference to race or class. But however this argument comes out, there remains the implacable fact that the discrimination of Christians by Christians has hurt Negroes in many ways and continues to do so, thus stirring a variety of emotional responses in white Christians when this comes home: guilt, discomfort, shame, or the search for self-justification,

[19] Joseph Washington, Jr., *Black Religion: The Negro and Christianity in the United States* (Boston: Beacon Press, 1964), pp. 234, 249–50.

[20] Charles R. Lawrence, "The Separated Darker Brethren," *Christianity and Crisis*, 25 (Feb. 22, 1965): 19. Dr. Washington is having second thoughts on his book, as is indicated in the new preface to the paperback (1966) edition of *Black Religion*. See also in that edition the penetrating review by Martin E. Marty, in which it is asserted that from each side there are distinctive and valid gifts which need to be brought together. On this point, as in many others in this paper, I am grateful for the wise suggestions of my colleague, Dr. Lawrence N. Jones.

or the desire to avoid the whole business. Hence when he deals with Negro Christian history, the white scholar must be extremely careful lest he unconsciously pass over or lighten the hard parts of the story, or lest he make the picture worse than it was in an effort to atone. Only the give and take of disciplined discussion from many points of view can set the whole matter into clearer perspective. Anyone who ventures judgments in this field will no doubt find someone to oppose him — and it is in ongoing debate that our understanding of a history in which all Americans participate can be made clearer.

If the white churchman finds deep emotional stirrings within him that make his work difficult, the Negro Christian also has to deal with deep feelings. The late E. Franklin Frazier set down flatly the way Negro hopes were frustrated in the later nineteenth and earlier twentieth centuries, after they had been raised briefly at Emancipation:

> But their hopes and expectations were rudely shattered when white supremacy was re-established in the South. They were excluded from participation in the white man's world except on the basis of inferiority. They were disenfranchised and the public schools provided for them were a mere travesty on education. The courts set up one standard of justice for the white and another standard for the black man. They were stigmatized as an inferior race lacking even the human attributes which all men are supposed to possess. They were subjected to mob violence involving lynchings and burnings alive which were justified even by white Christian churches.[21]

Who can escape emotional reactions to such realities, especially when he identifies himself with the victims, or when he feels the burden of discrimination almost daily himself? In many of his writings, W.E.B. Du Bois explained how it feels from the point of view of one imprisoned by racial barriers. For example, ". . . his attitude toward the environing race congeals into a matter of unreasoning resentment

[21] Frazier, *The Negro Church in America*, p. 45.

and even hatred, deep disbelief in them and refusal to conceive honesty and rational thought on their part. This attitude adds to the difficulties of conversation, intercourse, and understanding between groups." [22] Feelings of resentment and hostility are certainly understandable here, but they set difficulties in the path of the scholar.

Emotional overtones thus crowd into the study of **Negro** religion, whoever picks it up, at whatever point. As these are understood and compensated for — much easier to say than to do — then one confronts another set of closely-related difficulties. For the various historical matters that must be considered in order thoroughly to understand Negro Christianity are ridden with controversies — slavery, Civil War, Reconstruction, for example. To a considerable extent these controversies may root in the realms of feeling that have just been mentioned, but in the world of scholarship they appear as classic controversies. In a masterful survey, Elkins has shown that the study of slavery has largely been polarized between the positions epitomized by James Ford Rhodes and Ulrich B. Phillips. The debate between these main positions, presented with many variations, derives ultimately ". . . from the proslavery and antislavery debaters of ante-bellum times." [23] Of course the whole story of the Civil War has long been and continues to be hotly debated — with the role of the Negro largely left out on all sides.[24] As for Reconstruction, the standard account for many decades told the story in a way highly unfavorable to the efforts of

[22] W. E. B. DuBois, *Dusk of Dawn: An Essay Toward an Autobiography of a Race Concept* (New York: Harcourt, Brace & Co., 1940), p. 132.

[23] Elkins, *Slavery*, p. 23.

[24] Cf. Howard K. Beale, "What Historians Have Said About the Causes of the Civil War," Social Science Research Council, *Theory and Practice in Historical Study: A Report of the Committee on Historiography*, Bulletin no. 54 (New York: Social Science Research Council, 1946), pp. 53–102. Changing patterns of interpretation with respect to the Negro can be seen in James M. McPherson, *The Negro's Civil War: How American Negroes Felt and Acted During the War for the Union* (New York: Pantheon Books, 1965).

the radicals and their Negro allies. Kenneth Stampp has recently summarized the views reflected in dozens of histories of the period: the crafty and scheming northern carpetbaggers, the degraded and depraved southern scalawags, and the ignorant, barbarous, sensual Negroes who threatened to destroy the civilization of the South.[25] The accounts of the revisionists read quite differently. Stampp, for example, refutes the familiar legend point by point, and argues that of the few Negroes actually elected to high office, most were men of ability and integrity; they were seldom vindictive and were willing to defer social equality to concentrate on civil and political rights. Of course there was corruption in the South — but corruption then was a nationwide phenomenon, and some of the worst examples were northern. "Finally," Stampp concludes, "granting all their mistakes, the radical governments were by far the most democratic the South had ever known."[26]

Topic after topic that the church historian must at least touch on in doing justice to Negro Christianity has its own peculiar problems. The church history of the South has been neglected for many of the same reasons that Negro history has. Martin E. Marty has observed that ". . . Southern church history has until recently been written by processional historians who dealt with the church incidentally and by church historians hardly at all. . . . The South was dealt with negatively or incidentally in most of the general histories of religion in America from Robert Baird's in 1844 through Leonard Bacon's in 1898 down through Sweet's first edition in 1930."[27] To come down to date, controversies whirl around the way the various movements for civil rights are to be understood; one author deliberately dramatizes the controversial nature of the Student Nonviolent Coordinating

[25] Kenneth Stampp, *The Era of Reconstruction, 1865–1877* (New York: Knopf, 1966), pp. 3–23.

[26] *Ibid.*, pp. 167–85, quotation at pp. 185–86.

[27] Martin E. Marty, "Overcoming Southern History by Southern History: The Role of Church History," address to the American Society of Church History, Richmond, Virginia, April 15, 1966 (mimeographed), p. 10.

Committee by entitling his book on the movement *SNCC: The New Abolitionists.*[28]

The whole field of the history of Christianity among Negroes is thus a doubly difficult one, involving deep feelings and interlocking with many controversial topics. It is not hard to see why many have avoided it. But it is one that the historian of religion in America can no longer neglect, for it is part of his total responsibility. The thesis of this essay is that any effort at the general interpretation of Christianity in America must deal with the religion of Negroes, and that many periods and many subtopics of American church history which may often have been treated without reference to Negroes, or with only incidental reference, can no longer be so handled. It will no longer do for Negro church history to be treated as an option, or only as a "special interest" for the few. Of course, many specialists in this area will be needed, but their work must be taken seriously in general American church historiography. The American church historian has an obligation to provide his hearers and readers with a real sense of the religious and church life of the Negro (and of other minority groups) in whatever period of history he treats. No doubt part of the reason why this concern comes to the fore now is because many of us want to see those who have been treated unjustly and cavalierly given their due; in one sense, this effort is a scholarly side of the civil rights movement. I am arguing, however, that the church historian, whatever his viewpoints on current movements, needs to acquaint himself with the history of Negro Christianity and the many related topics in order to do adequately his work as historian. Benjamin Quarles opened an important article by declaring that "Just as the Negro's place in American life is now changing, so is his place in American history. The true role of the Negro in our country's past is

[28] Howard Zinn, *SNCC: The New Abolitionists* (Boston: Beacon Press, 1964).

emerging from the shadows." He concluded the article as follows:

> . . . the careful reader, of whatever hue himself, has a right to expect that the historian recognize that the record of the colored American has something to add to the knowledge and understanding of our country's past, something to add to the story of human collaboration and interdependence. Readers have a right to expect that the historian be led to examine more closely anti-minority assumptions that may have crept into his thinking.
>
> To say that the historian is morally accountable would be gratuitous. But to the extent that he helps to shape the national character in a pluralistic land such as ours, to that extent a special responsibility may inescapably be his.[29]

One way to get involved in the work here called for is to see the many topics normally discussed in church history as opportunities for the inclusion of Negro realities. No responsible interpreter of American religious history would leave out at least some consideration of immigration and its effects on church life. Yet the fact that the slave brought in "immigrants" too for two centuries has normally been thought of in different terms, yet important perspectives and fruitful comparisons can flow from this approach. "Americanization" was a stage in the experience of most immigrants, and was one in which the churches were deeply involved. The Americanization process for the Negro has gone on longer and has undergone more unfortunate limitations and crippling distortions than that of most other groups. Yet there have been prejudices toward other minorities, and the detailed explication of the parallels may prove to be fruitful. Daniel Boorstin has called attention to one aspect of the problem in a suggestive way:

[29] Benjamin Quarles, "What the Historian Owes the Negro," *Saturday Review*, Sept. 3, 1966, pp. 10, 13.

In the longer perspective of American history, it was perhaps less the institution of slavery (which most other European peoples had, in one way or another, experienced and then transcended) than the notion that there could be an indelible immigrant, which plagued the South and the nation. Even after the legal institution of slavery was abolished, Southern belief that there could be indelible immigrants would live on.[30]

When the church historian deals with immigration, he has an opportunity to stress the Negro experience.

Another important, closely-related topic is that of internal migration — the restless movement of Americans within their land. Church historians, especially since Mode and Sweet, have paid much attention to the westward migration. The migratory movements of the twentieth century have been of quite different character from those of the nineteenth, and they involve far greater numbers. One cannot discuss the modern migrations adequately without referring to the vast push of Negroes from South to North in the years of World Wars I and II, and after. For a time in the 1930's it looked as though the migration had stopped; but as one churchman exclaimed with genuine surprise early in the 1940's, ". . . we have the greatest and most complex migration in the history of the American continent."[31] We keep discovering more and more of what this vast migration means for the configuration of northern cities, and for the lives of Negroes. Before the outbreak of the first World War, Negro population was about two-thirds southern rural, while today it is about two-thirds urban. We are just beginning to understand what all this means for religious life; the present great theological interest in the secular almost certainly has this vast migration as one of its background factors. Years

[30] Daniel Boorstin, *The Americans: The National Experience* (New York: Random House, 1965), p. 189; Cf. Ira DeA. Reid, *The Negro Immigrant: His Background, Characteristics and Social Adjustment, 1899–1937* (New York: Columbia Univ. Press, 1939).

[31] G. Pitt Beers, in the Home Missions Council of North America, *Annual Report* (1941), p. 2.

ago J. Milton Yinger said, "It is a widely accepted generalization among sociologists that migration and culture con-
tact are an important cause of a 'secular' mode of thought
and a stimulus to the development of rationality, as con-
trasted with the 'sacred' traditional thought patterns of an
isolated culture group."[32] To probe the meaning of the migration of peoples for American religion is a continuing challenge for American church historiography; to try to do it
without the full inclusion of Negro movements would be
to overlook an important part of the whole story. Conversely,
to try to deal with Negro migration out of the context of
general migratory trends would be again to fall into com-
partmental thinking and to miss the possibilities of comparison which may give us much clearer perspectives in our efforts at interpretation. In writing and teaching American
church history, we can often illustrate the meaning and impact of such realities as urbanization and secularization by
reference to the experiences of minorities, thereby relating
them to the mainstream of interpretation, and also demon-
strating how pervasive such forces were.

The study of the history of Christian social movements in
the United States has attracted the attention of a number
of scholars, who have tended to be generally favorable to
the movements they have examined. One of the most important chapters in the larger history of social Christianity deals
with the liberal social gospel, which focused on the relations
of capital and labor and tended to accept the general perspectives of Progressivism with their limitations concerning
the Negro.[33] The whole story of American social Christian

---

[32] J. Milton Yinger, *Religion in the Struggle for Power: A Study in
the Sociology of Religion* (Durham, N.C.: Duke Univ. Press, 1946), p. 73.

[33] Cf. Thomas F. Gossett, *Race: The History of an Idea in America*
(Dallas: Southern Methodist Univ. Press, 1963), esp. chap. 8; see also
Reimers, *White Protestantism and the Negro*, pp. 53–54. There is some
danger that the fact that some social gospel leaders were in advance of
their time will be lost sight of in the recognition of the time-bound
nature of their attitude toward race. On the attitude of Washington
Gladden, cf. Robert T. Handy, ed., *The Social Gospel in America, 1870–
1920: Gladden, Ely and Rauschenbusch* (New York: Oxford Univ.
Press, 1966), pp. 29–30.

movements with their connections and discontinuities has yet to be told. It will involve reconsiderations of colonial-period and "benevolent empire" reform movements, treatments of the many strands of Christian social thought and action in the period of industrialization, and also analysis of movements for the betterment of the Negro, a number of which are related, directly or indirectly, to the history of Negro Christianity.

An important concern for the American church historian today is the burgeoning ecumenical movement in its many phases. The spread of Councils of Churches, the achievement of unions by once-divided churches and by denominations across confessional lines, the striking new ecumenical stance of Roman Catholicism, and the ongoing life of the Consultation on Church Union have thrust ecumenical prospects and dilemmas before us in dramatic ways. To deal with these matters without probing the extent and quality of the involvement of the churches of minority groups would be to overlook significant aspects of the total story.

The Federal Council of Churches was founded in 1908 at the time when Progressive thought was influential within Protestantism. The gradual overcoming of racial stereotypes was one of the significant internal developments of the Council's history. The call for racial justice in 1919, the formation of a Commission Race Relations two years later, and the declaration "The Church on Race Relations" in 1946 were milestones on this journey. The Federal Council passed this concern on to its successor in 1950, the National Council of Churches. In the 1960's it moved dramatically into larger participation in the movement for Negro freedom and equality.[34] The major Negro denominations are members of the National Council, but important questions as to the extent of their participation in its affairs and the impact of

[34] Cf. Robert W. Spike, *The Freedom Revolution and the Churches* (New York: Association Press, 1965); Anna A. Hedgeman, *The Trumpet Sounds: A Memoir of Negro Leadership* (New York: Holt, Rinehart & Winston, 1964).

such membership on the constituencies of both white and Negro denominations remain.

In the Consultation on Church Union, in which ten communions are working towards possible union, the African Methodist Episcopal Church, the African Methodist Episcopal Church Zion, and the Christian Methodist Episcopal Church are full members. Significant ecumenical advances at any level require real understanding of the history and traditions of other Christians. To see the Christian past as others see it is an important preliminary step to fuller cooperation and a larger Christian unity. The development of the ecumenical movement in a number of directions thus presses on the historian a responsibility to contribute to the deeper historical understanding of all of the many branches of the Christian church in America.

The discipline of American church history has probably not yet taken seriously enough the whole field of education. This involves Sunday, parochial, and secondary schools, collegiate, university, and theological education, and adult and continuing education. When the focus is on the Negro aspects of this whole story, some very interesting things come to light, and some tragic limitations are revealed. A number of white missionaries served effectively, often sacrificially, in helping able Negro leaders after the Civil War to build institutions of secondary and collegiate education. They were backed largely by mission agencies in the North. As a Southener admitted in a report to the Board of Education of the Methodist Episcopal Church South in 1907,

> Assistance in the education of the negro has been practically monopolized by boards, societies, churches and philanthropists of the North, and we have been disposed to let them have it, excusing ourselves with the claim that more is being done for the negro than for the poor white children of the South, and that we have more than we can do to look after our own.[35]

[35] Charles E. Bowman, quoted by H. Paul Douglass, *Christian Reconstruction in the South* (Boston: Pilgrim Press, 1909), p. 60.

Many of the colleges founded then later grew into distinguished institutions of higher education; for example, Talledega, Fisk, Tougaloo, Hampton, Morehouse, Howard. This story needs to be told again in the light of present perspectives, and while nothing can dim the luster of what was achieved, one must not be misled as to how representative of northern churches were the labors of the missionaries. Joseph Washington's strictures must be kept in mind:

> The white contributions in religion and education have been heroic. The products have often been splendid. But the anticipation that this education would lead the Negro into the full stream of American life was ill-founded — the Negro was not accepted in the North by the same societies who worked for his acceptance in the South.[36]

Theological education for Negro candidates for the Protestant ministry is currently in a state of transition. Many seminaries, North and South, once closed to Negroes now accept them, and some of the smaller ones that once served them have been closed or merged. The meaning of decades of discrimination, continued lack of opportunities, and minimal resources of Negro Christianity are reflected in a summary statement by Harry V. Richardson in the massive *American Negro Reference Book*: ". . . 92 per cent of the men entering the Negro ministry each year are professionally unprepared."[37] To say it another way, probably no more than eight per cent of the estimated 50,000 Negro pastors have both college and graduate-seminary education, and many of the rest have neither.[38] Until the educational background of more Negro candidates for the ministry come closer to standards

[36] Washington, *Black Religion*, p. 154.
[37] "The Negro in American Religious Life," in John P. Davis, ed., *The American Negro Reference Book* (Englewood Cliffs, N.J.: Prentice-Hall, 1966), p. 412.
[38] Walter D. Wagoner, *The Seminary: Protestant and Catholic* (New York: Sheed & Ward, 1966), pp. 172–75. As of Nov., 1965, there were 159 Roman Catholic Negro priests in the United States, all of them with full seminary education.

necessary for good performance in accredited seminaries, and until the churches become more genuinely interracial, certain seminaries primarily for Negroes would seem to be necessary.[39] The historical reasons and consequences of this "double standard" of Protestant theological education, and the record of sometimes heroic efforts to overcome it, need fuller interpretation than they have yet had. Researches into the general educational work of Christians that overlook aspects relating to Negro education will be incomplete.

This list of topics related to American church history which cannot be fully discussed without reference to Negro Christianity is meant to be illustrative, not exhaustive. Many more could be added. As has been implied, treatments of either rural or urban church history must involve Negro churches. Missions, both to and by Negroes, is an important field. In what ways has revivalism among Negroes been similar to and different from the revivalism church historians have usually considered? The topic of Negro cult and sect movements has been more fully examined than most others, and has perhaps received disproportionate stress in general interpretations.[40]

One way the church historian can get into the vast field of Negro Christian history has been suggested. It will also be important to understand more fully than we have the life and history of those denominations that are primarily Negro in membership, and also to learn more about Negro minorities in predominantly white churches. The *Yearbook of the American Churches* for 1966 reports membership statistics for six major Negro denominations, though the figures for

[39] Cf. Reimers, *White Protestantism and the Negro*, pp. 126–33.
[40] Cf. esp. Arthur H. Fauset, *Black Gods of the Metropolis* (Philadelphia: Univ. of Pennsylvania Press, 1944). There has been considerable attention to non-Christian Negro religious developments, especially the Black Muslim movement. Cf. C. Eric Lincoln, *The Black Muslims in America* (Boston: Beacon Press, 1961); and E. U. Essien-Udom, *Black Nationalism: A Search for Identity in America* (Chicago: Univ. of Chicago Press, 1962).

some of them are certainly outdated, and were probably rough approximations in the first place. The list, with estimates rounded off, are as follows:

National Baptist Convention, U.S.A., Inc. . .	5,500,000
National Baptist Convention of America . .	2,700,000
Progressive National Baptist Convention, Inc.	505,000
African Methodist Episcopal Church	1,120,000
African Methodist Episcopal Zion Church .	770,000
Christian Methodist Episcopal Church	445,000

There are about 780,000 Negro Roman Catholics; about 650,000 Negroes in primarily white denominations, of which the largest group is in The Methodist Church; and an estimated 725,000 in all of the other, smaller bodies.[41] The historical work done so far on the major Negro denominations has been scanty and uneven. A number of strands in the history of these groups runs back into slavery days when, as Boorstin aptly puts it, "The Negroes' religious life thrived in institutions that were often invisible to the white masters, and that are barely visible to the historian today."[42] There is much painstaking work to be done here — the location and preservation of collections of source materials, for example, and then their patient examination and interpretation. "Much of the historical information about Negroes must be dug out; it is not readily available in printed form . . ." Benjamin Quarles has said.[43] Hence the fuller understanding of an important aspect of American religious history, involving millions of Negroes, requires much careful digging in widely scattered sources, to be accompanied by thoughtful analysis and interpretation. Careful work in the history of the largely Negro denominations is important for its own sake, and for the light it can shed on the general story of Christianity in America.

[41] Benson Y. Landis, ed., *Yearbook of the American Churches, 1966* (New York, 1966), pp. 199–207; cf. Wagoner, *The Seminary*, p. 175.
[42] Boorstin, *The Americans*, p. 197.
[43] Quarles, "What the Historian Owes the Negro," p. 12.

More satisfying and complete interpretations of Negro Christianity, and hence of Christianity in general, can follow only on fuller study of many subtopics and of particular groups and denominations. A useful summary treatment, consolidating in compact form much of the work done so far, was prepared by the late E. Franklin Frazier, a sociologist, in his book, *The Negro Church in America.* In the course of supplying much information, Frazier has presented the thesis that the "invisible institution" of Negro religion in slave days merged with the "institutional church" in the post-Civil War period to form "a nation within a nation," the most important cultural institution created by Negroes. But this vast enterprise has become, he argues, ". . . the most important institutional barrier to integration and the assimilation of Negroes"; a once-needed refuge from white society has now become an obstacle. Frazier believed that Negro church life is authoritarian and anti-intellectual: "It is only as a few Negro individuals have been able to escape from the stifling domination of the church that they have been able to develop intellectually and in the field of art."[44] Generalizations such as those need much testing and discussion; on the basis of my own limited research and experience I'm not prepared to accept those judgments as the last word.

It is significant that the first two formally trained Negro historians in America, in their pioneering efforts to give satisfying general interpretations of Negro life, felt it necessary to write, among many other works, books on Negro church history. W.E.B. DuBois' *The Negro's Church* appeared in 1903; Carter G. Woodson wrote his important *The Negro Church* in 1921. So important has religion been in Negro history and life that efforts at responsible overall interpretation of that history require careful attention to religion. Today, as the Negro is increasingly taking his rightful place in American life, the story of his religious life and institutions needs to be more widely known in order that he may better understand himself and be better understood by others. This

[44] Frazier, *The Negro Church in America*, pp. 70–71, 86.

task of interpretation is now thrust on American church historians, white and Negro, Protestant and Catholic, Jewish and secular. Confident that human good is advanced by sound historical understanding, let us no longer neglect this important field of study.

5

Missionary Motivation through Three Centuries
R. PIERCE BEAVER

The task now needing to be done in the study of the history of American missions is not reinterpretation. First interpretation has not yet been achieved; even an adequate narrative of the development of the vast American Protestant missionary enterprise through three and a quarter centuries is still to be written. Analysis of most facets of the mission has not yet been undertaken, and the actual relationship of the expanding enterprise to many aspects of American religion and national life awaits explanation. These include revivals, nationalism, theological trends, Christian unity, and the ever-growing role of the United States in international affairs. General historians in the college and university history departments and students writing Ph.D. dissertations are currently producing most of the monographs on mission, but they seldom understand the relationship of the subject of their investigation to the total Protestant missionary enterprise, which until quite recently was characterized by an amazing sense of unity. The overseas mission was until well after the Civil War the most extensive and continuous expression of American philanthropy and altruism towards other peoples, the most potent form of American cultural impact on them at the grass-roots level, and the molder of the popular American image of the peoples of Asia, Oceania, Africa, and Latin America. It continued thereafter to be one of the chief factors in international relations. It was also the original wellspring of ecumenicity and the vehicle through which American initiative was contributed to the emerging ecumenical movement.

113

The efforts to evangelize the Indians in Massachusetts begun in the decade of the 1640's by the Mayhews, John Eliot, and their associates, inaugurated not only the permanent missionary endeavor of the American churches but the world mission of the European churches also. The simultaneous efforts by the chaplains of the Dutch East India Company are another foundation stone of the enterprise, but were far less influential. Statistical fruits of the mission were very meager by the time of the American Revolution, but the Indian mission had tremendous effect in providing inspiration and models for the great new overseas mission movement which began in Great Britain in 1792. Immediately after the Revolution a new nationalism, the challenge of the frontier, the effect of revivals, and the example of the English societies stimulated a tremendous missionary awakening in America. Between 1787 and 1810 a large number of missionary societies were founded in New England and the middle Atlantic states.[1] They all had a world-wide vision and objective, but they could not produce even enough men and money for the work in the frontier settlements and with the Indians. A student movement led to the formation of the first purely foreign missionary organ, the American Board of Commissioners for Foreign Missions, in 1810. By the end of the Civil War some fifteen boards and societies were serving the major denominations. The overseas mission so stimulated stewardship in the churches that home missions and an ever greater number of benevolent causes could be supported by the denominations.

India, Burma, and Ceylon were the chief targets of American Protestant foreign mission effort during the first half-century of the overseas venture. Then followed the Chinese in southeast Asia, west Africa, the southernmost tip of Africa, the Turkish Empire, and Hawaii, from which there was an extension into Micronesia. The missions in the Near East were intended to revive the ancient Eastern churches. By the end of the nineteenth century, China had become the major

[1] Oliver W. Elsbree, *The Rise of the Missionary Spirit in America* (Williamsport, Pa.: Williamsport Printing and Binding Co., 1928).

American field and Latin America had been added to the earlier spheres of interest.

The last thirty-five years of the nineteenth century were a period of tremendous expansion. By 1900 there were 52 mission boards in the United States and eight closely associated with them in Canada which directly sent missionaries. Women's boards which sent single women to work with women and children had come into being supplementing general denominational boards. There were also forty-nine auxiliary organizations. North Americans numbered 5,000 out of a total Protestant missionary staff of 18,164.[2] The agencies raised $6,616,096 in the last year of the century. The next decade rounded out the first century of the foreign mission, and it was the day of the slogan, "The evangelization of the world in this generation." More boards had been created. North American missionaries numbered 7,219 out of the total staff of 21,307. Contributions amounted to $18,000,000, compared with a world total of about $39,000,000.[3] North American missions had displaced the British from first place in the Protestant world mission.

The next half-century from 1910 to 1960 was a time of marked fluctuations due to two global wars, the depression, and the growing pressures of worldwide nationalism. Nevertheless, the churches of the United States and Canada continued to take a proportionately ever higher share of the total missionary enterprise. The 1925 statistics show that there were 14,043 North American missionaries out of 29,188 serving under all boards.[4] Then the depression struck, and the receipts of 97 boards reporting to the Foreign Missions Conference fell from $41,037,276 in 1928 to $22,525,556 in

[2] Derived from tables in James S. Dennis, *Centennial Survey* of Foreign Missions (New York: Revell, 1902).

[3] Derived from tables in *World Atlas of Christian Missions*, ed. James S. Dennis, Harlan P. Beach, and Charles H. Fahs, (New York: Student Volunteer Movement for Foreign Missions, 1911).

[4] Derived from tables in *World Missionary Atlas*, ed. Harlan P. Beach and Charles H. Fahs (New York: Institute of Social and Religious Research, 1925).

1933.[5] The staff was drastically reduced. Consequently the pre-Madras Conference statistics of 1936 revealed that the proportion was 11,289 for North America out of a world total of 27,577.[6] Rapid expansion followed the end of World War II, but the closing of China in 1950 eliminated the largest single body of North American missionaries. Nevertheless, in 1960 North Americans formed about 65 per cent of the total mission staff, and numbered 27,219. Four hundred twenty-one boards and societies in that year raised $170,000,000 for overseas missions in 146 countries and distinct territories.[7]

The avowed intent of this gigantic enterprise was the winning of the world for Christ through effecting individual conversions and planting new churches. The Anderson-Venn formula was throughout the last century the accepted strategy of the mission, namely, the planting and fostering of churches which would be self-governing, self-supporting, and self-propagating.[8] At present the work of the mainstream denominations is a vast system of interchurch aid without much of a real missionary thrust. However, the sectarian segment of American Christianity has produced a second force, numbering about 130 new non-denominational societies founded between 1940 and 1960, intent upon inducing personal conversions through methods in vogue a century ago.

What are the motives which originated, developed, and sustained this colossal enterprise? Limitations of space require this survey to end with 1910 or 1914, the close of what was hailed as "The Great Century," at the point where American missions had assumed first place in the Protestant world mission.

[5] Based on the *Annual Reports* of the Foreign Missions Conference of North America.

[6] Joseph I. Parker, ed., *Interpretative Statistical Survey of the World Mission of the Christian Church* (New York: International Missionary Council, 1938).

[7] Derived from Missionary Research Library statistical resources.

[8] R. Pierce Beaver, ed., *To Advance the Gospel: Selections from the Writings of Rufus Anderson* (Grand Rapids: Eerdmans, 1967); Peter Beyerhaus, and Henry Lefever, *The Responsible Church and the Foreign Mission* (London: World Dominion Press, 1964), pp. 25–33.

The Colonial Period

New England was the wellspring of American missionary concern and action. For a century and a half, the Puritan divines of that region were almost the only preachers and writers on missions. The entire planting of New England was in their estimation an act of mission, being the extension of the kingdom of God to the western far ends of the earth. Both the royal charters of Massachusetts Bay and Plymouth Colonies and the instructions of the directors of the Massachusetts Company imposed upon the settlers an obligation to evangelize the Indians.[9] Nevertheless, preoccupied as they were with the business of settlement, the colonists showed no disposition to discharge that obligation during the first generation. However, in the decade of the 1640's the mission was begun and since then has never been interrupted.[10] Both the missionary clauses in the charters and the Calvinist doctrine of the missionary obligation of Christian magistrates towards heathen subjects could justify some support by the state. Both may have been motives to mission, but the latter is never mentioned. There was some acknowledgment of the binding nature of the profession of the charters in the seventeenth century,[11] and Cotton Mather does say that John Eliot was "awakened by those expressions in the royal charter."[12] But it was in the eighteenth century

[9] *Records of the Governor and Company of Massachusetts Bay in New England*, ed. Nathaniael Shurtleff (Boston: William White, 1853), 1:17; New Plymouth Colony, *The Compact with the Charter and Laws of the Colony of New Plymouth* (Boston: Dutton and Wentworth, printers to the State, 1836).

[10] On the seventeenth- and eighteenth-century missions, see R. Pierce Beaver *Pioneers in Mission* (Grand Rapids: Eerdmans, 1966), *Church, State, and the American Indians* (St. Louis: Concordia, 1966), chap. 1, and, "American Missionary Motivation before the Revolution," *Church History*, vol. 31 (June, 1963); William Kellaway, *The New England Company, 1649–1776* (New York: Barnes and Noble, 1962); and Alden T. Vaughan, *New England Frontier, Puritans and Indians 1620–1675* (Boston: Little, Brown, 1965).

[11] Vaughan, *New England Frontier*, pp. 235–36.

[12] Cotton Mather, *Magnalia Christi Americana*, (Hartford: Andrus, Roberts, and Barr, from the 1st American ed. of 1702, 1820), 1:577.

that obedience to the charters was urged as a motive,[13] and Eleazar Wheelock regarded the depredations of the Indians as divine punishment for neglect of a main purpose of settlement.[14]

There was a prudential motive, at once religious and political, which played a part in the rise and development of the missions. Religiously this was the desire to emulate, surpass, and thwart Roman Catholic missions, while politically it was a calculated effort to establish Protestant missions as a barrier to French aggression from Canada in which the Jesuit missions were regarded as the front line of advance. That political-military motive appears strongest in the founding of the Anglican mission to the Mohawks in New York,[15] and it was frequently acknowledged in New England in the eighteenth century.[16] The French were supposed to instigate the attacks by the Indians.[17] Therefore, Joseph Sewall could assert that if missions should succeed, "the presence of Christ will be like a wall of fire" on the eastern and western frontiers.[18] Dr. Charles Chauncy instructed Joseph Bowman that his mission would equally serve God and country.[19] Wheelock held that conversion alone could "tame" the savages and induce them to keep treaties.[20]

[13] Solomon Stoddard, *Question Whether God Is Not Angry With the Country for Doing So Little towards the Conversion of the Indians?* (Boston: B. Green, 1723); Joseph Sewall, *Christ Victorious over the Powers of Darkness . . . , a Sermon preached in Boston, December 12, 1733, at the Ordination of the Rev. Mr. Stephen Parker* (Boston: S. Kneeland and T. Green, 1733), reprinted in Beaver, *Pioneers in Mission*, p. 57.

[14] Eleazer Wheelock, *A Plain and Faithful Narrative . . . of the Indian Charity School at Lebanon in Connecticut* (Boston: Draper, 1763); *Sermon Preached on the 30th of June, 1763, at the Ordination of the Rev. Mr. Charles Jeffry Smith, Missionary to the Indians*, reprinted in Beaver, *Pioneers in Mission*, p. 229.

[15] Beaver, *Church, State, and the American Indians*, pp. 14–20.

[16] Examples: Nathanael Appleton, Eleazer Wheelock, Joseph Sewall, Charles Chauncy, in Beaver, *Pioneers in Mission*, pp. 142, 148; 228; 42; 207 respectively.

[17] Cotton Mather, *Magnalia*, 2:610–12.

[18] Beaver, *Pioneers in Mission*, p. 62.

[19] *Ibid.*, pp. 206, 207.

[20] *Ibid.*, p. 229.

The religious opposition to Roman missions was a stronger motive than the political-military impulse in the earlier period. John Eliot regarded Jesuit missions as "a notable means of upholding Antichrist."[21] His friend, Cotton Mather, too, was concerned to "raise up a *bulwark* against the kingdom of anti-christ, which the Jesuits labour to rear up in all parts of the world."[22] Yet Mather was even more interested in emulating and surpassing Roman Catholic missionary action.[23] The influence of the Jesuits was blamed for the failure of the missions in Maine and on the upper Connecticut River.[24] The British victory in Canada, which ended the military threat to the colonies, was hailed with thanksgiving as providing a new grand opportunity for the advancement of the gospel.[25] Thereafter, and continuously until the very last Indian war on the western frontier at the end of the nineteenth century, the often reiterated prudential argument and motive for the Indian work was the cheapness and greater effectiveness of missions compared with military repression of the redmen and the protection that Christian Indians would provide their white brethren against the "wild men."[26]

It should be noted that a sense of indebtedness to the Indians for wrongs done them and a desire to make restitution by giving them salvation through Christ was never a motive in Puritan New England missions. English divines preaching before the Society for the Propagation of the Gospel in Foreign Parts for just a few years made this a motive for support of the Mohawk mission,[27] and Bishop Thomas

[21] Letter of Eliot to Baxter quoted from Baxter's Letters, vol. 3, 133a, in Sidney H. Rooy, *The Theology of Missions in the Puritan Tradition* (Grand Rapids: Eerdmans, 1965), p. 226.

[22] Cotton Mather, *Magnalia*, 1:69.

[23] *Ibid.*, "A Comparison between What the New Englanders Have Done for the Conversion of the Indians, and What Has Been Done Elsewhere by the Roman Catholicks," 1:521–24.

[24] Charles Chauncy, Sermon in Beaver, *Pioneers in Mission*, p. 201.

[25] *Ibid.*, p. 207; Nathanael Appleton, *A Sermon Preached October 9, Being a Day of Public Thanksgiving Occasioned by the Surrender of Montreal, and All Canada* (Boston: Draper, 1760).

[26] Beaver, *Church, State, and the American Indians*, pp. 181–82.

[27] But it was far more their motive for missions to the Negro slaves. See the Fleetwood, Secker, and Warburton sermons reprinted at the end

Wilson in the case of Georgia urged British merchants and stockholders in colonies to contribute to missions in restitution for the wealth derived from the labors of Indians and Negroes,[28] but New England parsons and laymen at no time felt any sense of guilt towards the displaced or subjugated Indians. Cotton Mather voiced the prevailing view when he lauded the unrequired kindness of the settlers who brought title to the land from the Indians despite the fact that it had been given them by royal grant.[29] Solomon Stoddard stated that the smallness of the sale price was not a matter of reproach, since the settlers met the Indians' price and gave them what they asked. Such other land as they took was empty, unoccupied, unused land which they possessed freely and improved on the basis of the divine warrant in Genesis 1:28.[30] It was not until half a century after the Revolution that indebtedness and restitution became motives to mission in the Indian work.[31]

Any indebtedness was on the side of the Indians for the blessings which Englishmen brought them. Thus Mather told the Indians:

> Behold, ye *Indians*, what care, what cost, has been used by the *English* here for the salvation of your precious and immortal *souls*. It is not because we have expected any *temporal advantage*, that we have been thus concerned for your good; no, it is God that has caused us to desire his *Glory* in your salvation; and our hearts have bled with *pity* over you, when we have seen how horribly the Devil *oppressed* you in this, and *destroyed* you in another world. It is *much* that has been done for

---

of Frank J. Klingberg, *Anglican Humanitarianism in Colonial New York* (Philadelphia: Church Historical Society, 1940), pp. 195–249.

[28] Thomas Wilson, *The Knowledge and Practice of Christianity Made Easy to the Meanest Capacities, or An Essay towards an Instruction for the Indians*, 9th ed. (London: D. Dodd, bookseller to the S.P.C.K., 1759), p. xv.

[29] Cotton Mather, *Magnalia*, 1:523.

[30] Solomon Stoddard, *An Answer to Some Questions of Conscience Respecting the Country* (Boston: B. Green, 1722).

[31] Beaver, *Church, State, and the American Indians*, pp. 62–63.

you; we have put you into a way to be happy both on earth while you live, and in *Heaven* when you die.[32]

The foregoing quotation clearly sets forth the first and second most important motives of Puritan missions, both of them theological and Calvinian in origin.[33] The glory of God is the taproot of the mission. The second is Christian compassion for the perishing souls of the Indians, and a correlative of that is also humanitarian pity for their wretched physical, social, and moral condition. The mission is always regarded as God's own action — "the work of the Lord among the Indians for the forwarding of the publishing of the glad tydings of peace."[34] Eliot refused the title of evangelist, objecting that "it is the Lord who hath done what is done."[35] The eighteenth-century preachers continued this emphasis.

Eventually *gloria Dei* was developed by Samuel Hopkins into his concept of disinterested benevolence, which he combined with the idea of man being the coworker with God, producing one of the most powerful impulses to missionary vocation and support at the end of the eighteenth and beginning of the nineteenth centuries.[36] Adoration of God's glory and selfless love of Him require absolute submission to the will of God. The best manner in which to glorify and obey God is to serve Him in that way which produces the highest good and brings the least possible personal honor and profit, and that is missionary service and support of missions.[37] It is a recurring theme, and as late as 1834 Gardiner Spring voices its continuing appeal when he exclaims:

[32] Incorporated in "Life of John Eliot," *Magnalia*, 1:524–25.
[33] See Sidney H. Rooy, *The Theology of Missions in the Puritan Tradition* (Grand Rapids: Eerdmans, 1965).
[34] Commissioners of the United Colonies of New England, Letter to Robert Boyle, Sept. 10, 1668, in *Some Correspondence between the Governors and Treasurers of the New England Company in London and the Commissioners of the United Colonies in America . . .* , ed. John W. Ford (London: Spottiswoode, 1896), p. 18.
[35] Cotton Mather, *Magnalia*, 1:502.
[36] Beaver, *Pioneers in Mission*, pp. 18–19.
[37] Samuel Hopkins, *The Works of Samuel Hopkins in Three Volumes* (Boston: Doctrinal Tract and Book Society, 1854), 3:16, 147.

> There is no work so grand and glorious as this — in
> the purity, disinterestedness, and greatness of its aims —
> . . . — in the toil and self-denial with which it is
> carried forward — in the interests which are subservient
> to its advancement — in the loftiness and sublimity of
> its moral associations. . . .[38]

Love and compassion for the perishing souls of the Indians,
barbarous creatures enthralled and ruined by the devil but
yet human beings with immortal souls for whom Christ had
died, determined the strong soteriological direction of American missions from Eliot, Mayhew, and Mather until nearly
the end of the nineteenth century in the older churches and
continuing until the present in conservative and fundamentalist quarters. Evangelism was at the outset regarded as
God's own adorable "kindness . . . towards poore lost
soules, his great compassion in seeking and searching out his
sheepe, among the poore naked natives of the Wildernes, so
far removed from the sound of his glorious Gospell, and the
Wisdome of his unsearchable Counsells appearing in his pro-
vidences that have been very wonderful for handing the
word of life unto them."[39] This remains one of the dominant
notes of eighteenth-century preaching.[40] Wheelock calls this
motive "disinterested regard to, and compassion for, the
perishing souls of men."[41]

Humanitarian pity was derived from this spiritual love of
souls. The Puritans held that the gospel flowered in English,
and especially New England, civilization, and they saw in
the Indian way of life full proof of the redmen's vassalage
to Satan. Only Roger Williams in New England and Sir William Johnson in New York saw anything commendable in
Indian society.[42] Johnson and Charles Chauncy in Boston

[38] Gardiner Spring, *"The Will of God Performed on Earth,"* a Sermon
Preached at Utica, N. Y., before the A.B.C.F.M., Oct. 8, 1834 (Boston:
Crocker & Brewster, 1835), p. 27.
[39] Commissioners to Boyle, 1668, see note 34.
[40] Beaver, *Pioneers in Mission*, p. 20.
[41] *Ibid.*, p. 226.
[42] Beaver, *Church, State, and the American Indians*, pp. 18–19;
Vaughan, *New England Frontier*, p. 43.

were lone voices opposed to anglicizing the Indians through education.[43] The latter held that the gospel alone, once it took root among them, would change the character and life of the aborigines.[44] But others agreed with Mather that Eliot had to "make men of them, e'er he could make them saints."[45] During the next century only Eleazar Wheelock stressed the point that "their wretched outward condition should move our compassions towards them,"[46] but the extent of the educational programs indicates the continuing strength of this humanitarian concern.

Love of God and of Christ come more strongly to the fore in the second century of the mission.[47] Ebenezer Pemberton mentions ardent love to God as David Brainerd's most compelling motive.[48] Obedience to Christ's Great Commission becomes a powerful incentive in the eighteenth century,[49] and emulation of the pioneer missionaries is made a reason for both vocation and support. A growing ecumenical vision, so apparent in the diary and works of Cotton Mather, had its influence. Stephen Badger was ordained as the last missionary pastor of the Indian remnant at Natick in 1753 against a background of the urgency of a total world-wide mission for the conversion of the heathen.[50] Jonathan Edwards' book, *An Humble Attempt to Promote Explicit Agreement and Visible Union among God's People, in Extraordinary Prayer for the Revival of Religion, and the Advancement of Christ's Kingdom on Earth, Pursuant to Scripture Promises, and Prophecies concerning the Last Time*,[51] was

[43] According to Johnson, such Indians as were "brought up under the care of Dissenting Ministers become a gloomy race & lose their abilities for hunting" (quoted by Klingberg, *Anglican Humanitarianism in Colonial New York*, p. 96.

[44] Beaver, *Pioneers in Mission*, p. 200.

[45] Mather held that the procedure was first to civilize and then to Christianize (*Magnalia*, 1:580-81).

[46] Beaver, *Pioneers in Mission*, p. 232.

[47] *Ibid.*, p. 19.

[48] *Ibid.*, p. 421.

[49] *Ibid.*, p. 19.

[50] *Ibid.*, pp. 125ff.

[51] Boston: D. Hinchman, 1747.

most influential in lifting the eyes of churchmen to a world-wide horizon. It made the obedient Christian a co-worker with God in preparing for the coming kingdom, and it was the most influential factor in the promotion of the Concert of Prayer, which ultimately became the great instrument of missionary promotion.[52] It stimulated tremendously the eschatological motivation which had become powerful before the end of the seventeenth century. The continuing roles of eschatology and apocalyptic expectation require special attention.

Eschatology and the Perishing Heathen

Eschatology was a major motive to mission from the beginning, but it soon showed a tendency to degenerate into imminent apocalyptic expectation of the millennium.[53] The tract *New England First Fruits* of 1643 voices the genuine eschatological view of the meaning of the founding of New England. Scriptures show that

> God means to carry his Gospel westward, in these later times of the world; and . . . as the Sunne in the afternoon of the day, still declines more and more to the West, and then sets: So the Gospel (that great Light of the World) though it rose in the East, and in former ages, hath lighted it with his heavens, yet in the latter ages of the world will bend Westward, and before its setting, brighten these parts, with this glorious lustre also.[54]

God was moving history towards its consummation and the Indian missions were part of that design. The Father had promised the heathen to Christ for His inheritance, and that must be accomplished in the Indians.[55] However, very soon

[52] R. Pierce Beaver, "The Concert of Prayer for Missions," *Ecumenical Review*, 10 (July, 1958): 420–27.

[53] R. Pierce Beaver, "Eschatology in American Missions," *Basileia, Walter Freytag zum 60. Geburtstag*, ed. J. Hermelink and H. J. Margul (Stuttgart: Evang. Missionsverlag, 1959), pp. 60–75.

[54] First of the "Eliot Tracts," most readily available in Sabin's Reprints, Quarto Series, no. 7 (New York, 1865; orig. London: Overton, 1643), pp. 18–19.

[55] Cotton Mather, *India Christiana*, pp. 19, 22.

the millennial expectation distorted true eschatology, and the "signs of the times" were avidly read. This did make for increased urgency in enlargement of missionary efforts. Thus Cotton Mather exhorted all Christian nations to follow the example of Eliot and New England, for "I am well satisfied that if men had the wisdom to discern the signs of the times, they would be all hands at work to spread the name of our Jesus into all the corners of the earth. 'Grant it, O my God, and Lord Jesus, come quickly.'"[56] The very missionary societies founded in England and Scotland were themselves signs of the approaching return of our Lord.[57] Preoccupation with the signs increased in the next century. Let two examples suffice. Pemberton at David Brainerd's ordination encouraged the young missionary with the expectation that "the day draws near;"[58] and Samuel Buell at Occum's ordination in 1758 asserted:

> [This is] a Day in which we have Reason to believe from Scripture Prophecy, and the present Aspect of Divine Providence, that the Latter-Day Glory is dawning; a Day also, in which, by the Smiles of Heaven upon our Forces, and the Success of our Armies in *America*, a joyous Prospect opens to View, far beyond all that ever appear'd before, for evangelizing the Heathen in these Ends of the Earth.[59]

Jonathan Edwards in *An Humble Attempt* asserted that the terrible time of the Church's trials foretold by the prophets had already passed. The coming of the latter-day glory now awaited united action in prayer by the people of God. Here was a return to genuine eschatology. On the one hand, the witness of the Church was by God's own design made prerequisite to the End; and, on the other, the individual's concern for the End was directed away from his own personal

---

[56] Cotton Mather, *Magnalia*, 1:531.
[57] Cotton Mather, *Diary of Cotton Mather* (2:332–33, being Massachusetts Historical Society Collections, 7th series, vol. 7 (1912).
[58] Beaver, *Pioneers in Mission*, p. 122.
[59] *Ibid.*, p. 179.

fate to the gathering of all peoples unto Christ. Then Edwards' friend and pupil, Samuel Hopkins, published his *Treatise on the Millennium,* fostering preoccupation with millenarianism and stimulating speculation about the time soon to arrive.[60] Hopkins did not connect the mission with the millennium and in the matter of the time of the trials of the Church his pupils followed Edwards rather than him, but he so popularized speculation about the time of the millennium that it was soon to have a tremendous impact upon missionary motivation. Missionary sermons become increasingly numerous after 1787. Fifty-two sermons selected at random from seventy covering the next thirty or forty years give considerable attention to eschatology in the form of millenarianism. The French Revolution and the Napoleonic Wars are interpreted as the prophesied "shaking of the nations," the last days of the tribulation of the Church before the glorious era of peace.[61] After the Napoleonic Wars, the signs were interpreted to mean that the eve of the millennium had arrived. At the very least, navigation, commerce, speedier communications, scientific inventions, and the like were opening all regions of the world to the gospel. The "time" was now frequently fixed from the middle of the nineteenth to the middle of the twentieth century.[62]

The consequence of the expectation of the imminent advent of the millennium was the sentiment that since Christ was so soon to return and reign with His saints, only a few years remained for preaching the gospel to the whole world and for gathering souls into the fold. Compassion for the perishing heathen then took a sentimental turn, and became a feverish "plucking of brands from the burning." The abundance of references, too great to document, seems to indi-

[60] The *Treatise* is appended to *The Systems of Doctrines* (Boston: Lincoln and Edmands, 1811), 2:411–538.
[61] An early example, John M. Mason, *Hope for the Heathen: a Sermon . . . before the N. Y. Missionary Society, . . . 1797* (New York: T. & J. Swords, 1797).
[62] The contradictory predictions must have been bewildering, yet they all tended to fix the time within a century and so had the effect of stressing urgency.

cate that well into the 1830's and 1840's the salvation of the perishing was popularly the most important motive in vocations and support. Few doubted that the unbelieving heathen perished in everlasting torment. Alexander Proudfit asked his hearers:

> Who that rolls in affluence, can deliberately witness a fellow mortal perishing with hunger, and not administer a pittance to his wants? Who, possessed of the common feelings of humanity, could cooly view a fellow creature shivering in the blasts of winter, without endeavoring to afford him seasonable relief? But a thousand fold more pitiable is the spectacle here exhibited to our view. Not the body merely, it being perishable in its nature, its miseries, however exquisite, are of but momentary duration; it is the soul, the precious never, never dying soul, which claims our compassion and our aid. Do not your hearts melt within you?[63]

And hearts did melt, purses opened, intercessions were offered, and men and women went forth to rescue the perishing. They were overwhelmed by the spectacle of destruction. They exclaimed: "Ah! While the sentence is yet on my lips, they are passing by hundreds into that world unseen, with no renewing Spirit, and no atoning blood!"[64] The young founding American Board missionaries at Bombay, Gordon Hall and Samuel Newell, publicized the colossal magnitude of the host of the perishing through the wide circulation of their tract, *The Conversion of the World: or the Claims of Six Hundred Millions of Heathens.*[65] More than half a billion "who have never heard of the name of Jesus, who know not that a Saviour has bled for sinners, are rushing through pagan darkness, by millions, down to hopeless death." The statistics of hopeless mortality were given by the year, the

[63] Alexander Proudfit, *A Sermon, Preached before the Northern Missionary Society in the State of New-York . . . 1798* (Albany: Loring Andrews, 1798), p. 23.
[64] John M. Mason, *Hope for the Heathen*, p. 32.
[65] Andover, Mass.: Flagg & Gould, 1818.

month, the day, the hour, the minute: Fifty-five thousand
die daily without salvation (1837).[66]

Rufus Anderson, the great theoretician as well as admin-
istrator of American missions, sought to recall churchmen
to a more genuine eschatology and interpreted the signs of
the times in relation to it. In the *Promised Advent of the
Spirit*,[67] he states that a time is coming when the divine power
will be so manifested through the preached gospel as to make
that gospel triumphant throughout the earth. Scripture promises a great and general outpouring of the Spirit in the latter
days, and it will be to the whole Church what it was to the
small group of disciples in the upper room on Pentecost. The
kingdoms of this world will become the kingdom of Christ.
Even at this time the advent of the Spirit may be discerned
by preparatory measures, foremost of which is the success
of missions, accompanied by spiritual revivals in the young
churches among the Hawaiians, Karens, and Tamilians. The
Church is not to wait until this outpouring has become universal, but, looking to the End and obedient to God's will
and purpose, is to "go before the Spirit, and prepare the way
for his advent." It has the necessary endowments, the most
favorable circumstances, and Christ's command. In *The
Time for the World's Conversion Come*,[68] Dr. Anderson holds
that the mid-nineteenth century is a "fullness of time" similar
to the period of the advent of Christ, since for the first time
God has opened the way for the universal propagation of
the faith and also for the first time the churches were organized to conduct a world mission. Anderson in these two tracts
points away from the millennium to the kingdom and divorces
the signs of the times from millennial speculation and applies
them to the providential new opportunities for preaching
the gospel to all people. Each decade thereafter some promi-

[66] John McDowell, *A Sermon, Preached at Newark, N. Jersey,
Sept. 13, 1837, before the A.B.C.F.M. . . .* (Boston: Crocker & Brewster, 1837), p. 23.

[67] Rufus Anderson, *Promised Advent of the Spirit* (Boston: Crocker &
Brewster, 1841); reprinted as an A.B.C.F.M. Missionary Tract.

[68] Missionary Tract no. 10 (Boston: A.B.C.F.M., n.d.); also published
as *The Missionary Age* (Boston: T. R. Marvin, 1851).

nent voice or pen read the signs of the times to show the providential working of the Almighty in favoring the mission and to demonstrate a new readiness of the heathen to accept the gospel.[69] One of the last instances occurs as late as 1931 when John R. Mott interpreted the favorable omens of the day in his book *Present Day Summons to the World Mission of Christianity.*[70]

As preoccupation with the date of the millennium ceased, the urgency to "pluck brands from the burning" lessened. Moreover, even in missionary sermons doubts about the damnation of all heathen came to be voiced.[71] The Andover Controversy in the American Board of Commissioners for Foreign Missions is the dividing line in this matter.[72] A tremendous furor was raised when it was discovered on the one hand, that Robert A. Hume and some other missionaries who had graduated from Andover Seminary believed in second probation, and, on the other, that the home secretary was refusing to present to the Board candidates who did not firmly believe that only in this present life is there a chance to be saved and that unbelievers could not be saved. "Second probation," on the contrary, was the idea that those who did not hear the gospel and believe on Christ in this life might be given a second chance hereafter. Although the secretary was upheld, the result of the affair was that thereafter the Board accepted ordination by some church judicatory as evidence of satisfactory and acceptable faith.

The salvation of the perishing heathen then became less and less prominent as a motive in mainstream missionary

[69] Good examples are two papers by N. G. Clark printed and circulated by the American Board, *A Century of Christian Progress*, 1876, and *The Historical Position of Modern Missions*, 1880.

[70] Nashville: Cokesbury, 1931, pp. 11–50.

[71] One of the earliest liberal arguments is Cornelius R. Duffie, *The Salvability of the Heathen No Excuse for Neglect of Revealed Duty by the Christian* (New York: Daniel Dana, Jr., 1860). The preacher declares that heathen ignorant of Christ who live by the light of their religion are saved in that religion but not by it, their salvation being effected by Christ. Their salvability is no excuse for neglecting missions.

[72] Fred Field Goodsell, *You Shall Be My Witnesses* (Boston: A.B.C.-F.M., 1959), pp. 111–15.

vocation and support, and while salvation through Christ was vigorously affirmed, the fate of the unbeliever was no longer fully faced. Acquaintance with non-Christians, the development of the study of comparative religion, and even the studies of other religions by missionaries all dispelled the old views of heathenism. Christians became uncomfortable about consigning noble, righteous, humanitarian unbelievers to eternal damnation. By the second decade of the twentieth century it was widely agreed that every man needs Christ to live as well as die, that God can be known fully only in Christ, but that men are saved by God's gracious response to their reverent, positive attitude towards the best they know, since Christ is the "light which lighteth every man." The fact of a man's salvation can be left to God.[73] Nevertheless, the certainty of the damnation of unbelievers coupled with a powerful yearning to save the souls of perishing unbelievers remains a powerful incentive to missionary vocation and support in those conservative circles now called "the Evangelicals."

The Wheaton Conference Declaration of 1966 speaks for that large and growing portion of the American missionary enterprise when it states:

We therefore declare

That we will ourselves be more forthright and thorough in our preaching and teaching of the testimony of the Bible on the aweful reality of eternal loss through sin and unbelief.

That we will encourage all evangelical theologians to intensify their exegetical study of the Scriptures relating to eternal punishment and the call to redemption and reconciliation.

That since the mission of the Church inescapably commits us to proclaim the gospel which offers men the forgiveness of sins only through faith in Jesus Christ, our verbal witness to him should accompany our service to the poor, the sick, the needy, and the oppressed.

[73] Edmund D. Soper, *The Philosophy of the Christian World Mission* (New York & Nashville: Abingdon-Cokesbury, 1943), pp. 141–45.

That the repudiation of universalism obliges all evangelicals to preach the gospel to all men before they die in their sins. To fail to do this is to accept in practice what we deny in principle.[74]

Millennial speculation lost respectability after the Civil War and the prevailing view came to be: "To make his word of salvation known to the uttermost parts of the earth, relying on the power of the Spirit to insure it success, *and leaving the times of fulfillment to the sovereign purpose of God* — this we take to be the revealed philosophy of the Lord Jesus Christ concerning the work for which his Church is set in the world."[75] Millennialism, lost as a motive in mainstream missions, continued a lively existence in fundamentalist circles. Conflicting pre- and postmillennial theories join together in agreement that the present is the time of outgathering before the millennium.[76] This makes for urgency in evangelization. Stressing verbal proclamation and opposing service ministries as tending to delay the divine intervention, such views and policies gave a bad name to eschatology in the estimation of people within the church missions. Consequently after World War II it was difficult to get a hearing in the United States for German, Swiss, and Dutch mission theology, which has a marked eschatological character.

The kingdom here and now tended to displace the kingdom coming at the End from the center of concern. Moreover, the kingdom of God came to be confused with "progress" to a considerable degree, that is, with the development and extension of modern European technological civilization. James S. Dennis in 1897 published three huge volumes in which he claimed for Protestant missions the chief credit

[74] "The Wheaton Declaration, Subscribed by the Delegates to the Congress on the Church's Worldwide Mission, Convened at Wheaton, Illinois, April 9–16, 1966," *East Asia's Missions*, 74 (June, 1966): 88.

[75] Robert R. Booth, "The Relation of the Work of Jesus to Christianity," reprinted from *American Presbyterian and Theological Review*, 1867, p. 5.

[76] Wm. O. Carver, *Missions in the Plan of the Ages* (New York: Revell, 1909), chap. 11.

for progress in every aspect of society outside western Christendom.[77] Human nature was being transformed and society reformed and ennobled by the gospel working through mission churches, schools, presses, hospitals, and other service agencies. According to William O. Carver in 1909, there was still in 1909 a considerable number in missionary quarters who believed in the second coming of Christ, and who expected a gradual growth of the kingdom through faithful mission work until He should come. But Carver stated that there was a still larger party, actually absorbing the other, who had no place for the second coming and expected the new heaven and earth to be brought in by a gradual evolution as spiritual forces in society gain control.[78] A critic of the Student Volunteer Movement's motto, "The evangelism of the world in this generation," said: "I would substitute the motto 'World-wide Victory' — the world for Christ; the church in every land; every church a witness for Christ; every church more and more triumphant, till Christ through the church, shall rule over all!"[79]

Nevertheless, while missionaries were engrossed in "building" the kingdom of God on earth, the eschatological dimension could not ultimately be eliminated. Edmund D. Soper, whose writings voice the consensus of mainstream American missions in the 1930's and early 1940's, wrote:

> When the realization comes home to us that it is God's kingdom, that it is the actual rule of God in the hearts of men . . . the conviction must surely be borne in upon us that only God is sufficient for these things and that he must bring in the kingdom when it comes. In its final consummation it is a spiritual order quite different from anything connected with the present world order. . . . With all that we may do, it is God's kingdom after all, and the mighty changes which must be

[77] James S. Dennis, *Christian Missions and Social Progress* (New York: Revell, 1897–1906).

[78] Carver, *Missions in the Plan of the Ages*, p. 258.

[79] E. A. Lawrence, *Modern Missions and the East* (New York: Harper, 1895), p. 37.

brought about to make it a reality are so far beyond man's power that we must bow our heads in humiliation at the suggestion that it is our task to bring in the kingdom. There can be little satisfaction in thinking of our work. Nevertheless, there may come a deepening conviction that not only we ourselves but the work we are attempting to do are in his hands and that he is working out partly through us his purposes which in the end must prevail.[80]

Nationalism

Nationalism appears as a motive to missionary action immediately following the end of the Revolutionary War. It becomes increasingly stronger during the course of the nineteenth century and is clearly a religious expression of the concept of manifest destiny.

The Continental Congress and the Army employed missionaries and Indian Christians in the national interest during the war, and afterwards the War Department, which had charge of Indian affairs, enlisted the mission agencies in a partnership in civilizing the aborigines.[81] Nationalism was certainly an important factor in inducing the missionaries and their societies to enter into such collaboration. But the immediate effect of nationalistic sentiment at the end of the war was organization for missionary activity. The New England Company transferred its operations to New Brunswick, but the Society in Scotland for Propagating Christian Knowledge moved to reestablish its support of the Indian missions. It appointed a new Board of Commissioners or Correspondents, distinguished gentlemen living in and near Boston. However, those persons deemed it unpatriotic for them to serve a foreign agency. Therefore, in 1787 they organized and got chartered the Society for the Propagation of the Gospel among Indians and Others in New England.[82] This

[80] Edmund D. Soper, *The Philosophy of the Christian World Mission*, pp. 286, 288.
[81] Beaver, *Church, State, and the American Indians*, chap. 2.
[82] *The Society for Propagating the Gospel among the Indians and*

was the signal for the founding of numerous state, regional, and local societies.[83] The example and inspiration of the new English societies beginning in 1792 further stimulated the movement.

Jacob Norton in 1810 asked the members of the Massachusetts Missionary Society:

> Is the expectation, my brethren, visionary and unfounded, that the time is not far distant, when from the United States, missionaries will "go into all the world and preach the gospel to every creature?" Yes, my brethren, when men in the benevolent spirit and with the holy ardour of an Eliot, a Brainerd, a Tennent, will under the patronage of the Massachusetts Missionary Society, go forth into every region of the inhabitable globe, with the everlasting gospel in their hands, in their hearts, and upon their tongues, accompanied with the fervent prayers of thousands for their success?[84]

That very year the American Board was founded, and soon the overseas mission became the chief vehicle for exerting American benevolent influence abroad. Soon the preachers were declaring that the Almighty had especially raised up the United States to be the great evangelist of the faith and the teacher of democracy to the peoples of the world.

Jonathan Allen, preaching a farewell sermon to two of the first missionary wives, asserted: "It is well known that in England and America, pure religion has taken a deeper root, and has flourished more for some time past, than in any other part of the earth. In these climes then, we may expect the greater exertions will be made to enlighten the heathen."[85]

Others in North America, 1787–1887, The Society 1887, includes a historical sketch by J. F. Hunnewell; Frederick L. Weiss, "The Society for Propagating the Gospel among the Indians and Others in N. A." (Dublin, N. H.: [the author], 1953).

[83] Elsbree, *The Rise of the Missionary Spirit in America.*

[84] Jacob Norton, *A Sermon Delivered before the Massachusetts Missionary Society . . . 1810* (Boston: Lincoln & Edmands, 1810), p. 25.

[85] Jonathan Allen, *A Sermon Delivered at Haverhill, Feb. 5, 1812, on the Occasion of Two Young Ladies Being about to Embark as the*

Gordon Hall, one of the first missionary band sent to India, declared: God "hath exalted the Church and nation to their present eminence, in which they enjoy greater privileges, civil and religious, than any other portion of the globe. No other people under heaven, ever did, in an equal time, receive blessings so many, so great, and so signal, as this nation has received." Consequently God has imposed a peculiar obligation upon American churches to send the gospel throughout the world.[86] The *Panoplist* in 1817 described God's blessings on the land, asserted that "nothing can be plainer than that the abundant display of God's bounty to the people of the United States should be accompanied and followed by corresponding feelings and actions on their part," and that if such exertions would be made under the divine blessing the west would be Christianized and "the Gospel would be preached in every part of the heathen world."[87]

The missionary vocation of the nation was increasingly insisted upon. For example, Sereno Edwards Dwight declared that although the United States owned no colonies which might be mission fields, only this nation could produce the requisite number of missionaries for the worldwide task.[88] Dr. Edward D. Griffin stated that one-third the "efficacy of the whole Church" was to be found in the United States.[89] David Abeel in 1838 asserted that only first convert America and enlist her in the cause of Christ, and then the conversion of the world is practicable and easy.[90] Thomas Skinner ven-

---

Wives of Rev. Messrs. Judson and Newell . . . , (Haverhill, Mass.: Allen, 1812), p. 9; reprinted in Beaver, *Pioneers in Mission*, p. 272.

[86] Gordon Hall, *Duty of the American Churches in Respect to Foreign Missions*, 2nd ed. (Andover, Mass.: Flagg & Gould, 1815), pp. 8–9.

[87] *Panoplist*, 18 (1817): 3.

[88] Sereno E. Dwight, *Thy Kingdom Come; a Sermon Delivered* . . . *before the Foreign Mission Society of Boston* . . . *1820* (Boston: Crocker & Brewster, 1820), pp. 26–27.

[89] Edward D. Griffin, *A Sermon, Preached May 9, 1819, at the Anniversary of the United Foreign Missionary Society* . . . *New York* (New York: Seymour, 1819), pp. 15–16.

[90] David Abeel, *The Missionary Convention at Jerusalem, Or an Exhibition of the Claims of the World to the Gospel* (New York: John S. Taylor, 1838), p. 28.

tured to say in 1843 that "the moral condition of the United States is to decide that of the world," that the spirit of evangelism cannot be confined, and that if it were not exported it would become weak and invalid at home.[91]

A passage in a sermon by Leonard Bacon is typical of the mid-century.

> In this land of ours it is especially incumbent on Christ's followers to appreciate their relations to the Gospel as designed for the world, and to Christ's great enterprise of saving the world by the publication of his Gospel to every creature. God has given us a country such as was never before given to any people; a country which he reserved till these last days as if for some great and peculiar purpose in his providence over the world. Here, for the first time in eighteen centuries, Christianity holds its legitimate position in respect to political institutions — subject neither to state persecution on the one hand nor to state patronage on the other. The consequence is that here the genius of Christianity, in every form, and under every circumstance, shows itself active and aggressive. . . . Meanwhile every citizen, and especially every thoughtful Christian citizen, is constrained to feel the relations of his country to the world. . . . The consciousness that our country is destined to act upon the world, not by conquest and dominion, but by moral influences, has come to be one of the elements of our moral character. Surely, then, we as American Christians are summoned as by a peculiar call, to enter with all our hearts and all our energies into sympathy with the spirit of the Gospel as designed for universal diffusion and universal conquest. In the position in which we stand, enjoying such freedom, and conscious of such relations to the world and the world's destiny, it becomes us above all other men to feel that the Gospel which we have received is, in the plan of its great

[91] Thomas Skinner, *Progress the Law of Missionary Work* (Boston: Crocker & Brewster, 1843), p. 44.

Author, the common heritage of all nations, and to put
forth our utmost efforts, that the great design of the
world's Redeemer may be speedily accomplished.[92]

Perhaps the most full and outspoken exposition of the
manifest destiny theme is the sermon, *God's Purpose in
Planting the American Church,* preached before the annual
meeting of the American Board in 1860 by Samuel W. Fischer,
president of Hamilton College.[93] He reasons that God has
sometimes selected special instruments for the enlargement
of his kingdom and Church, peoples as well as individuals. So
it is that "God has formed us as a nation to exert a special and
vast influence in the evangelization of other nations." On the
foundation of the extraordinary and splendid character of the
Anglo-Saxon race, which had been especially equipped and
trained for His divine purposes, He further raised up an elect
people in America. Here by the very vastness of the land and
through the conquest of a virgin continent, God has educated
the American for his peculiar world mission, in which he "is to
form men, to give laws to nations, and to interpenetrate the
souls of missions with the truth as it is in Jesus."

It is to this end that the Almighty has developed American
individuality and character.

Now in this process of national culture, you see the
development of just those qualities which, when conse-
crated by the spirit of the gospel, are to constitute the
finest missionary race in the world. They are positive
qualities; they constitute the energy that impresses —
the power that subdues and moulds other minds by a
law as certain as that which bids the flowers open, and
verdure crown the hills beneath the kiss of the sunshine
and the rain. This hardy frame; this restless energy; this

[92] Leonard Bacon, *Christian Unity. A Sermon . . . Before the Foreign Evangelical Society . . . New York . . . 1845* (New Haven:
printed for the Society by B. L. Hamlen, 1845), pp. 34–36.
[93] Samuel W. Fischer, *The Obstacles and Encouragements to Missionary Effort, in the Ancient and Modern Church* (Boston: Tappan & Den-
nett, 1842).

indomitable perseverence; this practical tact; this productive invention, not spending itself on minute forms
of embellishment, but exerting its genius along the line
of those practical combinations which multiply the
power of the hand a thousand-fold, and change, as if by
magic, the aspect of a country in a single year; this stal-
wart growth of individual power which makes man the
sovereign of nature; — these constitute a race which, informed by religion, is prepared, yea necessitated, to lead
the van of Immanuel's army for the conquest of the
world.[94]

Our constitutional principles, Dr. Fischer states, are further preparation for the American missionary role, and our
adventurous enterprising is another. Moving ever westward
on the frontier, each generation going onward to establish
new homes, we have been rendered mobile and adaptable,
and can cross the oceans to conquer the world for Christ. The
process of self-development along the line of material interests is necessary "to unfold the attributes which give us the
power to impress ourselves upon men." This material education but leads on to the spiritual. Further, "the character and
position of the Protestantism we possess constitutes our most
vital, substantive efficiency." Our very religious liberty and
pluralism "contribute not a little to our power as a missionary
race." Thus Americans have been well prepared for "the
grand work which this race is to effect in the conversion of
the world." Add to this divinely directed education "the remarkable character given to [American Christianity] by the
revivals of religion." And finally, "for full half a century, God
has been organizing the American church for the work of
foreign missions and training it, in actual service, for this
great object. . . . And now *the hour* has come."
Given the reiteration of such views, it is not strange that
American churchmen should regard the acquisition of the
Philippines and Puerto Rico and the independence of Cuba,
by the treaties ending the Spanish-American War, as the di-

[94] *Ibid.,* p. 16.

rect intervention of divine providence. A conference of representatives of mission boards prepared to respond to God's challenge, met in New York on July 13, 1898, and prefaced their resolutions with this statement:

> It is the judgment of this conference that the political and military relations into which the United States has been so strangely forced with reference to Cuba, Porto Rico and the Philippine and Ladrone Islands, involve certain moral and religious responsibilities — responsibilities which are, perhaps, quite independent of the precise character of the political relationship which may hereafter be formed with them — and that the Christian people of America should immediately and prayerfully consider the duty of entering the doors which God in His providence is thus opening. We believe that this feeling represents the deep and solemn Christian patriotism of the country, and that support will be given to the boards for this purpose.[95]

Thereupon the participating boards entered upon comity agreements for the division of territory, agreed upon federation of their missions, and began work simultaneously in the God-given new fields.[96]

Foreign Missions through the Nineteenth Century

Nationalism provided a powerful incentive to the development of the missionary movement, but, nevertheless, it was secondary to spiritual and theological motivation. Between the organization of the first societies in 1787 and the foundation of the American Board in 1810 the motives of the colonial era remained dominant, that is, *gloria Dei* first and compassion second.[97] Obedience to the Great Commission, however,

[95] *Report of the 7th Conference of the Officers and Representatives of the Foreign Mission Boards and Societies in the United States and Canada, 1899*, p. 118.

[96] R. Pierce Beaver, *Ecumenical Beginnings in Protestant World Mission* (New York: Thomas Nelson & Sons, 1962), pp. 134–40.

[97] *Gloria Dei*: Proudfit, *A Sermon . . . 1798*, pp. 21–22; John L. Livingston, *A Sermon Delivered before the New York Missionary So-*

now ranks close to the glory of God.[98] A sense of indebtedness to the heathen carries compassion somewhat deeper.[99] A desire to emulate and match the British in their efforts in mission forms a lesser motive.[100] Finally, there appears motivation much more glad and spontaneous: the Christian proclaims the gospel to all men simply because he has to share the blessings which God has given him, the greatest of which is salvation through Christ,[101] and because his heart is filled with gratitude to God.[102]

How is one to explain that with the advent of the overseas mission *gloria Dei* as a motive vanishes almost overnight? Only two sermons out of 126 between 1810 and 1850 mention it.[103] The mission is still God's will and God's

---

ciety . . . *1804* (New York: T. & J. Swords, 1804), p. 3 (several times reprinted); compassion: John M. Mason, *Hope for the Heathen*, p. 29; Wm. Linn, *A Discourse 1800 . . . before the New-York Missionary Society* . . . (New York: Isaac Collins, 1800), pp. 10–11; Solomon Williams, *A Sermon Preached at Northampton . . . 1802* (Northampton, Mass.: Wm. Butler, 1802), p. 17; Levi Frisbie, *A Discourse before the Society for Propagating the Gospel among the Indians and Others in N. A.,* . . . *1804*, pp. 27–28.

[98] Proudfit, *A Sermon . . . 1798*, whole; Linn, *A Discourse . . . 1800*, p. 8; Samuel Spring, *A Sermon Delivered before the Massachusetts Missionary Society . . . 1802* (Newburyport: E. M. Blunt, 1802), pp. 13, 30, 32; Samuel Austin, *A Sermon Preached before the Massachusetts Missionary Society . . . 1803* (Salem: Joshua Cushing, 1803), pp. 7–8; John Williams, *A Discourse Delivered April 5, 1803 . . . before the New York Missionary Society* (New York: Isaac Collins & Son, 1803), p. 13; Levi Frisbie, *A Discourse . . . 1804*, p. 26; Thomas Barnard, *A Discourse before the Society for Propagating the Gospel among the Indians . . . 1806* (Charlestown, Mass.: Samuel Etheridge, 1806), p. 4.

[99] Samuel Austin, *A Sermon*, pp. 5–6.

[100] Elihu Thayer, *A Sermon Preached at Hopkinton at the Formation of the New-Hampshire Missionary Society . . . 1801* (Concord: Geo. Hough, 1801), p. 16.

[101] Joseph Lathrop, *A Sermon Preached to the Hampshire Missionary Society . . . 1802* (Northampton, Mass.: Wm. Butler, 1802), p. 18.

[102] John M. Mason, *Hope for the Heathen*, pp. 23–24; Lathrop, *A Sermon . . . 1802*, p. 18; Eliphalet Porter, *A Discourse before the Society for Propagating the Gospel among the Indians . . . 1807* (Boston: Munroe, Francis, & Parker, 1808), p. 83.

[103] Samuel Spring, the *Charge* at the ordination of Judson, Hall, Newell, etc., in Leonard Woods, *A Sermon Delivered at the Tabernacle*

work,[104] but gratitude for God's saving grace is mentioned only twice.[105] The imitation of Jesus as the first and model missionary comes into prominence.[106] Apart from the frantic efforts to save the perishing heathen, the all-compelling motive is now obedience to Christ's Great Commission. Thirty of the sermons of the period make it fundamental, and eight others regard the mission as inescapable Christian duty, ultimately derived from the will of Christ.

During the half century from 1830 to 1880, Rufus Anderson was the great architect of mission theory and practice, and almost all followed his lead.[107] For him, obedience to Christ is the foremost motive and mission is the central function of the Church of Christ.[108] Seeking the salvation of

---

in Salem, Feb. 6, 1812, on the Occasion of the Ordination, etc. (Boston: Samuel T. Armstrong, 1812), p. 33; Wm. Hervey, *The Spirit of Missions, a Sermon Preached in Williamstown, Dec. 13, 1829* . . . (Williamstown, Mass.: Bannister, 1831), pp. 17–18.

[104] Isaac Knapp, *The Zeal of Jehovah for the Kingdom of Christ* (Northampton, Mass.: Wm. Butler, 1813), pp. 3ff; Bennett Tyler, *A Sermon Preached at Litchfield* . . . *1813* (New Haven: Eli Hudson, 1813), p. 4; James Bradford, *The Presence of the Lord Sufficient Grounds for Encouragement and Exertion* (Stockbridge, Mass.: Stockbridge Star, 1816), p. 7; John Codman, *Idolatry Destroyed and the Worship of the True God Established* (Boston: Lincoln & Edmands, 1818), p. 24; Gardiner Spring, *The Will of God*, whole; Samuel Spring, "Charge," in Woods, *A Sermon Delivered at the Tabernacle*, p. 36; Elias Cornelius, *A Sermon Delivered at the Tabernacle Church, Salem* . . . *1823, at the Ordination of the Rev. Edmund Frost* . . . (Boston: Crocker & Brewster, 1823), p. 21.

[105] Richard Furman, Substance of Sermon in *Proceedings of the Baptist Convention for Missionary Purposes, 1814*, p. 24; Wm. Hervey, *The Spirit of Missions*, pp. 19–21.

[106] Diodate Brockaway, "A Missionary Sermon . . . Delivered . . . 1812, at the Request of the . . . Missionary Society of Connecticut . . . ," *Conn. Evangelical Magazine and Religious Intelligencer*, 5 (June, 1812): 215; Samuel Austin, *Paul, an Example . . . of the Missionary Character* (Boston: Crocker & Brewster, 1824), pp. 3–4; Jeremiah Chaplin, *A Sermon Preached at North Yarmouth* . . . *1825, at the Ordination of the Rev. George D. Boardman* . . . (Waterville, Me.: Wm. Hastings, 1825), p. 23; Ed. D. Griffin, *A Sermon Preached Sept. 14, 1826, before the A.B.C.F.M., at Middletown, Conn.* (Middletown: E. & H. Clark, 1826), pp. 5, 23.

[107] R. Pierce Beaver, ed., *To Advance the Gospel*, pp. 9–38.

[108] *Ibid.*, especially pp. 17, 47, 49, 57, 60, 61, 63ff, 68, 73, 182–183.

souls because of love of Christ — not sentimental "plucking the brands" — is his second motive, and the opportunity of meeting the greatest need of the world is the third.

Anderson's fellow secretary in the American Board, S. L. Pomroy, published a very influential tract, *The Grand Motive to Missionary Effort*, which attempted to set all secondary motives in proper relation to what he thought the primary one.[109] He lists the prevailing popular motives as compassion for the physical, social, and temporal wretchedness of the heathen, pledges and resolutions, the success of missions, and the aweful doom of the pagan idolator. Yet there is one grand motive which includes every other good one. It is as powerful as it is simple: *love to Christ*. This is the only true motive. "It is to all secondary motives what the central sun is to the planetary system — 'the eye and soul of all.'"

> The love of Christ shining out from the cross, has enkindled a responsive love in the heart of the Christian. And one of the earliest emotions of the regenerate soul, commingling itself often with the first swelling tide of gratitude for its own deliverance, is the desire to speak of Christ to others. In this simple desire lies the germ of that great enterprise which carried the gospel through the Roman empire, and is now sending it through the world. . . . It never paralyzes or weakens any subordinate motive; but on the contrary, gives strength and tone to every chord of sympathy, whether for the body or the soul.[110]

Obedience and love contended and combined as motives. But obedience took first place and tended to be expressed as duty, — military duty of the soldiers of Christ obeying their General. The Third Conference of Officers and Representatives of the Foreign Mission Boards and Societies of the United States and Canada in 1895 by official action "Re-

[109] S. L. Pomroy, *The Grand Motive to Missionary Effort* (Boston: A.B.C.F.M., 1853), Missionary Tract no. 13.
[110] *Ibid.*, p. 9.

solved, that emphasis is to be placed first of all on our loyal obedience to the command of the Master as the highest motive in foreign missions. His command to 'go' is our imperative order and our highest inspiration."[111] A highly legalistic response to these "marching orders of the Church" was tied to the insistence that these were the *ipsima verba* of Jesus. As late as 1943 Samuel M. Zwemer was basing duty on "the authenticity and genuineness of the Great Commission" in his book, *"Into All the World," The Great Commission: a Vindication and an Interpretation.*[112]

However, such legalism offended the warm hearts, deep personal faith, and prized freedom in Christ of many persons, and higher criticism made the almost military duty derived from these Scripture passages questionable. Better grounds for obedience were advanced. Even Arthur T. Pierson, editor of the influential *Missionary Review of the World*, foe of higher criticism and new theological trends, staunch believer in the damnation of unbelievers, had to base duty in love. He wrote in 1886: "The principle of missions is not enough, however, without the *spirit* of missions; a law of labor for souls will not suffice without the love for Christ and for souls, which is the life secret of such labor."[113] Similarly E. K. Alden, a secretary of the American Board, explained:

> The impelling force underlying and pervading the missionary activity of the Church of Christ is the Spirit of Christ, its living Head. Whatever moved the Lord of glory to leave his heavenly home, to be "formed in fashion as a man," to humble himself and become "obedient unto death, even the death of the cross," is what now most profoundly moves the disciple precisely to the degree in which he possesses the mind of his Lord. He will think the Lord's thoughts after him, will be possessed by the same convictions of truth and duty, and

[111] *Report of the 3rd Conference of Officers and Representatives of Foreign Mission Boards and Societies of the United States and Canada, 1895,* p. 66.
[112] Grand Rapids: Zondervan, 1943, pp. 91–92.
[113] *The Crisis of Missions* (New York: Robert Carter, 1886), p. 305.

will be impelled in the same direction. In other words, *the love of God in Christ*, who gave up his only begotten Son, who gave up himself in sacrificial offering, will take control of a finite spirit and send it forth to similar service, *this love* continuously fed and sustained by a vital connection with its exhaustless Source.[114]

The most influential American teacher of missionary principles after Rufus Anderson has been Robert E. Speer. No one else made greater impact upon both students and mission executives in the last decade of the nineteenth and first third of the twentieth century. He successfully counteracted the legalism of others. Typical of his view is this passage.

> The last command of Christ is often set forth as alike the primary and conclusive argument for missions. What was the last command of His lips must have been one of the nearest desires of His heart. But the work of missions is our duty, not chiefly because of the command of Christ's lips, but because of the desire of His heart. He bade His Church evangelize the world because He wanted it evangelized, and He wanted it evangelized because He knew that it needed to be evangelized. Our duty in the matter is determined, not primarily by His command, but by the facts and conditions of life which underlie it. Even if Jesus had not embodied the missionary duty of the Church in the "great commission," we should be under obligation to evangelize the world by reason of the essential character of Christianity and its mission to the world.[115]

Speer adds that it is never wise to rest duty upon mere enactment, and that the spirit of Christianity is higher than legalism. The repetition and affirmation that "these are the Church's marching orders, and that's an end of it," is not enough. What is needed is that "we appreciate the funda-

[114] *Missionary Motives*, Boston: A.B.C.F.M., 1890. pamphlet.
[115] Robert E. Speer, *Missionary Principles and Practice* (New York: Revell, 1902), p. 9.

mental place missions hold in Christianity, and that our hearts respond warmly to the essential principles of the spirit of Christ, which are inseparably interwoven with missionary obligations." Added to this is the dynamic of love.

> For us love will suffice, the love of Christ, the love which Christ feels for us, the love which He has placed in us, the kind of love which we discern in Him, the love which is life. Surely if there is one thing needed in this missionary enterprise it is this, in the enterprise as a whole, in the councils . . . , in our own personal life of service.[116]

This impulse of duty became highly personalized and is the force behind the Student Volunteer Movement, to which attention will be given in the final section of this article.

Other powerful motives were operative towards the end of the nineteenth century. The opportunity for worldwide evangelization opened by divine providence was a powerful inducement to action. What was to be known in secular history as "the century of science" would be known in sacred history as "the century of evangelization."[117] A "century of Christian progress" was ending, but it was merely preparatory to the next and greater century to come.[118] The word "progress" is the key to understanding much of the enthusiasm for missions on the part of theological conservatives and liberals alike and of the humanitarians. There was the remarkable progress of the missions themselves,[119] but still more exciting and inciting to action was the progress which missions had wrought in formerly benighted lands in social change, civilization, economic betterment, and moral improvement.

A mere listing of some of the social achievements of mis-

[116] Robert E. Speer, in *Report of the 15th Conference of the Foreign Mission Boards in the U.S. and Canada, 1908*, p. 134.

[117] Bishop Cyrus D. Foss, *The Conversion of the World: A Call to Advance*, p. 15.

[118] N. G. Clark, *A Century of Christian Progress* (Boston: A.B.C.F.M., 1876), a printed paper.

[119] A. T. Pierson, in *Crisis of Missions*, reviews them; James S. Dennis, *Foreign Missions after a Century* (New York: Revell, 1893), chap. 6.

sions by James S. Dennis is enough to show why Americans were enthusiastic supporters of the overseas work.[120] Achievements in the transformation of personal character include temperance, opium reform, restraint of gambling, higher standards of personal purity, repression of pessimistic and suicidal tendencies, cultivation of habits of industry and frugality, replacing of barbarian pride and social conceit by Christian humility and self-respect, and cultivation of personal virtues. Nothing is of higher importance than the elevation of women through missions by the checking of divorce, abolition of child marriage, alleviating the plight of widows, improving domestic life, diminishing infanticide, and protecting and aiding children. Other achievements are the abolition of the slave trade, slavery, and forced labor; the abolition of cannibalism, human sacrifices, and inhuman sports; reforms as in footbinding in China, prison conditions, inhuman punishments, and ending of blood feuds. Famine relief, help to poor and dependent persons, and the mitigation of the brutalities of war were extolled as fruits of missions. The introduction of modern medicine, clinics and hospitals, and leprosy work were noted along with promotion of public and private hygiene and sanitation. Orphanages and work with youth are other credits to missions. Education from kindergarten to the university along with industrial and technical schools ranks high. Caste was disintegrated. Freedom and patriotism were cultivated. Missions caused laws to be reconstructed, judicial procedure to be reformed, and the standard of governmental administration to be elevated. Great contributions were made to intellectual and scientific progress, to better methods of transacting business, and to developing worldwide trade.

One other factor which motivated many and reinforced other motives at the end of the century was the conviction that the new "science" of comparative religion proved the superiority of Christianity and its unique character as the

[120] James S. Dennis, *Christian Missions and Social Progress*, 3 vols., (New York: Revell, 1897–1906).

one religion suited to all men. Thus N. G. Clark of the American Board, for example, hailed the timely aid and encouragement to evangelization afforded by the new "Science of Religion." He declared:

> By such inquiries Christianity is seen to be something not foreign to the human mind. There has been a development of religious systems — the expressions of man's moral and religious nature among the different races, in some measure correspondent to the development of the chosen people in preparation to receive the gospel. Christianity joins on to and supplements whatever is best and worthiest in all — the culmination of all, as man is the culmination of the animal kingdom. It is in its favor that many of its doctrines are found in other systems, its moral code only the higher and more complete.[121]

He quotes approvingly Max Müller: "Nothing would more effectually secure to the pure and simple teaching of Christ its true place in the historical development of the human mind than to place it side by side with the other religions of the world."

The Evangelization of the World in This Generation

The final decade of the first century of American foreign missions was also the last one of the great century of Christian expansion, both Protestant and Roman Catholic, during which Christianity actually became the most universally diffused religion. The year 1910, the year of the World Missionary Conference at Edinburgh, and the year 1914, the beginning of World War I, together usher in a distinctly new era in the Protestant world mission, and at that point this survey ends. Tremendous enthusiasm during this significant decade carried American missions to first place in the total Protestant enterprise with respect to the number of missionaries, the amount of money raised and spent, and

[121] N. G. Clark, *The Historical Position of Modern Missions* (Boston: A.B.C.F.M., 1880), reprinted from the *New Englander*, Sept., 1880.

the diffusion of the work. It is a period dominated by enthusiastic adoption of the watchword of the Student Volunteer Movement — "The evangelization of the world in this generation." A highly individualized and personalized sense of missionary obligation or duty, combined with the conviction that God in His providence had now prepared all things for success, was the power behind the slogan. This was equally true with regard to personal vocation and lay support of the work.

The Student Volunteer Movement had its genesis in a student conference at Mr. Hermon School with Dwight L. Moody in 1886 when one hundred of the two hundred fifty-one participants volunteered for overseas service. Under the impact of a tour of the campuses made by Robert Wilder and John N. Forman, 2,100 volunteers were enrolled in the academic year 1886–87. The movement organized in 1889 and was soon carried to Great Britain and Europe. It immediately became the most effective recruiting arm of the boards and societies, which quickly admitted that it brought them the majority of their candidates and improved the quality of them. It was at the same time a mighty educational force in the colleges, and its members and friends who did not go abroad after graduation infused greater missionary dedication and zeal into the churches. It had tremendous power and influence in the United States and Canada until about 1920 and then declined. It is estimated that by 1945 some 20,500 of its volunteers actually served overseas.[122] Certainly from 1900 to 1910 the S.V.M. slogan, "The evangelization of the world in this generation," well represented the mood and zeal of the mission agencies, their constituencies, and the Christian students. It also reflected the prevailing motivation.

The Movement did not spring full blown out of nothing. Behind it on the one hand, was the already proclaimed call for the evangelization of the world in this generation. For

[122] Ruth Rouse and Stephen Neill, eds. *History of the Ecumenical Movement* (Philadelphia: Westminster, 1954), p. 328.

example, after specifying the favorable circumstances, Dr.
N. G. Clark in 1877 wrote: "It is, therefore, in no spirit of
mere enthusiasm or foolhardiness that we claim it to be the
duty and privilege of this generation to secure the evangelization of the world."[123] There was, on the other hand,
the powerful influence of the foremost missionary motive
of the day, duty or obedience. Moreover, this obedience had
been placed by the teaching of Rufus Anderson squarely
upon the individual disciple before resting on the Church.[124]
The giving of the Great Commission preceded the emergence
of the Church. Each Christian under the guidance of the
Holy Spirit must decide whether his personal duty lies overseas or at home. An extraordinary call is not required. Careful study of the situation of mankind and of Christ's provi-
sion for the salvation of the world should convince anyone
looking objectively at the question. It is remaining at home
that is to be justified. "The command to 'preach the gospel
to every creature' comes to us with distinct specification of
the unevangelized world as our field; and we rest in this
decision, till unanticipated, unsought-for events change the
ground of our decision and call for reconsideration, and perhaps for a reversal."[125] Robert E. Speer took up this thesis
of Anderson, proclaimed it from thousands of platforms, and
eventually expounded it in his tract, *What Constitutes a Missionary Call?*. The tract was reprinted in many editions and
helped thousands of later Student Volunteers to make their
decisions.[126] But it was the contagious dedication and zeal
of the leaders, including Wilder, Forman, and Speer, and the
generalship of John R. Mott which fanned these embers into

[123] N. G. Clark, *Claims of the Unevangelized World on the Christian
Church* (Boston: A.B.C.F.M., c. 1877), p. 14.
[124] Beaver, ed., *To Advance the Gospel*, p. 132.
[125] Rufus Anderson, "On Deciding Early to Become a Missionary to
the Heathen," reprinted in *To Advance the Gospel*, ed. Beaver, pp.
186–87.
[126] Robert E. Speer, *What Constitutes a Missionary Call?* (New York:
Association Press, 1918), and reprinted many times by the S.V.M. and
others.

the flaming wildfire of the movement within the colleges and the churches.

John R. Mott in his apology for the idea and the Movement, *The Evangelization of the World in This Generation,*[127] made it clear that the whole Church was to be enlisted and that the duty rested on the entire body of Christ. He wrote:

> It is indispensable to the world's evangelization that the churches on the home field become filled with the missionary spirit. A task so vast cannot be accomplished by the leaders of the Church at home alone, nor by the representatives of the home Church on the foreign field. The cooperation of a great multitude of the members of the Church is essential. This means that the churches in Christian lands must become missionary churches.[128]

The members of such a church recognize and accept their responsibility with a deep conviction that this is their duty and with an ardent desire to perform it.

William O. Carver, the first full-time professor of missions, on the eve of the Edinburgh Conference in 1910 wrote:

> Beyond all question new elements have entered into the motive and new conceptions have entered into the aim. New factors and increased knowledge modify the method. We do not send missionaries to the heathen for exactly the same reasons now that moved our fathers, nor do our missionaries approach their task with the same conceptions that their forerunners entertained, nor pursue it by the same methods that were employed by their predecessors. In some respects the changes have been great. They would even be revolutionary but that they have come by way of evolution. And we would affirm that they have come by evolution.[129]

[127] New York: Student Volunteer Movement for Foreign Missions, 1901.
[128] *Ibid.*, pp. 179–80.
[129] William O. Carver, *Missions and Modern Thought* (New York: Macmillan Co., 1910), p. 264.

The evolution, or at least the course, of motivation with continuity and with marked change has been traced in this article. Limitations of space have allowed little attention to the causes of the changes. Moreover, British and American missions formed a single enterprise, and no exploration could here be made of the effect of British influence upon Americans. The thread of love — love of God, of Christ, of fellow men — runs throughout the whole story. But what had begun by giving glory to God, three hundred years later has become doing one's duty to Christ.

6

How American Is Religion in America?
WINTHROP S. HUDSON

> Everybody says
> I look just like my mother.
> Everybody says
> I'm the image of Aunt Bea.
> Everybody says
> My nose is like my father's
> But I want to look like me.[1]

What is true of individuals is also true of nations. Canadians do not want to be thought of as Americans. Americans do not want to be identified as Englishmen. Englishmen do not regard themselves as Europeans. Europe is across the Channel. And on the Continent people think of themselves as belonging to distinctive and self-contained national cultures — a French culture, a Norwegian culture, a Spanish culture. This emphasis on individuality has often fostered a false sense of separation and autonomy by obscuring the interrelations and reciprocal influences that have bound these nations together. There are, of course, differences within the common culture we designate as European or Western. There are differences of region and locale even within the various national boundaries. Since none of these regional and national cultures are exact duplicates, they do have a separate identity. On the other hand, none of them are wholly separate and self-contained. They have a family resemblance. In Europe the differences have been accentuated by language

[1] Dorothy Aldis, *Everything and Anything* (New York: Balch and Co., 1925), p. 89.

153

barriers, but even this isolating factor has been denied Americans.

In view of the common human quest for a separate identity, it is not surprising that Ralph Waldo Emerson should have issued a declaration of American intellectual and cultural independence in his Phi Beta Kappa Address ("The American Scholar") of August 31, 1837.

> Our day of dependence, our long apprenticeship to the learning of other lands, draws to a close. . . . We have listened too long to the courtly muses of Europe. . . . We will walk on our own feet; we will work with our own hands; we will speak our own minds.[2]

Nor is it surprising that in the course of the address Emerson should have documented the dependence by quoting or citing Socrates, Plato, Cicero, Locke, Bacon, Shakespeare, Chaucer, Marvell, Dryden, Goldsmith, Burns, Cowper, Wordsworth, Carlyle, Pope, Johnson, Gibbon, Goethe, Swedenborg, Newton, Flamsteed, Herschel, Macdonald, Linnaeus, Davy, Cuvier, Pestalozzi, and an Arabian proverb. And his allusions were to the Greeks, the Troubadours, the Savoyards; to Palestine, Algiers, Etna, Vesuvius, Naples, and Provence. What is surprising is that subsequent interpreters of the American scene should have taken Emerson's boastful declaration that the day of dependence was drawing to a close as a statement of an accomplished fact.

One gains the impression from most treatments of American history that the life of the nation developed in a vacuum, being almost wholly self-contained and self-determined. There was, to be sure, an initial European heritage, but thereafter, sheltered and secluded by a broad expanse of ocean, the United States went its own way untouched and uncontaminated by any stimulus from abroad. We commonly suppose that the Baltimore and Ohio was the world's first railroad, that "Fulton's folly" was the pioneering application of steam to water navigation, that the horseless carriage, with its

[2] R. W. Emerson, *Nature, Addresses, and Lectures* (Boston: Houghton Mifflin, 1888) pp. 83, 113–14.

chassis, tonneau, chauffeur, and *garage,* was the product of American inventive genius. The truth, of course, is that we have never been as cloistered as many of us have been led to believe.

The fact that Asians and Africans have tended to call us Europeans (the "Europeans Only" sign was no bar to an American)[3] should have reminded us that we are Europeans in almost all respects — not only in ancestry, but in language, religion, legal institutions, diet, clothing, and household furnishings, as well as in our most characteristic proverbs, our most familiar nursery rhymes, and most of our literature, music, art, philosophy, and science. We have been and are a part of Europe, drawing most heavily — as the mere fact of language so eloquently testifies — from the English-speaking segment of European society. While there are differences in spirit, temper, emphasis, and detail, there is little that we can call exclusively our own.

In the field of church history, our provincialism has obscured many of the interrelationships that have bound us to Europe. As is true of more general accounts of the American past, church historians have tended to depict the European heritage in terms of the initial colonial settlements, and largely ignore any continuing interplay of influence, as though there was no larger Christian community to which we belonged. The impact of German biblical and theological studies in the late nineteenth century has been generally acknowledged, for this was easily recognized as a "foreign" intrusion. But little note is taken of a Samuel Coleridge or a William Wordsworth as an "alien" influence, presumably because one almost automatically regards any Englishman as one with Shakespeare and Milton and, thus, as one with us. On the other hand, when one does become self-conscious and begins to examine the larger context of American religious life, he is astonished to discover how continuous and intimate have been the interplay of influences. A comparative study of religious developments at home and abroad

[3] Native dialects in Nigeria, for example, have no word for "American." Consequently even Negro Americans are called Europeans.

quickly reveals that there is scarcely anything in the whole gamut of religious life in America that does not have its equivalent and usually its antecedent in Europe, and most often in the British Isles.

The origin of the various American denominations is obvious. Most of them are European imports. The few that are not — Mormons, Christian Scientists, Seventh-day Adventists, Jehovah's Witnesses, Pentecostals, Disciples of Christ — have established, by a sort of reverse lend-lease, bridgeheads abroad. Even so, the inspiration for several of these diverse American contributions came from across the Atlantic. Thomas and Alexander Campbell were not wholly unaffected by the new current of religious life they had encountered in Scotland. Mary Baker Eddy owed more than perhaps she knew to Franz Anton Mesmer. William Miller of Adventist fame appears to have derived his biblical arithmetic from the calculations of the British Continental Society for the Diffusion of Religious Knowledge. Of a still later movement, Moral Re-Armament, who is wise enough to say whether it is English or American in origin? Must not the same be said of the quickening of religious life which came to be known as Evangelicalism? Was the initial spark ignited by Theodore J. Frelinghuysen in New Jersey, by Howell Harris in Wales, or by some other quickening preacher? Jonathan Edwards' account of the awakening in Northampton had a marked effect on the British scene; John Wesley's influence was great in America; and George Whitefield operated with telling effect on both sides of the Atlantic.

Reference to the transatlantic character of Evangelicalism calls attention to broader religious movements than those represented by individual denominations. Puritanism and Neo-Orthodoxy immediately come to mind as similar phenomena. But what of revivalism? Is this something peculiar to America? Did Whitefield operate in different ways in Britain and America? Was the Wesleyan revival not really a revival? The modern foreign missionary movement among English-speaking Christians found part of its initial inspiration from David Brainerd's *Journal*, but the trailblazer was William Carey of Leicestershire. The Sunday School movement was the product of the stimulus provided by Robert Raikes of Gloucester. The whole humanitarian and reform thrust of the American churches in the first half of the nineteenth century — prison reform, temperance, education, peace, the care of the orphan, the abolition of slavery — owed much to British precept and example. Indeed, so great was the prestige and authority of the British anti-slavery movement that its American counterpart felt obliged to adopt the British motto, "Immediate Emancipation," even though this necessitated considerable reinterpretation. And when the Americans sought to implement their missionary, humanitarian, and reform concerns, they did so by duplicating the system of voluntary societies which had been fashioned in England.[4] Later in the century, the transatlantic character of the quest for Christian unity was symbolized by the so-called Chicago-Lambeth Quadrilateral, as well as by the Evangelical Alliance which found a ready enough response in the United States to permit the formation of an American branch. Nor was Fundamentalism restricted to the American environment. In fact, to the extent that Fundamentalists insisted upon Dispensationalism as a criterion of self-identification, the movement may be said to have its roots in the teachings of J. N. Darby in England. And Fundamentalism was nourished, with a "holiness" emphasis, on both sides of the Atlantic by the annual Keswick conferences in the Lake Country near the Scottish border.

Institutionally, it is the same story. The voluntary societies, the Sunday school, and the Evangelical Alliance have been mentioned. But the Y.M.C.A., perhaps the most vigorous arm of the churches in the latter half of the nineteenth century, was also imported from Britain. The Salvation Army emerged from "darkest England." The "settlement houses" were modeled after Toynbee Hall.[5] Another British export was the

---

[4] For the relationships of the voluntary societies both in England and America, see Charles I. Foster, *An Errand of Mercy: the Evangelical United Front* (Chapel Hill, N.C.: Univ. of North Carolina Press, 1954).

[5] For the "social settlements," see Robert A. Woods and Albert Kennedy, *The Settlement Horizon* (New York: Russell Sage Foundation,

"labor church." The more successful "institutional church," with its wide-ranging ministry of social service, was equally prominent in both Britain and America. Even that familiar feature of American church life, the Boy Scout troop, was a product of British "muscular Christianity" as represented by Sir Robert Baden-Powell, the founder of the movement. Wherever one looks, the influence is apparent. In America, Frederick W. Robertson, James Martineau, C. H. Spurgeon, John Watson (Ian Maclaren), Alexander Maclaren, Joseph Parker, and John Henry Jowett were among the most admired and emulated preachers, while in England, Henry Ward Beecher and Phillips Brooks were equally admired and emulated.

How does one account for this intimacy of relationship? A common language is the most obvious answer. No interpreter or translator was required; no second language needed to be mastered. But the interplay of influence was sped by constant visits across the Atlantic. Billy Graham's campaigns in England and Scotland broke no new ground. Charles G. Finney toured England as an evangelist in 1849–50 and again in 1859–60. Dwight L. Moody visited England in 1867 and 1870 to get acquainted with Christian leaders and to study their methods, returning to England in 1873 to conduct a two-year campaign that established his reputation at home as well as in Great Britain as the preeminent revivalist of his time. He led two other British campaigns from 1881 to 1884 and in 1891–92. Lesser lights, such as Reuben A. Torrey, made evangelistic tours of the British Isles, and British evangelists came to the United States to lend aid in American efforts. But the revivalists were not the only American representatives who went abroad. Henry Ward Beecher, who made speaking tours of Britain in 1863 and 1886, was typical of many American churchmen. Matthew Simpson, for example, first went to England in 1857 to attend the British Wesleyan Conference in Liverpool. In 1870 and 1875 he was again in England. And in 1881 he delivered the opening sermon at the Ecumenical

---

1922), and K. S. Inglis, *Churches and the Working Classes in Victorian England* (Toronto: Univ. of Toronto Press, 1963).

Methodist Conference in London. Phillips Brooks first visited England in 1865, and in 1880 he preached in Westminster Abbey and in the Royal Chapel at Windsor. Five years later he received an honorary D.D. degree from Oxford University. Washington Gladden made repeated trips to England, announcing on his first visit that he was "coming home."

The traffic across the Atlantic, of course, was not one-way. Perhaps this can best be illustrated by the Lyman Beecher Lectures at Yale. The first lecturer, after the inaugural lectures of Henry Ward Beecher, was a transplanted Britisher, John Hall, and R. W. Dale's name appears early in the list. During the twenty-two years from 1892 to 1914, no fewer than ten of the lecturers — James Stalker, A. M. Fairbairn, R. F. Horton, John Watson, George Adam Smith, John Brown, P. T. Forsyth, H. H. Henson, J. H. Jowett, and C. Silvester Horne — were from Great Britain. Then in 1919, as soon as the war was over, John Kelman was the lecturer. Equally impressive evidence of European influence could be accumulated by an analysis of the personnel of American theological faculties, many having been recruited abroad. Nor should the astonishing numerical contribution of Canada to the theological faculties of the United States be forgotten.

Important as were these constant personal contacts, they were far outweighed in influence by the printed page. Most American periodicals, including the denominational weeklies, carried "religious intelligence" from Great Britain. Even more impressive was the circulation of British periodicals in the United States. Of the general literary magazines which frequently carried articles on religious subjects, the *Edinburgh Review*, the *Fortnightly Review*, the *Nineteenth Century*, and the *Westminster Review* all were published in American editions. This too was true of *Christian Literature*, the *Christian Observer*, and, for a period, the *Expositor*. The back files in American theological seminaries also indicate that the *British Weekly: a Journal of Social and Christian Progress*, the *Christian World*, the *Christian World Pulpit*, the *Church Quarterly Review*, the *Critical Review of Theological and Philosophical Literature*, the *Expository Times*, the *Guardian*, and the *Lon-*

don Quarterly Review were almost everywhere available and supposedly being read. And equally conspicuous in seminary libraries were such general literary publications as the *Contemporary Review* and the *Spectator*. Furthermore, because of the absence of proper safeguards in the copyright laws,[6] almost any book of consequence was published simultaneously in Great Britain and the United States. For this reason, many British works in American libraries published prior to the twentieth century bear an American imprint. This act of self-protection meant that full-scale elaborations of the latest British thinking were immediately available in the United States. Books by American authors that gave promise of being of interest to a British audience were smaller in number, but when they did give such promise, they likewise were published at the same time in Great Britain. Thus Josiah Strong's first book and most famous work, *Our Country*, received delayed publication in England, but the same mistake was not made with his subsequent volume, *The New Era*. Washington Gladden's early writings [7] were imported and were on sale in London almost immediately, but the others, beginning with *Applied Christianity* in 1886, were published simultaneously in both countries.[8]

The debt of American churchmen to German biblical critics and theologians in the decades immediately before and after the end of the nineteenth century should not be minimized,

[6] Until 1891, only American citizens or residents could obtain a copyright in the United States but there was an informal understanding that the first American publisher to place a British work on the market secured a copyright by "courtesy." This explains the practice of simultaneous publication. Even after 1891 when foreign authors could obtain a copyright, the book had to be manufactured in the United States.

[7] *Plain Thoughts on the Art of Living* (1868), *Working People and Their Employers* (1876), *Things New and Old* (1884), and *The Christian League of Connecticut* (1883) were imported.

[8] Gladden's books prior to 1900 that were published simultaneously were: *Applied Christianity* (1886), *Burning Questions* (1889), *Who Wrote the Bible?* (1891), *Tools and the Man* (1893), *The Church and the Kingdom* (1894), *Ruling Ideas of the Present Age* (1896), *Seven Puzzling Bible Books* (1897), *The Christian Pastor and the Working Church* (1898), *Social Facts and Forces* (1898), *England and America* (1898), and *How Much Is Left of the Old Doctrines?* (1899).

but neither should it be allowed to obscure the much greater debt to British scholars. The standard commentaries and biblical analyses of an American clergyman's library were apt to be those of William Sanday, Samuel R. Driver, F. J. A. Hort, B. F. Westcott, John W. Colenso, George Adam Smith, Joseph B. Lightfoot, Arthur S. Peake, T. K. Cheyne, William Robertson Smith, Archibald Duff, A. B. Davidson, W. T. Davison, and H. Wheeler Robinson. And while many American scholars did study in Germany, the German influence was often mediated through British scholars, and German books were generally available to the English-speaking world only in British translations.

Among the theologians, F. D. Maurice, Charles Gore, R. W. Dale, A. M. Fairbairn, Robert Horton, Henry Drummond, R. J. Campbell, John Oman, and others rivaled the earlier influence of Joseph Butler and William Paley. Of the non-theologians who were theologically important in nineteenth-century America, first place must be given to Charles Darwin and Herbert Spencer. In the first part of the century, Samuel Coleridge had exerted a decisive influence on such diverse personalities as Horace Bushnell, J. W. Nevin, Ralph Waldo Emerson, and John Henry Hobart; and at the same time Thomas Arnold was making his contribution to the untheological religiousness which was increasingly to characterize church life first in England and somewhat later in the United States. In both countries a formless spirituality developed, and books written on both sides of the Atlantic could easily have been interchanged.

What was called "spiritual religion" first made a public stir among English Congregationalists in 1877. "No authoritative statement," R. W. Dale reported, "was made to explain what range of belief the phrase was intended to cover," but "the world at large interpreted it as indicating a departure even from Liberal theology." Within a decade Spurgeon had become alarmed at the inroads the new spiritual religion was making in Baptist ranks.

> A new religion has been initiated which is no more Christianity than chalk is cheese; and this religion, being

destitute of moral honesty, palms itself off as the old faith with slight improvements, and on this plea usurps pulpits which were erected for gospel preaching. The Atonement is scouted, the inspiration of Scripture is derided, the Holy Spirit is degraded into an influence, the punishment of sin is turned into a fiction, and the resurrection into a myth, and yet these enemies of our faith expect us to call them brethren, and maintain a confederacy with them.

Spurgeon then defined the issue in a way that anticipated the Fundamentalist controversy in twentieth-century America. It becomes a question, he declared, "how far those who abide by the faith once delivered to the saints should fraternize with those who have turned aside to another gospel." [9]

By 1890 the revolt against dogmatic theology had swept the theological colleges. In 1893 A. M. Fairbairn noted that whereas the old theology was "primarily doctrinal and secondarily historical," the new was "primarily historical and secondarily doctrinal." And in 1898 Alfred Rowland reported a further shift. "The truth is that . . . dogmatic theology has been deposed by two forces, the one ethical, the other scientific." Another Congregationalist rejoiced that the Congregational church had become "the most democratic and undoctrinal of all Christian churches," and that prospective members "are not asked to define or dogmatically state their beliefs as to the 'Incarnation,' the 'Atonement,' or the 'Resurrection'." They are only expected to believe "the spirit" of these latter doctrines. [10]

In 1907, with the movement at full tide, a spate of books was issued to publicize what was now being called the "New Theology." [11] R. J. Campbell defined the New Theology as

[9] J. W. Grant, *Free Churchmanship in England, 1870–1940* (London: Independent Press, 1955), pp. 91, 93.

[10] *Ibid.*, pp. 115–18.

[11] R. J. Campbell, *The New Theology* (London: Chapman and Hall, 1907); K. C. Anderson, *The New Theology* (London: A. H. Stockwell, 1907); T. R. Williams, *The New Theology* (London: Lund, Humphries & Co., 1907); and Joseph Warschauer, *The New Evangel* (London: James Clarke & Co., 1907).

"the attitude of those who believe that the fundamentals of the Christian faith need to be rearticulated in terms of the immanence of God." He called his message "the gospel of the humanity of God and of the divinity of man" and announced that "Jesus was and is divine, but so are we." The true church, he declared, consists of "those, and those only, who are trying, like their Master, to make the world better and gladder and worthier of God." Any organization, including the Labor Party, that strives for human betterment, he insisted, is a church.[12] Similar sentiments were shared by American churchmen.

If the rise of religious "liberalism" or "modernism" in the United States has been viewed in relative isolation from the larger context of a common religious life within the English-speaking community, there has been an equal misreading of the developing interest in social Christianity in America at the close of the nineteenth century. One of the clearest consequences of our parochialism has been the claim that the "social gospel" represents an "indigenous and typically American movement" and constitutes "America's most unique contribution to the great ongoing stream of Christianity."[13]

The social interest of the Protestant Episcopal Church was an obvious exception, for it was deeply influenced by Anglican views and activities. F. D. Maurice and Charles Kingsley were key influences, as was John Ruskin. Current literature from England was widely read, and American Episcopalians imitated their Anglican colleagues by duplicating in the United States the instruments of social concern that had been fashioned abroad, including, Church Congresses for discussion of social issues, the Church Association for the Advancement of Labor, the Christian Social Union, and the Christian Socialist League.

[12] Grant, *Free Churchmanship*, pp. 135–36, 141.

[13] C. H. Hopkins, *The Rise of the Social Gospel in American Protestantism, 1865–1915* (New Haven: Yale Univ. Press, 1940), p. 3. This was a preliminary study, and Hopkins noted that "no systematic study" had been made of "the influence of English social-gospel thought upon American social Christianity" in connection with his research (*ibid.*, p. 151 n.).

The Episcopalians, however, were not alone in being influenced by Maurice, Kingsley, and Ruskin. Alexander Mackennal, the eminent English Congregationalist, thought that when the influence of Maurice was fully assessed it would be found to have been greater on English Congregationalists than on Anglicans,[14] and the debt owed to Maurice by American social gospel leaders of every denomination was widely acknowledged. In the *Andover Review* of 1884, Julius H. Ward wrote that in making possible the development of a sense of social responsibility Maurice's contribution was analogous to that of Schleiermacher but that Maurice was of greater importance in America because "for English-speaking people there is something far-off in the operations of German thought." It was John Ruskin, however, who had stirred A. M. Fairbairn in England to an interest in social Christianity,[15] and his *Unto the Least* (1860) and *The Crown of the Wild Olive* (1866), both of which were published in the United States, had a similar effect upon Americans. Sir John R. Seeley's *Ecce Homo: A Survey of the Life and Work of Jesus* (1866) seems to have been of even greater importance in giving impetus and inspiration to social concern. Seeley was regarded by Francis G. Peabody as marking the real beginning of the "new appreciation of the social teachings of Jesus," while Vida D. Scudder reported that many had found it a "most stirring and disturbing" book.[16] Seeley's thought was elaborated in another book of decisive importance, W. H. Fremantle's *The World as the Subject of Redemption* (1885). Richard T. Ely, in his *Social Aspects of Christianity* (1889), asserted that Fremantle's book was "as suggestive a work as I ever read," and Gladden called it "one of the most inspiring books of this generation."[17] Ely also had been reading B. F.

[14] Alexander Mackennal, *Sketches in the Evolution of English Congregationalism* (London: J. Nisbet & Co., 1901), p. 202.

[15] W. B. Selbie, *The Life of A. M. Fairbairn* (London: Hodder and Stoughton, 1914), p. 49.

[16] F. G. Peabody, *Jesus Christ and the Social Question* (New York: Macmillan, 1901), p. 38. V. D. Scudder, *Father Huntington* (New York: E. P. Dutton & Co., 1940), p. 63.

[17] R. T. Ely, *Social Aspects of Christianity* (New York: T. Y. Crowell & Co., 1889), p. 51. Washington Gladden, *The Christian Pastor and the*

Westcott, *Social Aspects of Christianity* (1887); W. J. Richmond, *Christian Economics* (1888); and Hugh Price Hughes,
Social Christianity (1889). A more stirring summons from
England was provided in 1883 by Andrew Mearns in *The
Bitter Cry of Outcast London,* three pages of which were reprinted in Josiah Strong's *Our Country* (1885). A similar impact was made by William Booth's *In Darkest England*
(1890), and a massive collection of source material was made
available by Charles Booth and others in the seventeen-
volume *Life and Labor of the People of London* (1891–1903).
As Henry F. May was to note, "almost no important" American Protestant "religious writer" dealing with social issues
"failed to mention English precedents," although May failed
to take into account the influence R. W. Dale, Andrew
Mearns, A. M. Fairbairn, C. Silvester Horne, John Clifford,
Hugh Price Hughes, and many others, who were not "handi-
capped by ties with an aristocratic and partly feudal Establishment." [18] Washington Gladden's writings clearly reveal his
indebtedness to current British literature and sociological
investigation. And Graham Taylor went to England in 1903
to study the training methods of the English settlements,
returning to teach with Charles R. Henderson at the University of Chicago the first course for social workers.

The relationship between Britain and America, of course,
was reciprocal. The "institutional" church may have been an
American contribution,[19] just as the Student Volunteer Movement had been introduced into England by Robert Wilder in
1892. When W. T. Stead of London aroused many Americans
in 1894 with his book *If Christ Came to Chicago,* he inspired

Working Church (New York: Charles Scribners' Sons, 1906), p. 38. For
an assessment of Freemantle's influence in America, see Shailer Mathews,
"The Development of Social Christianity in America," in G. B. Smith,
ed., *Religious Thought in the Last Quarter-Century* (Chicago: Univ. of
Chicago Press, 1927), p. 231.
[18] H. F. May, *Protestant Churches and Industrial America* (New York:
Harper, 1949), pp. 149, 150.
[19] For the "institutional churches," see Washington Gladden, *The
Christian Pastor and the Working Church* (see footnote 17); Edward
Judson, *The Institutional Church* (New York: Lentilhon & Co., 1899);
and C. Silvester Horne, *The Institutional Church* (London: James
Clarke & Co., 1906).

WINTHROP S. HUDSON

Charles M. Sheldon to write *In His Steps: What Would Jesus Do?* (1896).[20] And Sheldon's book, without copyright protection, was to be printed by thirty different British firms. Gladden's books also were widely read in Britain, as were those of Josiah Strong. In 1914 Strong went to England and took the lead in organizing the British Institute of Social Service. When Paul Monroe wrote an article in 1895 on "English and American Christian Socialism" for the *American Journal of Sociology*, he treated his subject as constituting a single movement. Much the same verdict would be reached by anyone who deals with the larger field of Christian social thought and activity in the two countries.

There were differences of spirit and emphasis and detail in the religious life of Britain and the United States. No two individuals are ever exactly alike, nor are two local communities ever exact duplicates. In the same way, religious life in the two countries was not identical. The denominational balance from the beginning had been reversed. In England the majority of the people were at least nominal members of the Church of England, while in America the "Dissenting" interest represented by Congregationalists, Presbyterians, Baptists, and Quakers was predominant.[21] The separation of church and state was a powerful conditioning factor in the United States, as was the presence of an established church in both England and Scotland. The presence of continental Protestant groups also was an energizing feature of American religious life, and the later massive Roman Catholic and Jewish immigration was to give the American religious scene a different cast. Nonetheless religious life in America prior to World War I can best be understood only when it is viewed

[20] Hopkins, *Rise of the Social Gospel*, pp. 146–47. For the impact of Stead's account on American opinion, see H. F. May, *Protestant Churches and Industrial America*, pp. 118–19. Edward Everett Hale also published a response, *If Jesus Came to Boston* (Boston: J. S. Smith & Co., 1894).

[21] Formal membership of an established church, of course, is an inadequate index of relative strength. By the middle of the nineteenth century, the membership of the English "free churches," excluding Roman Catholics and minor religious groups, was roughly equal to the communicant membership of the Church of England.

as an integral part of the developing life of the larger English-speaking community and not unrelated to European society as a whole.

After World War I, the continental influence became much more prominent and much more direct. Several factors contributed to this shift: (1) There was a growing tendency among Americans to think of themselves as members of a pluralistic rather than an Anglo-Saxon society. (2) Religious groups of continental origin emerged from their former isolation and began to participate in the general religious life of the nation. (3) American scholars began to play a much more active role in translation projects. (4) The United States increasingly became the senior partner in the English-speaking world. Instead of British periodicals publishing an American edition, American magazines began to publish British editions. The alliterative list of Barth, Buber, Brunner, Bonhoeffer, and Bultmann serves to illustrate the shift in influence that took place, with Alfred North Whitehead serving as the major symbol of continuing British influence.

What difference does it make, beyond service to truth, to remember that we are Englishmen and Europeans as well as Americans in our religious life? First of all, the search for uniqueness leads to a narrow and provincial understanding of ourselves, to a turning inward at a time when eyes should be on events and developments beyond our national boundaries. Second, the recognition that we are part of a larger community serves as a counter to the sense of difference and superiority which accompanies efforts to prove that we represent an indigenous spirit that has developed independently of outside influences. Without this counter, we become easy prey to the nativism and jingoism which too often has found expression among us. Thus it both guards us against cultural and intellectual isolationism, and serves to restrain messianic impulses. Lastly, such a recognition gives us a sense of continuity, perspective, and insight, and at the same time gives us an awareness of being related in intimate fashion to the whole church of Christ both past and present.

7

Reinterpretation in American Church History

SIDNEY E. MEAD

Because the word "reinterpretation" in the title suggests the propounding either of a new interpretation or of a new manner of interpreting American church history, I hasten to say flatly that I make no such claim, and that I am somewhat weary of hearing others make such claims. An epidemic seems to be raging in our seminaries that perhaps descended to them from ancient Athens where, Scripture tells us in parentheses, all "spent their time in nothing else, but either to tell, or to hear some new thing" (Acts 17:21). Fads follows one another in rapid succession. One week it is *Honest to God,* the next, *The Secular City,* and the third, the "death of God" and *The Gospel of Christian Atheism. Life, Look,* and *Playboy* supplant the staid old theological journals, and being sandwiched in between bunnies is the puberty rite of the avant-garde. Meanwhile, concentration on these waves on the surface of the vast ocean of civilization distracts attention from the cultural winds that create them and the massive human continuities in the unfathomed depths beneath them. Defenders of the faith seem rapidly to be beating their battleships into surfboards and their submarines into waterskis.

In our old academic world the claim to have a "new" approach usually reveals the parochial orientation of its author. I remember the day in 1940 or 1941 when Professor K. S. Latourette came riding out of the east like a misdirected Lochinvar to tell those of the "Chicago school" about his "New Perspectives in Church History."[1] His "new perspective," he

[1] Published in *The Journal of Religion,* 21 (October, 1941): 432–43.

said, resulted in "a transition from the history of the Christian church to the history of Christianity." Concentration on the former, he argued, tended to separate the institution "from its environment," while his "new" approach would emphasize the effect of the environment upon Christianity and "the effect of Christianity upon its environment." The trouble was that he expounded this to a group of Chicagoans who, with what they called their "social-historical methodology" had been writing the history of Christianity in that fashion for a quarter of a century, and had just published an inclusive example of their views in a symposium entitled *Environmental Factors in Christian History*.[2] After the first flurry of dialogue Professor Latourette was candid enough to confess that his perspective was not new after all. I have never forgotten that lesson, or my youthful amazement that one who seemed to know so much about what was and had been going on all over the world apparently did not know what was and had been going on in Yale's backyard west of the Hudson River. I am almost persuaded that "The Preacher" was right so far as "new" interpretations are concerned:

> The thing that hath been it is that which shall be;
> and that which is done is that which shall be done:
> and there is no new thing under the sun.
> [Ecclesiastes 1:9]

In this perspective my more modest claim is only to have pulled together some observations on interpreting, on interpretations, and on the interpreters.

I suppose that "to interpret" means to explain rationally or to represent artfully the meaning[3] of something. It is implied

[2] Chicago: University of Chicago Press, 1939. Edited by John T. McNeill, *et al.*, the work contained twenty-one essays in honor of Dean Emeritus Shirley Jackson Case, and was collectively "designed to illustrate an approach to the history of Christianity" which illustrates "the impact of non-Christian and non-religious elements in culture and society upon the historical development of Christian thought, life, and institutions."

[3] Of course "the meaning of meaning" is no simple matter. See, e.g., C. K. Ogden and I. A. Richards, *The Meaning of Meaning* (New York: Harcourt, Brace & World, 1923).

that three elements are always necessarily present if interpretation is to take place: an interpreter, a reasonably receptive audience, and something of common interest to be interpreted. To "reinterpret" means, literally, merely to interpret again — the thing we teaching professors do year after year for the benefit of the hopeful neophytes in our introductory survey courses. More commonly in academic circles the word suggests a new and different explanation or representation of known "facts" — the communication of how this particular constellation of "facts" looks from a perspective other than the one commonly held. I have placed "facts" in quotation marks to indicate that of course an observed or experienced event looked at from different perspectives does not "mean" quite the same thing in each of the possible conceptual contexts in which it may be placed. This, for example, is why I have often advised students to study their teachers as well as the subject content of their courses. For one cannot understand a person's interpretation of a subject until and unless one understands the perspective from which he views it.[4]

In other words, a thinker must be grasped as a whole before his arguments and the details of his system can be seen to make consistent sense. Of course it is possible in our pluralistic culture that a theologian's or historian's perspective cannot be grasped as a whole because there is no wholeness there to be grasped. And there is no wholeness in the man because his mind, thanks largely to our modes of education, is cluttered up with unorganized snippets of accumulated information, and the only thing the snippets have in common is that they are all entertained in the same head. From such a mind a man's pronouncements and writings will be little more than the premature regurgitation of identifiable lumps of the intellectual food he has ingested. Technically the lumps are commonly known as "footnotes." Usually, I suppose, we teachers, even in what is called "higher education," communicate what we have learned with the hope that it will be digested. But many things in our multiversity systems militate

[4] I think I learned this from Horace Bushnell.

against this hope — for some of which we teachers are responsible.

Of course we are not primarily responsible for what has been called the "knowledge explosion." But we are partly responsible for overpublication and for the fact that much of what is published can hardly be considered a contribution to the explosion of knowledge. And we are most responsible for drenching our students with too much information until some of them experience "a total communications overload" and blow their intellectual fuses. I, like A. N. Whitehead,

> In my own work at universities . . . have been much struck by the paralysis of thought induced in pupils by the aimless accumulation of precise knowledge, inert and unutilised.[5]

By clogging his system, the sheer amount of material the student is sometimes required to ingest under the pressures of time makes digestion almost impossible. At best he ends up knowing practically everything about a subject, and understanding nothing. At worst he ends up under the expert custodial care of the men and women in white. And probably somewhere in between are those who drop out after their wrestle with the angels of higher education, thereafter to be marked by a limping conception of what the intellectual life is all about.

Perhaps even more insidious in our era of specialists is the exposure of a student simultaneously to the conflicting perspectives of a number of experts without any serious attempt to help him to see the pattern of coherence and integrity of the whole program. Seminaries seem to me especially culpable in this respect. For a seminary is a university in microcosm, its four to seven or more "fields" analogous to the university's schools and departments. But there is one big difference between the seminary and the university, namely, the seminary commonly labors under the illusion that its degree program is a unit. Therefore, while in the university

[5] A. N. Whitehead, *The Aims of Education* (New York: New American Library, 1949), p. 48.

the graduate student may usually concentrate in the work of one discipline, in the theological school the preliminary or comprehensive examinations are usually compounded of the several fields. It is as if the graduate student in history were required to take preliminary examinations, not only in history but also in anthropology, psychology, sociology, philosophy, and, perhaps, law, medicine, and astronomy.

Commonly, also, the seminary student is exposed each term simultaneously to professors in several different fields, no two of whom may be operating on the same set of premises or viewing the overall purpose of the school in the same way. The professors are also likely to be competing, each trying to convince the students that his perspective is the only up-to-date and therefore viable one. Indeed, a professor who is not doing this, is by implication hiding behind a misconception of "objectivity" while really teaching that what one believes and how one thinks does not make any difference.

In this situation, which is not entirely unknown today, one would suppose that a consuming passion of faculty members would be to explore their conglomeration of outlooks to ascertain if perchance it might be possible to come to some common understanding of their joint enterprise, and develop a common language with which to articulate it. But seminary faculty members, as I have known them, have usually exhibited a strong resistance to this venture. I have been told by a most able theologian, who professionally was busily engaged with proclaiming how Christianity ought to be understood and unified, that "We cannot discuss that! It would disrupt the faculty." The result is that a faculty often appears to be merely a gathering of highly independent entrepreneurs, each paid to operate his own private concession stand in a "plant" maintained by a board of trustees with funds the president can persuade or coerce "the constituency" to contribute. Each belongs to his own national association of the manufacturers of knowledge in his speciality, in whose meetings he finds consolation with those who speak his dialect and refuge from his immediate colleagues who do not. Meanwhile the student is largely left on his own intellectually and emotionally to integrate as best he can what the faculty members cannot or will not demonstrate can be integrated.

Here may lie one explanation of the appeal of a philosophy of "the absurd" to many seminary students. For while the professors may be claiming that Christianity is a — or the — unifying force in their society, their inability to come up with even the appearance of agreement among themselves makes their claim absurd.[6]

Such a concept has meaning only in relation to its opposite.[7] I suppose that the opposite of "the absurd" is "the reasonable" or rational. In our culture, then, "the absurd" would not make sense to intellectuals today unless they were nourished in the long tradition of the assumption that an inherent rationality characterizes their universe.[8] This, I think, is ploughed into their conceptual order, and dominates what they expect of all aspects of their experienced and observed order.[9] Therefore they tend to confront the task of

[6] From the perspective of those concerned with preserving social order, "religion" as exemplified and defended by the churches has — for almost 500 years — been primarily divisive.

[7] "To itself, no life lacks meaning, even if, like some professors and poets, it cultivates its own meaning by charging everybody else's life with lacking any" (Horace M. Kallen, "How I Bet My Life," *Saturday Review*, October 1, 1966, p. 80).

[8] For example: "And yet the one insistence that rings through history, the one plain platitude on which angry and arrogant philosophers instantly agree, is that in all of this festering turmoil, this implacable tragedy, this cynical comedy of clinging indecency, we are in the constant presence of order. From Plato to T. S. Eliot the refrain varies little. Plato, never quite certain whether he trusted artists or not, was nevertheless willing to explain that 'we are endowed by the Gods with vision and hearing, and harmony was given by the Muses to him that can use them intellectually' in order to 'assist the soul's interior revolution, to restore it to order and concord with itself.' T. S. Eliot, wanderer of the wasteland, remains certain that 'it is ultimately the function of art, in imposing a credible order upon ordinary reality, and thereby eliciting some perception of an order *in* reality, to bring us to a condition of serenity, stillness, and reconciliation . . .'" Walter Kerr, *The Decline of Pleasure* (New York: Time Inc., 1966), p. 155. See also Michael Polanyi, *Science, Faith and Society* (Chicago: Univ. of Chicago Press, 1964).

[9] I am invoking here A. N. Whitehead's concept of ". . . the meeting of two orders of experience. One order is constituted by the direct, immediate discrimination of particular observations. The other order

trying to understand any one of their inherited institutions with the assumptive premise that it is a rational structure.

What happens? Interpretation begins at home, and the seminary is the primary actual household in which the theologue and his professor live. If in trying to understand *its* institutionalized structure one begins with the premise that he is dealing with a rational structure, he is likely to be frustrated, because there is little in his experience and observed order to bear out any such supposition.

Suppose, for example, we observe a faculty meeting called to discuss what is to go into the general curriculum, or into the requirements for a degree. The meeting is more likely to resemble a clash of interest groups, each bargaining to get the most, than it is a dialogue between rational scholars, each concerned first, to be sure that he understands the common enterprise and second, to understand how what he has to offer may be fitted into it. Naturally the outcome is seldom a rationally coherent and understandable program. Rather, from the viewpoint of each participant, it is a compromise of his ideal forced by the actualities of the possible rooted in the obtuseness of his colleagues.

If now the faculty members persist in trying to convince the students, the constituency, and perhaps themselves, that the program is a rational structure — as they seem to do in announcements, catalogues, and other promotional literature — the recognized gap between what is observed and experienced and what is claimed is likely to lead to the conclusion that the claim is absurd. This conclusion, the result of observation and experience at home, then tends to be generalized and projected as the primary premise to be invoked for an understanding of all institutions — churches included — past and present.

I suppose that through most of Christian history one primary and perennial task of the theologian was to examine, explain, and defend the premises of the intellectual structure

---

is constituted by our general way of conceiving the Universe. They will be called, the Observational Order, and the Conceptual Order" (*Adventures of Ideas* [New York: New American Library, n.d.], p. 158).

explanatory of the modes of thinking and acting that characterized the church-community of which he was an actively participating and responsible member. In this situation the nature of his responsibilities and the purpose of his school were reasonably clear. But few theologians today are practicing and responsible churchmen. Most appear to belong to the highly abstract and conveniently "invisible" church whose fulfillments are "beyond history" and not of this world. Hence, they tend to be at best tolerant, at worst contemptuous of the actual institutional incarnations of this church in our denominations and congregations. Therefore, much of their written work is addressed only to their fellow denizens of the self-made ghetto in which they live, and is almost totally unrelated to the experienced order of the mill run of pastors and church members. Chicago's ubiquitous, prolific, and penultimately infallible Marty noted that one might "attend a discussion of theological educators talking about improving the ministry" and discover that "they can talk for a week and not mention preaching and parish routine." And Fairchild and Wynn, delving into the understanding of *Families in the Church*, concluded that theologians who write books about "the church" seem to be talking about something that even better than average members of the congregations simply do not recognize as part of their experience.[10]

But if the theologian today seldom lives responsibly in the church as institutionally incarnated and therefore can hardly be expected to understand it existentially, he does live in and with the actualities of the seminary as institution — in fact he runs it. One would expect him to be quite self-conscious and realistic about the presuppositional premises on which *his* institution actually operates. But is he? What are these premises?

One seems to be the principle of "automatic harmony" — the idea that each professor may go his own highly individ-

[10] Roy W. Fairchild and John Charles Wynn, *Families in the Church: A Protestant Survey* (New York: Association Press, 1961), p. 174: "Theologians who write books about Christian doctrine have one type of definition of the church; but parents, we were to learn, have quite another."

ualistic way because the "invisible hand" postulated by Adam Smith sees to it that "'the private interests and passions of men' are led in the direction 'which is most agreeable to the interest of the whole society.'"[11] It follows that collectively, in concocting programs, they may concentrate on technical means and gimmicks, for there is a destiny that shapes their ends and one cannot do anything about destiny. They may be exquisitely critical of laissez-faire as a philosophy to guide the social, economic, and political affairs of their "secular" community, while implicitly defending it for the guidance of their own institution, usually under the aegis of academic freedom covertly understood to mean theoretical anarchy.

Meanwhile, the palpable inconsistency of their dichotomous stance probably leaves a deep impression on students that ought to be examined by those interested in finding out what students are actually being taught in the school. For what they are actually being taught will determine how they will interpret and reinterpret not only American church history but everything else.

I think they must be learning that at least the institution that most directly impinges upon their lives at the moment is not subject to rational understanding, and that there is not necessarily any relation between the ideas academics expound, and the institutions academics run. To be sure, administrators and professors may be always ready "to give a reason" for every thing in the program. But the reasons given, and the way they are given, are apt only to convey an impression of the truth of Benjamin Franklin's dictum that it is a wonderful thing to be a rational creature for it enables one to make or find a reason for everything he is inclined or has to do.

From one perspective, the students' conclusion is essentially correct. But this does not mean that the institution is necessarily absurd in the sense that it cannot be rationally understood. For it can be, provided one begins, not with the

[11] Robert L. Heilbroner, *The Worldly Philosophers: The Lives, Times, and Ideas of the Great Economic Thinkers* (New York: Time Inc., 1962), p. 47.

premise that he is dealing with a rational structure, but with the premise that he is dealing with a historical structure. The Ford Motor Company, at least in origin, was a rationally structured institution — that is, its purpose, conceived largely in a single mind, was to turn out Model T Fords, and all its structure from mines to the rattles built into the finished product was rationally built to order means to this end.

A seminary, on the other hand, is not today a rationally structured institution in this sense, but a historical structure. By this I mean, that for about three quarters of a century in the United States most seminaries have just "growed" like Topsy, without any clear purpose or commonly held conception of the end for which they existed. The Niebuhr, Williams, Gustafson three-volume study of *Theological Education in the U.S. and Canada* fairly well documented this. The net results of that extensive study on the thinking of the conductors of seminaries are fairly well summarized in Alice's exchange with the Cheshire Cat:

> "Cheshire Puss," she began, rather timidly. . . . "Would you tell me, please, which way I ought to walk from here?"
>
> "That depends a good deal on where you want to get to," said the Cat.
>
> "I don't much care where —" said Alice.
>
> "Then it doesn't matter which way you walk," said the Cat.
>
> "— so long as I get *somewhere*," Alice added as an explanation.
>
> "Oh, you're sure to do that," said the Cat, "if you only walk long enough."
>
> Alice felt that this could not be denied, so she tried another question. "What sort of people live about here?"

Because few seminaries have an idea of where they want to get to, they cannot be understood in terms of the rational ordering of means to an end. Nor can it be supposed that there is a rational coherence of the diverse parts.

Students should be helped to understand this intellectually

and accept it emotionally. First, for the simple and immediate reason that if they begin with the premise that the program is a rational structure, they may waste a great deal of time and energy butting their inherently rational heads against its obvious irrationalities.

But second, and much more important, because this is the immediately perceptible prototype of all institutionalizations of religion — especially in our democratic setting where government is projected on the principle of consent, and society is organized in purposeful voluntary associations — including of course, the religious groups.

From the perspective of the discipline of history, such associations are institutionalized attempts to incarnate in actuality some ideal conceptualized in the mind — what Whitehead called a "great idea." But religious ideals are of necessity on the level of very high generality — ideas "expressing conceptions of the nature of things, of the possibilities of human society, of the final aim which should guide the conduct of individual men."[12] As such, they "rarely receive any accurate verbal expression. They are hinted at through their special forms appropriate to the age in question."[13] Therefore, the purpose of a religious institution can never be as clear, definite, and tangible as that of the institution designed for the production of Model T Fords. To argue, as did H. Richard Niebuhr in *The Purpose of the Church and Its Ministry*,[14] that the goal of the Church is "the increase among men of the love of God and neighbor" is to suggest an extremely broad generalization under which innumerable specific notions respecting its abstract meaning and its implications for practice may legitimately be entertained. No one could rationally entertain all these specific notions, for some pairs of them are mutually exclusive. So from the perspective of any one person among those who readily accept the high generalization, some of the specific notions respect-

[12] *Adventures of Ideas*, p. 19.
[13] *Ibid.*, p. 13.
[14] New York: Harper & Brothers, 1956, p. 31.

ing its meaning and practical implications will be extremely repulsive.

This, I suppose, is what A. N. Whitehead had in mind when he wrote that "Great ideas enter into reality with evil associates and with disgusting alliances."[15] As the author of *The Last Temptation of Christ* (Nikos Kazantzakis) reminded me, a truly human body will smell of the flesh even though the one who is truly God dwells in it. Almost all of the divisions among Christians, often devastating and bloody, have been created by conflicting specific notions respecting the meaning and practical implications of the high generalities held and professed by all. What Thomas Jefferson said of the political conflicts that attended his election to the Presidency, could as well be applied to religious controversy between Christians—they are rooted in a confusion of principles with opinions.[16] It is difficult even for perceptive intellectuals to recognize the ideas for which they are contending when they are expressed by another person in somewhat different terminology.

Man, who is fearfully and wonderfully made, whatever else he may be is the animal that entertains high ideals, on the basis of which he adumbrates aspirations respecting his ultimate goals, and devises as best he can from the materials that Providence provides him in his generation, the means for their attainment.[17] His basic drive is to incarnate in actuality his image of the ideal situation—the world he sees beyond this world—that can now only be hoped for.[18] His assurance

[15] *Adventures of Ideas*, p. 26.

[16] Jefferson said in his First Inaugural address, "But every difference of opinion is not a difference of principle. We have called by different names brethren of the same principle. We are all Republicans, we are all Federalists."

[17] Compare Whitehead's, "And yet the life of a human being receives its worth, its importance, from the way in which unrealized ideals shape its purposes and tinge its actions" (*Modes of Thought* [New York: Capricorn Books, 1938], pp. 37–38).

[18] Compare Tillich's, "The form of religion is culture. This is especially obvious in the language used by religion. Every language, including that of the Bible, is the result of innumerable acts of cultural creativity. All functions of man's spiritual life are based on man's power to speak

that the ideal hoped for, his conviction that the things not seen will be "tangibilicated" (to use Father Divine's wonderful word) is called faith. Anyone who has ever tried to make anything is aware of the painful gap between the ideal conceived in the mind of the maker and the actual finished product — between, for example, the ideally conceived purpose of an institution and its tangible results as seen in its everyday practices. But in faith man asserts that those who cherish the ideal "shall overcome."

It is not, therefore, legitimate to judge a religious institution solely on the basis of the shapes it assumes in its everyday practices with their "evil associates and . . . disgusting alliances." These are unavoidable and, like the poor (at least until we win the War against Poverty) will be ever with us. Nor is it legitimate on the other hand to judge it solely on the basis of the great ideas and aspirations it cherishes and perpetuates in our culture — as many pious people are inclined to judge their chuches. This would be to judge it solely by its good intentions, and among us it is axiomatic that good intentions without works pave the road to hell. Such people in discussing Christianity and democracy often judge the former by its great ideas, and the latter by the smelly shenanigans that characterize its current political operations.

Rather, an institution is to be judged by the amount and quality of the awareness of the tension between its ideal and its actuality that its members exhibit, and by the realism of the efforts they are making to reduce the gap. This "critical discontent, which is the gadfly of civilization"[19] and of all the religious denominations is the hallmark of the prophetic posture, and the source of the perennial renewal of the life of institutions.

So in judging our religious and democratic institutions

---

vocally or silently. Language is the expression of man's freedom from the given situation and its concrete demands. It gives him universals in whose power he can create worlds above the given world of technical civilization and spiritual content." *(Theology of Culture,* ed. Robert C. Kimbal [New York: Oxford Univ. Press, 1964], p. 47.

[19] *Adventures of Ideas,* p. 19.

(and I cannot separate the two), we note first that "the ulti-mate ideals, of which they profess themselves the guardians, are a standing criticism of current practices.";[20] and second, that in this perspective no matter how disgusting and evil some of their earthly associates and alliances may now be, nevertheless, of the aspirations which they perpetuate it may still be said that their "greatness remains, nerving the race in its slow ascent."

This is what I mean by historical understanding. It is an attempt to understand when and where and how great ideals enter into the minds of men with such compulsive motiva-tional power that they are often called "revelations," and gradually through the years and the centuries they get in-carnated in the social arrangements of a people goaded by that "critical discontent" which results from man's gift to be self-consciously aware of the discrepancy between what is and what he thinks ought to be. All religious activity is devoted to reducing the distance between the actuality and the ideal, and an essential purpose of all preaching is to keep alive the sense of tension between the "ultimate ideals" and the "current practices."[21]

This is the foundation, compounded of images and ideas, upon which I would attempt to build an interpretation of our American denominations and their place in our society. It leads me to suppose that one loves an institution both *as it is* and, for what it could be. This, I think, is the way we love people; certainly it is the only way we can love students. From this stance it is highly irrational to suppose that a person or an institution must be rational in our way, and to judge him or it solely on that basis. Yet this expectation seems often to form the premise of critics of our congregations and denominations.

So, for example, a bit of an earthquake was created five years ago on the tight little island inhabited by the semi-naries' elite, by the noise of a solemn Berger who crashed in from the hills of New England to tell the American religious

[20] *Ibid.*, p. 26.
[21] *Ibid.*, pp. 18–19.

"Establishment" that "I take no delight in your solemn assemblies." Proclaiming in a gross understatement that he was "not concerned . . . with historical explanations,"[22] and in the context of a grotesque caricature of what the discipline of history is all about for which I would flunk an undergraduate, this self-chosen assumer of the mantle of Amos candidly detailed what was left out of his analysis. The list is so revealing that I quote it at length:

> We have left out a complex intellectual development among the best minds of American Protestantism, a development which represents a steady advance towards greater realism concerning the nature of society. The name of Reinhold Niebuhr may serve as a symbol for this development. We have also left out the frequent attempts of denominational and interdenominational bodies to speak relevantly on specific social issues. These attempts may often have been naive, but they have almost always been well-intentioned. We have left out the courageous attempts of Protestant ministers and laymen to witness to the social implications of their faith in local situations of crisis or conflict. Finally, we have left out completely the question of what the churches have meant to many individuals in their search for religious truth, beyond and even within the functionalities that we have analyzed.[23]

In other words, left out of consideration was the work of the "best minds" (except perhaps his own), the relevant pronouncements on social issues, the instances of courageous witness to the social implications of the faith, and consideration of the "religious truth" many individuals found in their churches. In brief, he built his case against the "Establishment" by refusing to consider the evidence of intelligence, of the judgment of the actual by the ideal, of courageous wit-

---

[22] Peter L. Berger, *The Noise of Solemn Assemblies: Christian Commitment and the Religious Establishment in America* (Garden City, New York: Doubleday & Company, Inc., 1961), p. 60.

[23] *Ibid.*, p. 106.

ness in practice, and of the religious commitment of many of its members. From my perspective this was to leave out all possibility of understanding either the institutions or one's self as a historical being shaped by the constellation of ideas and standards with their consequent customs that give his culture and himself a distinguishable identity.[24] The result seems to me to have been a loud and fantastically individualistic burp, reminding one of Henry David Thoreau's cynical suspicion that what really bugs every reformer is the pain in his own digestive tract.[25]

The obvious question left unanswered by this approach is: if the Establishment is as stupid, defensive, and worthless[26] as pictured, how is it that it has not only nourished but also supports, listens to, and rewards such sharp critics? In other words, how do you account for your origins; how do you think you were shaped to such acute insights, except by, and

[24] Ruth Benedict, *Patterns of Culture* (Boston: Houghton Mifflin, 1959), pp. 2–3: "No man ever looks at the world with pristine eyes. He sees it edited by a definite set of customs and institutions and ways of thinking. Even in his philosophical probings he cannot go behind these stereotypes; . . . The life-history of the individual is first and foremost an accommodation to the patterns and standards traditionally handed down in his community. From the moment of his birth the customs into which he is born shape his experience and behaviour. By the time he can talk, he is the little creature of his culture, and by the time he is grown and able to take part in its activities, its habits are his habits, its beliefs his beliefs, its impossibilities his impossibilities. . . ."

[25] "I believe that what so saddens the reformer is not his sympathy with his fellows in distress, but, though he be the holiest son of God, is his private ail. Let this be righted, let the spring come to him, the morning rise over his couch, and he will forsake his generous companions without apology" (in *Walden*, 3d from the last paragraph of chap. 1).

[26] "The sharp edge of the Christian engagement with the modern world is not likely to be in the parish. We might possibly make some hopeful concessions about the potentialities of the local congregation in the task of personal conversion and of the accustomed church institutions in the task of theological construction. But even this becomes hard to do when we think about the task of social engagement, especially in the active varieties that we discussed in the preceding chapter. We would contend that these will have to occur in 'supraparochial' settings, some of them to be created as new forms of the Church in the modern world" (*The Noise of Solemn Assemblies*, p. 167).

in the context of, the Establishment in which intellectually and sociologically you always have and do still live, and move, and have your being? That is the historian's question, namely, what is it in the institutionalized church that perennially produces these prophets afflicted with such "critical discontent" with its current practices as to bring about continuous evolutionary change and periodically to create constructive revolutions in its life?

In its more general form, the question is the relationship between ideas and institutions — between the pregnant ideals adumbrated in the high myths of a culture ("expressions of the ultimate meaning of man's existence" as Paul Tillich called them[27]) and the intricate complex of customs, habits, and organizational forms developed by its people.[28] In this context, and from this perspective, the history of religion has to do primarily with the motivations of men.[29] It follows that we do not interpret the nature and place of religion in our culture merely by writing stories about the development of religious institutions where "secular" historians write similar stories of voluntary associations, and of political, economic, or military institutions, but by assessing the place religious beliefs and convictions played in affecting what men did in all their societies, and in their political, economic, and military activities.[30]

[27] *Christianity and the Encounter of the World Religions* (New York: Columbia Univ. Press, 1963), p. 97.

[28] Compare Tillich's observation that "Religion as ultimate concern is the meaning-giving substance of culture, and culture is the totality of forms in which the basic concern of religion expresses itself. In abbreviation: religion is the substance of culture, culture is the form of religion. Such a consideration definitely prevents the establishment of a dualism of religion and culture. Every religious act, not only in organized religion, but also in the most intimate movement of the soul, is culturally formed" (*Theology of Culture*, p. 42).

[29] Cf., "You cannot write the history of religious development without estimate of the motive-power of religious belief. The history of the Papacy is not a mere sequence of behaviours. It illustrates a mode of causation, which is derived from a mode of thought" (A. N. Whitehead, *Modes of Thought*, p. 25).

[30] This statement is a paraphrase of a statement by my colleague, Professor Stow Persons: "A convincing demonstration of the pervasive

185

There is suggested here an approach to what in the semi-naries has commonly been called "American Church History" that has far-reaching implications. I would not claim that it is "new" — and below I shall note that in the context of this outlook a reinterpretation of religion in American history has been going on among the "secular" historians of the United States for more than a generation.

In this approach, the guiding motif is the incarnation of ideals in practices; institutions are seen as the shape given the ideals in the history-that-happens. The shape that any incarnation of an ideal takes in any particular place and era is determined first by the specific notions respecting its meaning that dominate the thinking of the period. H. Richard Niebuhr exemplified this in his book, *The Kingdom of God in America*, in which he argued that the kingdom of God had indeed been the dominant ideal throughout the history, but that it had not always meant the same thing.

> In the early period of American life, when foundations were laid on which we have all had to build, "kingdom of God" meant "sovereignty of God"; in the creative period of awakening and revival it meant "reign of Christ"; and only in the most recent period had it come to mean "kingdom on earth." Yet it became equally apparent that these were not simply three divergent ideas, but that they were intimately related to one another, and that the idea of the kingdom of God could not be expressed in terms of one of them alone.[31]

In the second place, the shape is determined by the finite number of practical possibilities that the people of an era and place have at hand, and in the third place, by the in-

effects of religion in its peculiar American forms will be made not by stressing formal religious history where secular historians talk about politics or economics, but by showing how religious convictions have had their effects upon politics and economics. . . ." *William & Mary Quarterly*, 3d Series, 9 (October, 1952), 558–61.

[31] *The Kingdom of God in America* (Chicago: Willett, Clark & Co., 1937), p. x.

genuity they can muster in manipulating these possibilities into furthering the attainment of the ideal.

On each level, the essential quality determining achievement is imagination. In this context, imagination means the complex ability intellectually to conceive and emotionally to entertain the possibility of what A. N. Whitehead called the "vast alternatives"[32] to one's cultural and hence personal ideals, and to the current specific notions about the limits of what is possible, and the means available. Hence the perennial enemy of achievement is a hardened orthodoxy which maintains conformity to accepted ways of thinking and acting by overt coercive power or through social and economic pressures. Such orthodoxy is the last refuge of the unimaginative, who fear nothing more than the "critical discontent, which is the gadfly of civilization" and of religious institutions.

Guided by this motif, two opinions form the premises on which I would rest an interpretation of the significance, nature, and place of religion in the United States. The first is that this "critical discontent" with things as they are, which motivated the launching of our republic and still keeps it alive, is not only rooted in the Jewish-Christian tradition derivatively but is therein and thereby given elemental religious and metaphysical sanctions of tremendous motivational power. The second is that the forms of our democratic government that were delineated and put into practice during the eighteenth century were deliberately shaped to prevent any unimaginative orthodoxy from ever again gaining control over the society. So long as the system is working, heteronomy is prohibited. In this sense, the civil authority guards institutionalized religion against its traditionally most common temptation and tendency.

That is what the Bill of Rights and the elaborate legal structure which protects the free expression of all minorities are all about. It is this that has kept our social, religious, and civil institutions fluid enough to adjust to the changing con-

[32] *Modes of Thought*, pp. 62–63.

tours of the history-that-happens. And upon such fluidity the continuous renewal and maintenance of their lives depends. In defending the right of all minorities to be heard, the civil authority protects that gadfly of its civilization — that imaginative grasp of possibility viable alternatives to current patterns of thinking and acting. For the critical discontent which provides the motivational impetus necessary for developmental change always sprouts in a minority. The prophet is always a lonely figure.

In this perspective the relationship between the religious groups which in the society continually nourish and provide divine sanctions for "critical discontent" with things as they are, and the civil authority which protects the right of the discontented to be heard, is of tremendous importance. The two are inseparable aspects of our system — of our "American way of life," if you please. But the understanding of the relationship is commonly confused and the discussion of it obfuscated, by insisting upon discussing it under the traditional but obsolete and inapplicable categories of "Church" and "State,"[33] "The difficulty in the use of church-style terminology" was clearly stated by Paul G. Kauper in his book, *Religion and the Constitution*. It "is that it at once creates a picture of two competing power structures and suggests a clear line that marks their separate functions." This made sense in the England of Henry VIII, but it has made no sense in the United States of George Washington to Lyndon B.

[33] See, e.g., Paul G. Kauper, in his *Religion and the Constitution* (Baton Rouge: Louisiana State Univ. Press, 1964) pp. 3–4: "Although this terminology has its usefulness as a shortcut and as a symbol of current problems, it suffers from weaknesses and inadequacies. Church-state terminology comes to us from Europe and recalls a background which is quite unlike the American scene. It has its origin in a time when the church was indeed a single monolithic Church and governmental power was centered in a single ruler. It is inadequate to describe the American situation because of both the multitude of churches in this country and the dispersion of governmental power among the federal government, the states, and the local communities.

"In our situation, it is more illuminating to call them problems of the interrelationship of the civil and religious communities. This phrase at least makes clear that we are discussing communities that embrace in part a common membership."

Johnson. Adherence to the church-state terminology suggests a paralysis in the conceptual order which prevents understanding of the actual experienced order in which we live
and the history behind it.

Closely related is my long-standing critical discontent with
the phrase "American Church History" to designate the
hunting grounds allotted to our discipline. For if the words
"Church history" are understood to mean, as they appear to,
the history of *"the* Church" in the United States, then — at
least so far as Protestants are concerned — its subject content
is ambiguous to a point of being undefinable. For, granted
the facts of religious freedom and its consequent pluralism,
the words "the Church" do not point in our society to any
tangible historical entity but, at best, to a highly abstract
theological assertion better dealt with in histories of Christian thought — at worst, to a verbal tranquilizer used to assure
undisturbed dogmatic sectarian slumber in the midst of the
clanging symbols of the high clerical sounding brass of the
competing denominations. The once popular slogan, "Let
the church be the church," provided for some a way of
deadening "the sense of vast alternatives, magnificent or hate-
ful, lurking in the background, and awaiting to overwhelm
our safe little traditions."[34] The Psalmist walked through the
valley of the shadow of death, and the Christian "looked for
a city which hath foundations, whose builder and maker is
God (Hebrews 11:10). Both saw, and stood with fear and
trembling before "vast alternatives" to their "safe little traditions." Bunyan's Pilgrim was never closer to hell than when
he finally touched the gate of the celestial city. But Whitehead was not just being petulant when he complained that
most of

> the liberal theology of the last two hundred years . . .
> has confined itself to the suggestion of minor, vapid rea-
> sons why people should continue to go to church in the
> traditional way.[35]

[34] Whitehead, *Modes of Thought*, pp. 62–63.
[35] *Adventures of Ideas*, p. 174.

I would, then, drop the confusing phrase "American Church History" in favor of "The History of Christianity in the United States," or "Religion in American History." These titles have the immediate virtue of suggesting awareness of the continuity of developments in this country with those of the whole Christian past. America, said Philip Schaff, presents "a motley sampler of all church history, and the results it has thus far attained." But, he added, these results "must be regarded on the whole as unsatisfactory, and as only a state of transition to something higher and better"—thus exhibiting that "critical discontent" with things as they are in the light of the ideal nourished in and by the institutions.[36]

This is in keeping with the overall interpretive motif noted above, namely, the incarnation in actuality of ideals and aspirations nourished in and by the religious tradition of the culture. In this context, the history has to do with the relation between the activities of people and the ideals that motivated them. If, then, we are dealing with the history of Christianity in this country, the attempt is to delineate the place Christian beliefs and convictions played in affecting what men thought and did in *all* areas of their lives, not just in their ecclesiastical organizations. This approach enables one to distinguish between conceptions of the ideal character of Christianity and of the particular shapes it has assumed in theological structures and institutions in our society. Ability to make this distinction provides a guard against judging it solely on the basis of its current institutionalized forms. To be sure, there is a sense in which an institution is what it does. But religious and democratic institutions do more than can be ascertained by mere observation of the everyday shenanigans of their members. For these institutions are the vehicles through which the ideals of the culture are carried to the people of each successive generation, creating in them that "critical discontent" with things as they are which sparks all change. The egregious blunder of Will Herberg in his *Protestant, Catholic, Jew* was to equate

[36] *America: A Sketch of Its Political, Social and Religious Character*, ed. Perry Miller (Cambridge, Mass.: Harvard Univ. Press, 1961), p. 80.

the American faith or "common religion" with the outward manifestations of "the Amercian Way of Life," and to confuse specific notions with high generalities.[37] He, and that other academic burgher noted earlier, fail to give due credit to the institutions in which their prophetic posture is rooted. Both present a view of institutions comparable to a paper-doll cut out of a newspaper — it is flat, has no depth, and they read only what happens to be written on the surface.

The approach I have suggested also enables us to understand the emergence of our democratic ideals and institutions out of the complex of the culture of Christendom, and thus stimulates study of the continuity of democratic ideas and ideals with those of the Jewish-Christian traditions. But, and more important, I think, it enables us to see how our American conception of the relation between the civil authority and religious institutions was deliberately intended and has effectively worked to prevent any religious group, or any combination of religious groups, from becoming heteronomous in our society. In this context we can understand that the neutral civil authority is not anti-religious, but must be anti-sectarian — neither favoring nor hindering any religious group. It seems to be anti-religious only to those who cannot distinguish between the "religious," or generic Christianity, and the particular theological and institutional shapes of their sect. Perhaps this might be designated as a confusion of ultimate with penultimate things.

I had fun above in describing the collection of entrepreneural specialists who commonly constitute a seminary faculty. But I was serious in suggesting that while the situation they represent has no rational order, it can be understood historically. Now I would add that the general approach I have adumbrated could provide, if not a basis for unifying the enterprise, at least a context in which the situation might be understood and hence discussed to some purpose. My criticism of the seminaries is not that the professors are at present woefully divided as specialists, but that so many of them are

[37] *Protestant-Catholic-Jew: An Essay in American Religious Sociology* (Garden City, N.Y.: Doubleday & Co., 1955), pp. 88–91.

apparently content to have it so. They have anesthetized the gadfly of their own institution while often presuming — in the ecumenical and civil rights movements — to be the gadflies of "the Church" and the social order. This is why some professorial ecumenical leaders are much more honored when far away from home than they are in their own seminary-country.

Finally, I emphasized above[38] that the approach of which I have spoken is neither new nor original with me. There would be something wrong with a historian who supposed he had originated a new approach to his subject. He appears original only to those ignorant of his history — as Horace Bushnell intimated.

It is not easy for one to delineate the men and movements that have influenced his thinking. Surely having passed through the Divinity School of this University during the twilight years of the "Chicago school" with its social-historical methodology, the intended thrust of the movement was indelibly impressed upon me. I remember especially the freedom I felt in the presence of such men as Shirley Jackson Case and William Clayton Bower — men who demonstrated a willingness to shed all defensiveness in examining the record. It was of course their general intention and stance that impressed me, more than the specific notions they came up with. It was from the Chicago group, and not from Professor Latourette's "New Perspectives in Church History," that I learned that the subject was the history of Christianity, not the history of "the Church." This view, of course, was exemplified in the work of my special mentor, William Warren Sweet.

Much later, after a reviewer of my work said that I had been greatly influenced by A. N. Whitehead, I began seriously to read Whitehead's works, and found — especially in the *Adventures of Ideas* — an overall view of historical development that greatly enlightened my understanding of what I was trying to do. A concurrent influence was R. G. Collingwood's *The Idea of History*, which idea I found most congenial.

[38] See pp. 169–70.

But the context in which I have primarily operated is that delineated by Henry F. May in his article, "The Recovery of American Religious History," published in *The American Historical Review* of October, 1964. May argues that

> For the study and understanding of American culture, the recovery of American religious history may well be the most important achievement of the last thirty years,

because this

> has restored a knowledge of the mode, even the language, in which most Americans, during most of American history, did their thinking about human nature and destiny.

The recovery came about as the subject matter of the history was broadened to include what is variously called cultural, social, or intellectual history. Analysis of intellectual developments tends to push one to awareness of the common presuppositions upon which the intellectual structures of an era are built — and to the realization that the presuppositions that undergird American thinking have been largely derived from the Jewish-Christian tradition. Hence May's second point, that American religious history provides about the only way fully to understand the continuity of American with European thought. These historians are, of course, little concerned with the abstract truth of the ideas held by the people they are studying, but they are greatly concerned with trying to understand how the ideas motivated them. Hence May's third point is that religious history provides a readily available way of studying the relation between ideas and institutions.

These "secular" historians during the past generation have been, from their perspective, reinterpreting what in the seminaries is commonly called "American Church History." During that period, almost two hundred articles on religious developments in the United States have been published in *The American Historical Review* and the *Mississippi Valley Historical Review* (now *The Journal of American History*) alone. This means that because of the sheer number of studies published by the "secular" historians, the loci of the reinterpretation of "American Church History" has shifted out of the seminaries and into the history departments of the private and state universities. I will not attempt a comparison of the relative quality of the studies emanating from seminary and "secular" sources — although I have my impressionistic opinion. But the shift does suggest that the church historians have lost the initiative in communicating an understanding of religious developments in the United States to the coming generations, and, perhaps, they are becoming relatively irrelevant so far as directing the main stream of the historical discussion of matters pertaining to religion in the United States is concerned.

I am tempted to advise the able young student who aspires to achieve in what is called "American Church History" to take a long look at the work these "secular" historians are and have been doing. A basic dictum of the discipline of history is: if you can't lick 'em you have to join 'em — or become a candidate for academic oblivion.

8

Reinterpreting American Religious History in Context
MARTIN E. MARTY

Those who study America's religious history in divinity schools associated with universities experience jostling and pressure from two directions. To the theologians and churchmen who are their colleagues in divinity, they must justify the validity of historical research and give evidence that its testimony helps provide understanding in today's world of religion. To the historians and humanists who are their colleagues in their own discipline, they must justify the validity of the religious community on whose language they draw and give evidence that that language does not control their assumptions in such a way as to distort historical understanding. Meanwhile, the humanist historians themselves are called to justify their enterprise in a time of "crisis in the humanities." They are aware that "the powers that be are not at present much interested in" humanities or in anything that does "not make anything explode or travel faster."[1]

Since the central discipline of a divinity school is ordinarily theology, such a school will tend to attract specialists in systematic or constructive theology. If a divinity school is then viewed as a microcosm of a university, one gains an almost medieval view that theology is the queen of sciences. Sometimes theologians act as if this is the case and they speak in imperial terms:

> There is some evidence to suggest the possibility that
> American theology is now living in the present. First of

[1] Graham Hough, "Crisis in Literary Education" in J. H. Plumb, ed., *Crisis in the Humanities* (Baltimore: Penguin, 1964), p. 96.

195

all, there is very little theology in America today: dogmatic theology has virtually disappeared, biblical scholarship is largely archeological and philological, church history barely maintains its existence as a discipline. . . . The very least that can be said is that there seems no possibility that American theology will once again return to the past.[2]

Admittedly these words come from a radical iconoclast who has a private definition of theology, its task, and its future. but this anti-historical mood is not new. In 1847 the editor of *The Biblical Repertory and Princeton Review* was already complaining:

> Our national tendency . . . to slight the past and overrate the present . . . is nowhere more conspicuous and more imperious than in our theology. Hence the perpetual resuscitation of absurdities a thousand times exploded, the perpetual renewal of attempts which have a thousand times proved abortive. . . . Hence, too, the bareness and hardness by which much of our religious literature is distinguished, because cut off from the inexhaustible resources which can only be supplied by history.[3]

University historians do not spend much energy criticizing theological assumptions in the work of church historians. Where their work measures up to the needs and interests of the historical fraternity it is regarded with respect; where it serves interests of apology or piety it is casually dismissed.

The setting of historical work tends to determine its shape. In his study of the sociology of the discipline, James Hastings Nichols noted that "teachers in theological faculties related to universities" form one of three categories of religious his-

[2] William Hamilton and Thomas J. J. Altizer, *Radical Theology and the Death of God* (New York: Bobbs Merrill, 1966), pp. 17–18. This quotation is from an essay by Prof. Altizer.

[3] Archibald Alexander, *The Biblical Repertory and Princeton Review*, 19 (1847): 105.

torians; this group "is the smallest"; in proportion "it produces
the great bulk of the solid scholarship." While the churches
fail to subsidize the second category enough to permit much
original work (he is referring to teachers in denominational
seminaries), the sheer weight of numbers and the disciplinary
possibilities established by colleges and universities makes
another category, university teachers, the most productive:

> The better part of American scholarly writing about the
> history of Christianity, however, has come from outside
> the ranks of the professional church historians altogether.
> Church history has profited notably from the rise of inter-
> est in history faculties in the last generation of the history
> of ideas.[4]

This recent phenomenon has tended to push church history
in a "secular" direction. Perhaps the majority of divinity
school Ph.D. graduates are preparing to teach in such history
departments. During their training they spend as much time
in the history department classrooms as in those of the theological school. Even in divinity school, their courses will tend
to be shared almost equally with students from history departments. They find themselves studying and writing history on
assumptions similar to those held in their cognitive "secular"
field.

If there has been a tendency for such church historians to
feel more at home with historians than with theologians, this
is not to say that the formation of a historian-church historian
coalition by itself solves part of the crisis in the humanities
and thus helps all the world immediately to see what cognitive
import church historical studies possess. First, it is the sciences
that claim to change life:

> The humanities don't claim to alter the conditions of our
> life: they claim to enhance the quality of the life we al-
> ready have. And the second, far deeper crisis [than the
> one which puts humanities on the defensive in techno-

[4] James H. Nichols, "The History of Christianity" in Paul Ramsey,
ed., *Religion* (Englewood Cliffs, N. J.: Prentice-Hall, 1965), p. 161.

logical culture] is that we are beginning to doubt whether the claim is true.[5]

In a "humanist culture" ("'Humanist' concerns now embrace the divine. [Both speak the same language.]"), a culture based on literacy, "the notion of the Priest or the Scholar, or even the Clerk, evokes an image which is not without dignity" but today we ask "how seriously does one now take the *cognitive* equipment of the *clerk?*" Ernest Gellner answers, "Alas, not very." He admits that the one obvious exception to the cognitive downgrading of the humanist intellectual is the field of history, but even there the humanities scholar "has lost much of his standing now as a source of *knowledge* about the world. The educated public in developed countries turns to the scientific specialist when it wants information about the world. It does so even in spheres (e.g. psychiatry) where the record of the scientific specialist is not beyond all challenge."

> The deprivation of the humanist intellectual of his full cognitive status has happened fairly recently . . . almost within the last few decades. The magnitude and profundity of this social revolution can scarcely be exaggerated.[6]

We picture church history in a crisis, then. In its bearing toward "church" it "barely maintains its existence as a discipline." In its stance toward "history" it carries the burden of some sort of theological or ecclesiastical concern in a secular environment and shares with all the humanities a crisis of status and role. Therefore, this is a promising time to study religious history, to examine its roots and its goals, to engage — in the rubric of this volume — in reinterpretation. Why?

The situation in the humanities and in religious history today is not too different from that in which American history first began to become sophisticated; R. W. B. Lewis writes concerning William Prescott and his age (the 1840's):

[5] Graham Hough, "Crisis in Literary Education," p. 96.
[6] Ernest Gellner, "Crisis in Humanities and the Mainstream of Philosophy," in Plumb, *Crisis in the Humanities*, pp. 71–73.

Prescott was the most notable and impressive of those who responded to the forward-looking enthusiasms of the age by looking backward with compensatory vigor. . . . In doing so, he illustrated the later insight of Nikolai Berdyaev in *The Meaning of History*: that historical research is apt to flourish not during periods when the human mind exercises itself in a deep, organic communion with actual, concrete history but precisely during periods when the mind has been jolted out of such communion, when it is sufficiently detached from the continuing flow of history to reflect self-watchfully upon it.[7]

Insofar as our culture is technologically future-oriented, and to the degree that the religious community is uncertain about its continuity with the past, such a moment now exists. Like Prescott, a new generation of historians is looking backward "with compensatory vigor" though not necessarily do they all share his disdain for "the forward-looking enthusiasms of the age." They are forced to ask, as did their teachers before them, what bearing their story has on the quest for self-understanding in culture today, what cognitive import their research has, what knowledge they can transport and transfer. Since their contemporaries in an industrialized affluent culture ask different questions than did their teachers' contemporaries, it is only natural that their studies will carry them in different directions, that their stories will have somewhat different themes, that some measure of reinterpretation does exist.

Under pressure, jostled and jolted and self-watchfully reflective, then, some of us are coming to see several main themes in the reinterpretation today. I shall summarize these as a turn from "innocence" to the acceptance of complexity; from "isolation" of American religious history to its location in an Atlantic community; from obsession with themes of "voluntaryism" and "revivalism-expansion" to preoccupation with the effects of industrialization on religion and the reli-

[7] R. W. B. Lewis, *The American Adam* (Chicago: Univ. of Chicago Press, 1955), p. 160.

gious interpretation of industrialism's contribution to the process or the event often called "secularization."

From the beginnings in Cotton Mather and Jonathan Edwards and then down through the long period of the writing of American religious history in relative isolation from the rest of the West, "innocence" has been a theme which provides continuity for the historians. Not only did it pervade the communities concerning which they wrote; it often was worked into the controlling assumptions of the writers. This is true even through the generations of William Warren Sweet and Sidney E. Mead at Chicago. By reference to innocence I do not mean naïvete or lack of sophistication in dealing with the sources; these historians were not "born yesterday." Rather, they tended to accent the simplicity and newness of American religious life and to shun complexity, the longer history of Christianity and of Europe, or the realities of urbanization and pluralism. Their thematic preoccupation is not unjust to the community concerning which they wrote and by no means all of their efforts have to be reworked — to say nothing of repudiated. Rather, building on their foundation, historians are asking what they overlooked, what their approach failed to explain concerning the religious and secular cultures we have inherited, what can be gained by seeing American history in relation to that of other cultures.

By "innocence" I mean something of what Lewis implies in his work on *The American Adam*, on the new kind of man "whose moral position was prior to experience," and whose newness itself "was fundamentally innocent. The world and history lay all before him."[8] Applied to the historical fraternity, innocence helped produce what David W. Noble called *Historians Against History*.[9] Whether or not he accurately relates that phrase to the men he studies, it can be applied with

[8] *Ibid.*, p. 5.
[9] David W. Noble, *Historians Against History* (Minneapolis: Univ. of Minnesota Press, 1965); Noble regards historians as the "Jeremiahs" of American life, calling the nation from complexity to simplicity and thus, in effect, away from history.

considerable accuracy to the American religious historians. It is significant that Sidney E. Mead calls his summary work *The Lively Experiment*; that Jerald C. Brauer found "a constant free experimentation and search for a fuller manifestation of God's truth and will" to be one of two major emphases in American religion; [10] that Winthrop S. Hudson had found at the end of his story of *American Protestantism* only "the form of surviving memories and a lingering identification with the resources of historic Christianity." [11] Peter Mode — to stay within the Chicago tradition — devoted himself to the enterprise of American Christians and concluded his work with an expression of faith in "the challenge of the heroic." [12] William Warren Sweet's life work was devoted to the turn from history, from Europe, from complexity, to the new man of the frontier. Mead, Brauer, and Hudson, of course, moved far beyond Mode and Sweet in their preoccupation with qualifying the innocent anti-historical interpretation, but the thrust of their work has been toward accent on the novelty of the American experience.

The roots for this approach are deep. In the cosmic vision of Cotton Mather, one begins:

> I write the *Wonders* of the CHRISTIAN RELIGION, flying from the Depravations of *Europe*, to the *American Strand*: And, assisted by the Holy Author of that *Religion*, I do, with all Conscience of *Truth*, required therein by Him, who is *Truth* it self, Report the *Wonderful Displays* of His Infinite Power, Wisdom, Goodness, and Faithfulness, wherewith His Divine Providence hath *Irradiated* an *Indian Wilderness*. [13]

[10] Jerald C. Brauer, *Protestantism in America*, rev. ed. (Philadelphia: Westminster, 1966), p. 7.

[11] Winthrop S. Hudson, *American Protestantism* (Chicago: University of Chicago Press, 1961), p. 171.

[12] Peter G. Mode, *The Frontier Spirit in American Christianity* (New York: Macmillan, 1923), chap. 9, pp. 165 ff.

[13] Cotton Mather, *Magnalia Christi Americana; or the Ecclesiastical History of New England* (London, 1702), reproduced in Perry Miller and Thomas H. Johnson, eds., *The Puritans*, rev. ed., (New York: Harper & Row, 1963), 1:163.

Flying from the Depravations of Europe becomes the grand and familiar theme of the church historians. Indeed, they occasionally remind us that the fathers in the colonies only wanted to continue the reform of European religion and that they hedged a bit by looking backward from their boats as the English shore receded. But the detail of life in Europe, the idea that one could draw models from its depraved and weary religious life, or the prospect of painstaking research concerning the whole Christian past — these tend to disappear from view.

Only the bliblical period was presumed to offer guidance for later ages. "In short, the *first* Age was the *golden* Age: to *return* unto that, will make a man a Protestant, and, I may add, a Puritan . . ."[14] continued Mather. When he celebrates a departed brother he resorts to rhyme:

> The ancient apostolic Age of Gold,
> Obscured so sadly in the mists of Time,
> Our WILSON, cast in apostolic mould,
> Seems to restore in all its pristine prime.[15]

If — and let us strain here a bit — Cotton Mather was the American Eusebius, chronicling events from the seat of power itself, Jonathan Edwards was the Augustine, seeing the detail of day-to-day colonial life against a cosmic background. His *History the Work of Redemption* was to be "a body of divinity in an entire new method, being thrown into the form of a history."[16] He preached thirty sermons on the subject in 1739, though he was unable to work out the whole plan of his *Civitas Dei* on a Northampton scale.

Edwards, for all the sophistication of his theology, held to an innocent, optimistic, open view of his environment. In *Thoughts on the Revival* he could bring in the note of hope and reflect it backward on his time and place: "The latter-day glory, is probably to begin in America." The Sun of righteous-

[14] *Ibid.*, 1:166.

[15] Cotton Mather, *Magnalia Christi Americana*, (Hartford, 1853), 1:321.

[16] Perry Miller, *Jonathan Edwards* (Cleveland: Meridian, 1959), p. 307.

ness was to "rise in the west, contrary to the course of things in the old heavens and earth." God had opened the new world "in order to make way for the introduction of the church's latter-day glory — which is to have its first seat in, and is to take its rise from, that new world." It is not "agreeable to God's manner to introduce a new and more excellent state of his church" into England, which was old and corrupt. "When God is about to turn the world into a paradise," the new beginning is "in the wilderness." [17]

Mather and Edwards could import a whole philosophy of history to set America apart over against the old world. Near the end of the colonial period a gentler, more tolerant man, was more empirical. Wrote Ezra Stiles, President of Yale, concerning his researches:

> From the cursory View I made of Ecclesiastical History, I thot all the protestant Churches as well as all the Xtian Churches since the first Age, had many Usages and Doctrines which I did not find in the Bible — yet I found sincere good men in all Churches catholic and protestant. Hence I adopted and professed an extensive and universal Charity: I readily saw the Mode of Worship in the New England Churches was as conformable to the Bible as any in the World, and I thot more so. [18]

The themes of the many chronicles which pass for church history in the colonial era can be condensed into a few. The viewpoint, of course, was consistently Protestant. From the Spanish and French Catholic missions we have chiefly log books dealing with highly localized circumstances. American religious history on the grand scale came out of the thirteen colonies where the population was overwhelmingly Protestant, a circumstance which colored the writing of Christian history until a decade or so ago. That earlier Protestantism was militant in its repudiation of the Catholic past. It was largely English Protestant in outlook, and from such a vantage

[17] *The Works of Jonathan Edwards* (Andover, 1842), 1:381–82.
[18] Quoted in Edmund S. Morgan, *The Gentle Puritan: A Life of Ezra Stiles, 1727–1795* (New Haven: Yale Univ. Press, 1962), p. 72.

the religious experience of the continent could ordinarily be downgraded. There were some doctrinaire advocacies of exceptions: the Waldensians or Albigensians of the Middle Ages, or Luther and Calvin; but the contemporary continent was largely written off. The outlook was ordinarily Puritan, even when it came from Anglican Virginia. This religious viewpoint, with its long shadow over American history, tended to seek innocence, to despise externals and forms and complexity.

The colonial writing was often promotional, written to attract more colonists or to justify the migrations which had been made; this caused the historians to exaggerate contrasts between the old and the new world. Throughout the national period historians felt impelled to continue this exaggerated and promotional note. The concern for the primitive or pristine church might suggest that a complex historical model was presented as an exception to the rule. But the early church turned out to be a kind of doctrinal construct which coincidentally prefigured the polity of the communities which were producing colonial history. Over it all there arched a Providence, assuring colonists that their day-to-day activities were scrutinized and that a benediction could be pronounced on their doings, if they lived properly in their wilderness, their new world.

After the colonial era, the second great chapter in American church history offers some surprise: during the rise of denominations and the time of adaptation to voluntaryism or the spread of revivals, precious little overall interpretation of American religious life was being produced. From the Revolution until almost 1850 American Protestants tended to borrow from Europe. One would expect that such borrowing would have led to an involvement in the destiny of the European churches. However, the borrowed ecclesiastical history bore an anti-historical character of either an Enlightenment or a Pietist stamp. The works of Johann Lorentz von Mosheim and Joseph Milner were used wherever the ideal of a learned ministry was kept alive.

Mosheim, "the father of Protestant church history," (died

1755) wrote *Institutiones historiae ecclesiasticae antiquioris* as a "careful and true narration of all external and internal events in the society of men which takes its name from Christ," "in order that we may learn piety and wisdom." [19] His man-centered interpretation helped churchmen slide into the Enlightenment, where liturgical and ecclesiastical complexity were devastated. But his degree of enlightenment was disturbing to the more pious British evangelical, Milner (died 1797). Mosheim had even made too much of the church's heresies and faults. Milner would discuss continuity, but continuity only of piety and sainthood:

> The terms "church" and "Christian" in their natural sense respect only good men. Such a succession of pious men in all ages existed, and it will be no contemptible use of such a history as this if it proves that in every age there have been *real* followers of Christ.[20]

As full of detail as Mosheim and Milner were, the logic of their approaches led to enlightened or pietist reductionism, and models from the old world and from the whole past were few. The earliest, Golden Age survived, as did the sects of the Middle Ages, the main line of the Reformation, and selected moments of later history.

Near mid-century, in the time of nationalist awakenings, the Americans became more self-conscious again about their positive part in church history. Borrowed evangelically enlightened church history lived on in the seminaries but beginning with Robert Baird in the 1840's there followed a century of what might be called "the great tradition of American church history." Providence was transformed progressively into Progress in the hands of Baird, Daniel Dorchester, or Leonard Bacon by century's end. But English Puritan Protestantism provided the angle of vision as it had more than a century earlier.

[19] Quoted in Karl Baus, *Handbook of Church History: From The Apostolic Community to Constantine* (New York: Herder and Herder, 1965), p. 32.
[20] *Ibid.*, p. 48.

Two late nineteenth-century events served to add themes and to change methods. The introduction of *academic* history, especially through the imitation of the German historical seminars in universities during the secularization of the colleges and universities, and the development of the *frontier thesis* both helped bring the discipline into the twentieth century. In this time the subject of inquiry was not so consistently the New England origins; particularly under William Warren Sweet the American West came into its own. But that westward shift of focus only served to underscore the preoccupation with American innocence, enterprise, experiment, and freshness over against complex history. And the academic-secular imposition of the need to specialize meant that people who studied American religious history could not claim to be experts also on European history.

James Hastings Nichols, one of the men at Chicago (and one of the few men anywhere) who was interested in and capable of integrating the story of American Christianity into that of the West and the world has complained about the result:

> For four-fifths and more of the sweep of the life of Christianity one will find only a lonely handful of Americans scattered about, but when one comes to the church in America . . . the American historians are as crowded as trout fishermen on opening day . . . No one can quarrel with American interest in American topics. If Americans do not write the history of American Christianity, who will? But the American Christian experience is only a minor portion of the whole. . . . One who does not know the earlier story will not understand American Christianity.[21]

Thoreau's "beware of tradition" and "forget historical Christianity"[22] came easily to practical frontiersmen and ecclesiastics. In Nichols' telling, it worked its way into the presuppositions of the church historians, to the distortion of their

[21] Nichols, "The History of Christianity," pp. 158–59.
[22] Lewis, *The American Adam*, p. 23.

narratives. "The offal of history is good enough for worms and monks, but it will not feed a living man. Power moves in the direction of hope."[23] These words of Horace Bushnell at Yale in 1843 anticipate Thomas Altizer's would-be radical remarks of 1966, and characterize the attitude of many American church historians in the Baird through Sweet era. In the remaining two sections I shall point to two modes of overcoming "innocence;" one has to do with the scope of inquiry and the other with the subject matter.

The historian of religion in America today is beginning to find that he can best understand his culture and make a contribution to others' self-understanding by enlarging the milieu concerning which he asks historical questions. Ideally, the setting should be the whole world, but we are not talking about ideal circumstances, about supermen and superminds. Mastering even one brief period in one small plot of ground demands a life's work. Now and then someone from the sphere of Eastern religions or from the underdeveloped nations of "the Third World" will do a comparative study of religious ideas and institutions in America and elsewhere. These almost accidental and casual abrasions between two histories are illuminative. But to picture sustaining such an approach as a life work seems staggering and, in its own way, artificial. From the viewpoint of religion in general and Christianity in particular such attempts involve correlation of narratives concerning at least two whole and separate religious complexes. But is it not possible to find a larger-than-American province of which the American experience is but a part, one whose telling involves but a single story?

Now as we look back on the period of intense nationalism in society and provincial innocence in the church we find that there is such a province. One can call it "the West" and imply therein Western continental Europe and Anglo-America. Some word like "Atlantic culture" or "Atlantic community" or "Atlantic civilization" might serve as a provisional term,

[23] *Ibid.*, p. 68.

though there is no need here to debate all the dimensions of words like community or culture. During the past two centuries one part of the world moved from pre-industrial to highly industrialized existence. This change, which accounts for so much of the power balance of the world today, changed virtually every dimension of institutional life throughout those nations and helped people see reality—including religious reality—in a new way. Of course, geographical isolation prevented them from realizing at all times how much they had in common in their experience. And one common experience, that of the rise of modern nationalism, was divisive and led historians and the public to stress the private experience of the nations. But the events in the separate nations and especially the religious life in those nations can better be understood when they are seen to be part of a common story.

Throughout the century some American historians and religious leaders served as commuters. Robert Baird was one, and his transatlantic commitments provided perspective for his history. Philip Schaff, trained in his native Europe, towered over the other nineteenth-century historians, but his experience and equipment were virtually unique. Still, others who were unable to bring off the story provided the service of calling its importance to American attention. Speaking of Germany's reputation for flirting with dangerous theology, John Williamson Nevin wrote in 1845:

> It is preposterous to suppose that in the most speculative portion of the whole Christian world these errors stand in no connection with the general movement of the world's mind, or that they do not *need* to be surmounted by a fresh advance on the part of truth.[24]

The truth was to be found in intercontinental dialogue and sharing of resources. Nevin's phrase, "the general movement of the world's mind" has enough of a Hegelian hint to cause us ordinary historians to gasp. And, as with Hegel, he could

[24] From Nevin's introduction to Philip Schaff, *The Principle of Protestantism* (Philadelphia and Boston: United Church Press, 1964), p. 32.

not have meant "the world's mind"; he referred to a much smaller province. But that "mind" did have to do with events which were directly shaping American religion.

The narrative of American religious history by itself does not serve to explain enough concerning the American present. Friedrich Nietzsche, Karl Marx, Charles Darwin, and Sigmund Freud, from a problematic point of view, had more to do with the shaping of subsequent American religion than did any home-grown god-killers. Positively, some British forms of carrying on mission or responding to industrialization, or some continental experiments with new forms of church life have proved to be as durable as were many American enterprises.

How to tell the unified or interrelated story is the difficult question. The world is full of mere generalists, non-experts who can deal superficially with many stories including that of religious events of the past three centuries. The historical discipline demands the education of specialists, people who can impart some sort of knowledge about the past and who can speak with some confidence. I take it there are some good reasons for the rise and the durability of prevailing orthodoxies, and academic specialization in history has a plausible background. Church historians in particular have to resist the temptation to become experts on everything, because of the ways in which such superficiality can be misleading. So: students do and must specialize.

The question is, why should the partly accidental experience of national isolation and the ideology of innocence which grew up around its religious experience be determinative? Can one not specialize in parts of a whole story even if these have an international base? Indeed, in the end, almost every scholar will find that vocational pulls, the location of research centers, and his personal predilections will lead him to be thought of as primarily an American, or British, or Continental (of some sort or other) expert. But that expertise is best developed on a comparative basis.

In this argument I am echoing Page Smith's appeal to turn from the statesmen's and historians' myth that "the independ-

ent, aggressive, expansionist, self-centered state whose microcosm was the independent, aggressive, self-centered individual, indivisible and autonomous" was a viable model for
living or the only field for historical research. Smith saw this
myth reinforced by the Turner frontier hypothesis in America.

> It was . . . a myth, albeit a useful and appealing one
> and one which provided a framework for a host of Amer-
> ican historians. But the point is that once this law, or
> principle of interpretation, had been formulated, it
> closed the eyes of most historians to any facts which did
> not conform to it.

What if the national-monographic specialization were to be
changed? "What would then occupy the attention of historians?" "There are about fifteen trained and presumably
productive scholars for every year of our history as a nation,"
working and studying as Ph.D.'s in American national history.
"We have reached the point of diminishing returns in the research and writing of American history."[25] There is no need to
follow Smith in his positive argument, that historians should
trace stories which contribute to an understanding which
would promote the unity of mankind. But it does make sense
to argue that historians of what purports to be an ecumenical
and catholic reality should not be beguiled into seeing all religious history from the viewpoint of people who during one
century were undergoing ecumenical and international experiences without realizing it.

Methodologically, such an approach does not involve historians in a pathetic quest for scraps of evidence which prove
that there was influence of certain Americans on Europe, or
vice versa. Such an attempt would tend to have to confine
itself to straightline institutional history, as in the case of the
story of the old Evangelical Alliance, which was an ecumenical movement or moment. Or it might restrict itself to the pursuit of footnotes, suggesting that Bushnell did read Schleiermacher or that Schaff was noticed here and there in his old

[25] Page Smith, *The Historian and History* (New York: Knopf, 1964),
pp. 140, 150, 222–23.

German stamping ground. Stories based on such inquiry would be artificial and of little interest. More fruitful is the pursuit of historical events and narration based on that research, organized around a rubric stated so well by Jacob Burckhardt in the famous paragraphs in which he was shrugging off the centaur of philosophy of history. "We shall confine ourselves to observation, taking transverse sections of history (*Querdurchschnitten*) in as many directions as possible."[26]

Such observation is less difficult in the colonial era or after World War I than it is in the nineteenth century. Yet numbers of major events did occur, sometimes with similar and sometimes with vastly differing effects, in America and elsewhere in the Atlantic community. Just a mere citation of a few suggests the possibilities. These include: revolutions, the rise and fall of colonial and imperial projects, the development of constitutionalism, the progressive separation of church and state, kinds of romanticism and reaction to Enlightenment, industrial development and revolution, the actual interaction and transfer of people in emigration-immigration, religious revivals and awakenings, missionary expansion (for which this was "The Great Century"), the rise of humanitarianism and the abolition of human slavery, a variety of assaults on Christian dominion and ideas, the rise of cities and the accompanying problems for religious institutions, the growth of modern nationalism, the foretastes of Christian ecumenical movements, and some theological interaction.

In some instances the narrative would have to be restricted to a comparative study of reactions to an external brute force; in others there would be obvious, conscious, and sustained interaction. Methodologically, such pursuit of "transverse sections of history" on an international basis does nothing to minimize specialization or academic historical techniques. It makes intercultural and often multilingual demands on students and may be of profit to air lines and tourist agencies just as it may be a new plague to research foundations which are

[26] Jacob Burckhardt, *Force and Freedom* (New York: Meridian, 1955), p. 72.

appealed to for funds. But the results of such comparative and interactive studies should be rewarding.

In the epic of innocence and the epoch of isolation, two grand themes came to be explanatory of American religious development, once the determinative story of colonial arrivals and intentions had been told. These were the story of religious freedom (including the separation of church and state and voluntaryism) and of the expansion of the churches across the continent, particularly through various modes of revival. Sidney E. Mead creatively fused the two in his classic essay on "Denominationalism: The Shape of Protestantism in America." [27]

Both themes were dealt with on the cosmic scale foreseen by Cotton Mather and Jonathan Edwards. Jerald C. Brauer in *Protestantism in America* speaks of the event which produced religious freedom as "the great turning point both for the nation and the Church." [28] For Mead, "The Revolutionary Epoch is the hinge upon which the history of Christianity in America really turns." [29] Winthrop S. Hudson called his interpretive history of voluntaryism, *The Great Tradition of the American Churches*. Winfred E. Garrison, who taught at Chicago, called the separation of church and state one of "the two most profound revolutions which have occurred in the entire history of the church . . . on the administrative side." [30]

Meanwhile, William Warren Sweet wrote:

> The greatest accomplishment of America is the conquest of the continent, and the greatest achievement of the

[27] Sidney E. Mead, *The Lively Experiment* (New York: Harper & Row, 1963), Chapter 7, pp. 103 ff.

[28] Brauer, *Protestantism in America*, p. 88.

[29] Mead, *The Lively Experiment*, p. 52.

[30] Winfred E. Garrison, "Characteristics of American Organized Religion," *Annals of the American Academy of Political and Social Science*, 256 (March, 1948): 45.

American churches has been the extension of their work westward across the vast stretches of the continent, keeping abreast with the restless and ever moving population.[31]

And Peter G. Mode before him had stressed, "The Americanizing of Christianity has been the process by which it has been *frontierized.*" [32] While I have here restricted myself once again to Chicago historians, a report on the narrative of others would substantiate the contention that three themes — colonization, religious freedom, and the frontier — have dominated. Each of these served to underscore the themes of innocence and isolation. Today a fourth event or cluster of events can be added to this list: industrialization. Of all the experienes in late eighteenth- through early twentieth-century Atlantic culture, no other is so intricately involved with the record of religious response. My own explorations have been in this direction. Whitehead once said that the history of the modern world could be written around the terms "steam" (brute forces) and "democracy" (ideal expressions). The historians have done well and they continue to do so on the subject of religion and democracy. That drama of interaction still unfolds. They have done less with "steam," which is not *only* brute force but which also symbolizes a variety of ideal expressions and ideological constructs.

Historians are rightfully wary when they approach "the Industrial Revolution" as an event; in a way they know they are dealing with "symbolic" history. Yet more distortion results from overlooking the changes it symbolizes than from hazarding narration. I agree with E. J. Hobsbawm on this point:

> Some time in the 1780's, and for the first time in human history, the shackles were taken off the productive power of human societies, which henceforth became capable of

[31] William Warren Sweet, *The Story of Religion in America* (New York: Harper and Brothers, 1950), p. 3.
[32] Peter G. Mode, *The Frontier Spirit in American Christianity*, p. 14.

the constant, rapid and up to the present limitless multi-
plication of men, goods and services. This is now technically known to the economists as the "take-off into self-
sustained growth". . . . If the sudden, qualitative and
fundamental transformation, which happened in or
about the 1780's, was not a revolution then the word has
no commonsense meaning. . . . By any reckoning this
was probably the most important event in world history,
at any rate since the invention of agriculture and cities.[33]

The Industrial Revolution came slightly later to the United
States and to the continent, but it provided much of the plot
for religious institutions in the nineteenth century. We cannot
fault the earlier historians for neglect of industrialization —
they were writing before it arrived on a large scale. Nor has
there been total neglect of its effects, at least on a mono-
graphic level. After all, Father John Ryan's *Social Doctrine in
Action*, Henry May's *Protestant Churches and Industrial
America*, and Aaron Abell's *The Urban Impact on American
Protestantism* appeared in the 1940's and an impressive literature on industrialization in American religious life emerged
already around the turn of the century. But industrialization
as an ecumenical event in the Western world has not become
a main theme in the writing of American religious history.

Concentration on the religious involvement in industrialization on an "Atlantic" scale would be one of the ways of overcoming the attitude of innocence which more plausibly
marked earlier church history than later: such a narrative
necessitates a revisiting of Europe, a confrontation of the
urban reality, the dealing with complexity. If it is to be placed
in perspective (C. S. Lewis says that those who do not know
history are usually victims of recent bad history), the story
must also be seen against the background of many centuries
of Christian response to social change and of the church as
agent and victim of change. Not that religion-and-industrial-

[33] E. J. Hobsbawm, *The Age of Revolution* (Cleveland: World, 1962),
pp. 28–29.

ization would represent the end of the story, the ultimate version that leads to displacement of the earlier ones. Some might say that the only reason that we can now take up the subject is that we are in a post-industrial era and that historians can only comprehend a movement or an event (slavery, the frontier) after it has lived its vital life. For now, however, it provides a dramatic subject and angle of vision.

Most historians of religion in the modern world find themselves dealing with the concept or process of secularization. That process has to be faced through a study of events. Legal secularization, the separation of church and state, presented few durable problems to churchmen or historians. Through it the external construct as old as Augustine and Constantine broke up, but "the Protestant empire" lived on and even the most imperial churchmen like Lyman Beecher could report almost immediately that it was "the best thing that ever happened" to religion where they were. The frontier experience, because it relates to the mystique of the soil, was also exploited by churchmen and historians for its obvious spiritual potential. But the machine and the city, products of the industrial age, have been more problematic.

A comparative study of industrialization on the Continent, in Great Britain, and in the United States suggests different kinds of secularization. German and French transition was accompanied by a heavy burden of ideology: "God is Dead." In England, what H. G. Wells called "everydayishness" prevailed: people were practically preoccupied and religion seemed to make less difference. In the United States radical religious change — but under continuity of symbols — occurred. In all three instances, what Robert C. Binkley called "the pitiless and persistent rivals" of the Church [34] took form in this period, one in which I like to speak of *The Modern Schism* (a future book-title) as having occurred. The generalizations in this paragraph are comprehensive and demand scrutiny which I hope to give in the years ahead.

[34] Robert C. Binkley, *Realism and Nationalism 1852–1871* (New York: Harper and Brothers, 1935), p. 71.

Theologians have often remarked on the overall effects of industrialization on man and society. These include, using their words implying judgment, "depersonalization," the divorce of the worker from his product and the means of production, a change in his status, the necessity for more complex governmental life, an assault on the role of the family, an increase in personal mobility, "alienation," the rise of new leisure. For the churches, the old territorial parish lost meaning; the scientific-technological demands and practical necessity created new habits of mind, many of which resulted in assaults on time-honored theological world-views: one could extend the list indefinitely and then subject each effect to historical research.

The historian need have no interest in working out an ultimate synthesis or a philosophy of history which will tell with confidence where industrial or post-industrial man and his gods are going. As Ernest Gellner has argued concerning philosophy, one needs first and foremost to be able to cope with the ongoing experience of transition, an experience built into the logic of industrial and technological development. If you ask Gellner what philosophy is or ought to be about today, he would answer, "industrialization." As an historian I hesitate to condense so much into one term, but for exploration of American (and Atlantic nations') religious life for more than a century, no word serves better as an heuristic tool. With Gellner, I see considerable durability in that religious complex which helped Americans and other Westerners "over the hump of transition" into industrialized affluent life. As a social philosopher he can speak confidently about that concerning which the historian inquires:

> The ideology with which a society has passed the hump of transition is likely to remain its nominal doctrine, thereafter: indeed it is likely to become, locally, the symbol of that overcoming of the painful hump, of the achieved satisfactory order which is now the true "social contract." It seems as unlikely that the West will repudi-

ate its formal religious faiths, as that the Russians should disavow Marxism. The effective content may be eroded, becoming ever more selective, symbolic, "spiritual," etc.

There tends to be in modern society a dualism and sometimes a pluralism or a division of labor between

on the one hand symbolic, unifying ideas, communal banners, which once were full-bloodedly cognitive, but whose cognitive import is now shrouded in semi-deliberate ambiguity; and on the other hand, the cognitively effective but normatively not very pregnant or insistent beliefs about the world.[35]

The result: the symbolic world has become one of civic religions which can provide for a tolerant basis in a pluralist society. From the theological side, such ideology and religion may come under judgment as representing (from some normative angle or other) the wrong kind of secularization. From the historical side, they represent a process which can better be described as "radical religious change" and they provide a subject matter which shows few signs of disappearing in a world which we often call secular.

The *church* historian engaged in such reinterpretation has no interest in trying to "pull rank" on the historian who allows no adjective denoting such specialization before his name. He, too, remains a "mere" historian. If he wishes to be in the service of the church, that service is best carried out through faithful representation of history. Faced with "the forward-looking enthusiasms" of the age, he will "look backward with compensatory vigor." He cannot prophesy or predict, to satisfy forward-looking hungers and hopes. Edward C. Kirkland has said:

History cannot give certainties — I'm not certain it can even give probabilities — but most of all it can give possibilities when you are extrapolating about the future.

[35] Ernest Gellner, *Thought and Change* (Chicago: Univ. of Chicago Press, 1964), pp. 123, 125.

History points out the varieties of choices. I suppose that's what we mean by breadth. Wisdom, depth, urbanity, impartiality, detachment — these are the contributions historians and students of history can make.[36]

Kirkland's charter begins in modesty and ends in apparent grandiosity. But if "history points out the varieties of choices," it seems unreasonable to ask for more.

[36] David Hawke, "Interview: Edward C. Kirkland" in *History 4* (Cleveland: World, 1961), pp. 168–69.

Biographical Notes

R. PIERCE BEAVER has held the position of professor of missions at the Divinity School of the University of Chicago, since 1955. An ordained minister of the United Church of Christ, he was born in 1906 in Hamilton, Ohio. He was educated at Oberlin College, A.B. and M.A., 1928; Cornell University, Ph.D., 1933; and has studied at the University of Munich, Yale University, Union Theological Seminary, and Columbia University.

JERALD C. BRAUER was born in Wisconsin in 1921. He has studied at Carthage College, B.A., 1943; Northwestern Lutheran Theological Seminary, B.D., 1945; and received his Ph.D. in church history from the University of Chicago in 1948. Appointed dean of the Federated Theological Faculty in 1955, he has served since 1960 as professor of church history and dean of the Divinity School of the University of Chicago.

ROBERT T. HANDY was born in Connecticut in 1918. He graduated from Brown University, A.B., 1940; Colgate Rochester Divinity School, B.D., 1943; and received the Ph.D. in church history from the University of Chicago in 1949. He is author of *We Witness Together* (1956), *Members One of Another* (1959), co-author of *American Christianity* (1960–63), and editor of *The Social Gospel in America* (1966).

WINTHROP S. HUDSON, professor of the history of Christianity at the Colgate Rochester Divinity School, received the Ph.D. in church history from the University of Chicago in

1940. A native of Michigan, born in 1911, he is a past president of the American Society of Church History, and the author of several books, including *Religion in America, American Protestantism*, and *The Great Tradition of the American Churches*.

FREDERICK KIRSCHENMANN was born in 1935. He received his A.B. from Yankton College in 1957 and his B.D. from the Hartford Seminary Foundation in 1960. He received his M.A. (1962) and his Ph.D. in church history (1964) from the University of Chicago. In 1962 he began teaching in the Religion Department at Yankton College where he is now head of the department.

MARTIN E. MARTY is an associate professor of modern church history at the Divinity School of the University of Chicago, where he joined the faculty in 1963. He is also an associate member of the University's History Department, member of the Committee on the History of Culture, and chairman of the History of Christianity Field at the Divinity School. Born in 1928, Mr. Marty received his Ph.D. in church history in 1956 at the University of Chicago.

SIDNEY E. MEAD is professor of religion in American history at the University of Iowa. Born in 1904, he received his Ph.D. in church history from the University of Chicago in 1940 and taught American church history there from 1941 to 1960, being concurrently president of The Meadville Theological School, 1956–60. He taught at the Claremont School of Theology from 1960 before going to Iowa in 1964.

WILLIAM SPARKES MORRIS was born in 1916 in Cardiff, Wales. A professor of philosophy and religion at Huron College in Ontario, Canada, since 1955, he has studied at Corpus Christi College, Oxford, 1939–41; Wycliffe Hall, Oxford, 1941–43. In 1955 he was awarded the Ph.D. in church history by the University of Chicago. A contributor to various journals, he is the author of *The Unity We Seek*.

Acknowledgments

Many of the articles in this volume were first presented at the Alumni Conference of the Field of History of Christianity, October 6–8, 1966, celebrating the seventy-fifth anniversary of the University of Chicago and the hundredth anniversary of the Divinity School of the University of Chicago. The conference was greatly enriched by two public lectures by John T. McNeill and Sidney E. Mead. The first lecture appeared in Volume Two of *Essays in Divinity*, and the second is in this volume. Thanks are due also to those members of the conference who served as discussants on several of the papers in this book. Limitations of space made it impossible for their comments to be included.

Special thanks are due to Professor Trygve Skarsten of Sweet Briar College, who, as editorial assistant, offered many helpful stylistic suggestions and helped to prepare the manuscript for publication.

The excerpt from Dorothy Aldis' poem "Everybody Says" is reprinted by permission of G. P. Putnam's Sons from *Everything and Anything*, by Dorothy Aldis (copyright 1925, 1926, 1927 by Dorothy Aldis; renewed 1953, 1954, 1955 by Dorothy Aldis).

Index

Abeel, David, 135
Abell, Aaron, 214
Ahlstrom, Sidney E., 17, 25
Alden, E. K., 143
Allen, Jonathan, 134
American Board of Commissioners for Foreign Missions, 114, 127, 139, 142–43
American Colonization Society, 94
American Revolutionary War, 114, 120, 133, 204
Anderson, Rufus, 116, 128, 141–42, 144, 149
Andover Seminary, 129
Aristotle, 30, 32–33, 39, 44, 53, 61
Arminianism, 42, 45, 59, 61
Arnauld, Antoine, 32, 53, 56
Atlantic community, 15–16, 19, 153–55, 167, 207, 211, 214. *See also* Marty; Hudson
Augustine, 56 n, 63

Bacon, Leonard W., 4, 68, 101, 136–37, 204
Baden-Powell, Robert, 158
Badger, Stephen, 123
Baird, Robert, 2, 3, 6, 12, 14, 25, 101, 205, 207–8
Baptists, 96, 161, 166
Beecher, Henry Ward, 158–59
Beecher, Lyman, 159, 215
Berdyaev, Nikolai, 199
Berger, Peter L., 182–83
Bibliographical works, 5, 16, 91–92
Binkley, Robert C., 215
Boorstin, Daniel, 103, 110
Booth, Charles and William, 165
Bower, William C., 192

Brainerd, David, 123, 125, 156
Brauer, Jerald C., 201, 212
British Continental Society, 156
Brooks, Phillips, 158–59
Buell, Samuel, 125
Burckhardt, Jacob, 18, 211
Burgersdycke, Franco: influence of, 60, 64; logic of, 29–33, 35; philosophy of, 37–42, 44–45, 48–50, 56–57
Bushnell, Horace: interpreters of, 67–72; theology of, 67–70, 81, 88–89; theory of language, 69, 71–74, 76–82, 84–87; misc., 161, 171 n, 192, 207, 210
Butler, Joseph, 64, 161

Calvinism, 29–30, 34, 61, 63, 121, 204
Campbell, Alexander and Thomas, 156
Campbell, R. J., 161–62
Carey, William, 156–57
Carver, William O., 132, 150
Case, Shirley Jackson, 192
Chauncy, Charles, 41, 118, 122
"Chicago School," 5–6, 11, 13–15, 169–70, 192, 213
Church: concept of, 10, 12, 192; institutional, 62, 70, 138–39, 181, 184; life of, 9–10, 92–93, 95, 163, 166, 179; Negro, 91–112
Church history: American, 1, 6–7, 10–11, 18, 89, 91, 93, 102–5, 107, 109, 112, 155, 186, 189–90, 194; church historians, 6–7, 15–16, 19, 21–25, 104, 106, 109, 196–97, 206; discipline of,

223

Index

Sunday School Movement, 157
Swedenborgians, 3, 83, 154
Sweet, William Warren: church
historian, 5–7, 10, 12, 101, 200–
201; use of frontier thesis, 13–
14, 25, 104, 206, 212–13; misc.,
18, 192, 207
Symbolism, Religious, 22, 24, 28,
84

Tannenbaum, Frank, 93
Taylor, Graham, 165
Theological climate, 9, 195–96
Theological seminaries (educa-
tion), 108, 172–74, 178, 191,
195–97
Theology: Bushnell's, 67–69, 71,
73, 81, 85, 87–89; Edwards',
29–65 *passim*; systematic, 24,
29, 162–63, 189, 196
Thoreau, Henry D., 206
Tillich, Paul, 185
Torrey, Reuben A., 158
Trinterud, Leonard J., 20–21
Turner, Frederick J., 6–7, 11, 14,
210. *See also* Frontier thesis

Universals, 33–36, 61

Van Buren, Paul, 82
Voluntaryism, 3, 12–14, 199, 212

Ward, Julius H., 164
Washington, Joseph Jr., 97–98
Watson, John, 158–59
Weigle, Luther, 7
Wells, H. G., 215
Wesley, John, 156
Westcott, B. F., 161, 165
Wheaton Mission Conference Dec-
laration, 130
Wheelock, Eleazar, 118, 122–23
Whitefield, George, 156
Whitehead, Alfred North, 11, 88,
167, 172, 179–80, 187, 189,
192, 213
Wilder, Robert, 148–49
Williams, Roger, 122
Wilson, Thomas, 120
Woodson, Carter G., 96, 111
Wordsworth, William, 154–55
Wright, Benjamin F., 11

Yale College, 29–30, 203, 207
Yinger, J. Milton, 105
Y.M.C.A., 157

Zwemer, Samuel M., 143